Birds of Britain and Northern Europe

Field Guide to Birds of Britain and Northern Europe

DETLEF SINGER

Consultant Editor, David A. Christie

The Crowood Press

The Publisher would like to thank **Martin Walters** for translating the original German text and David A. Christie for adapting the text for the English language.

This edition first published in 1991 by
The Crowood Press Ltd
Gipsy Lane
Swindon
Wiltshire SN2 6DQ

British Library Cataloguing in Publication Data

Singer, Detlef
    Field guide to the birds of Britain and
        Northern Europe.
    1. Great Britain. Birds 2. Northern Europe.
        Birds
    I. Title II. [Vogel Mitteleuropas. *English*]
    598.2941

ISBN 1 85223 596 9

Original title: Die Vögel Mitteleuropas, Detlef

Illustrations:

Front cover photograph. Blue Tit (Maurice K.
Walker, Nature Photographers).
Back cover photograph. Avocets (Mike Lane,
Natural Image).

Title page: Gannet colony (Paul Sterry, Nature
Photographers).
Contents page: Bee-eater (Paul Sterry, Nature
Photographers).

Typeset by Chippendale Type Ltd, Otley, West
Yorkshire
Printed and bound by Times Publishing
Group, Singapore

Contents

How to Use this Book   6
Bird Song   9
Equipment for the Birdwatcher   12
Bird Protection   13
Key to Families   15
Eggs and Clutches
Nests and Nest-Holes
Young Birds
Signs
Feather Remains   53
Feathers   57
Pellets and Droppings   63
Further Reading   68
Important Addresses   68
Identification Section   69
Divers, Storks, Herons, Ducks and Allies   69
Birds of Prey   124
Gamebirds, Rails, Cranes, Bustards   147
Waders, Gulls, Terns, Auks   165
Doves, Owls, Kingfishers, Woodpeckers
and Allies   221
Songbirds   257
Flight Patterns of   370
Flight Patterns of   372
Flight Patterns of   374
Flight Patterns of Gulls   376
Flight Patterns of Terns   377
Index   378

How to Use this Book

This book describes the birds regularly found in Britain and northern Europe, as well as most of those occurring in central Europe south and east to Hungary. Most vagrants are omitted.

The birds are, with one or two exceptions, treated in systematic order, so that related species are dealt with together. However, this order is not exactly the same in all bird books, being based upon evolutionary relationships which are often incompletely known. The colour photographs were nearly all taken in the wild and show each bird in its typical habitat. Normally the male (♂) is shown in breeding plumage, but if the female (♀) or another plumage is shown this is pointed out in the text. Extra colour illustrations are used to show different plumages (such as female, winter or juvenile) where these are important in identification.

The birds are arranged in six colour-coded groups, as follows:

Divers, petrels, cormorants, herons, storks, ibises, swans, geese, and ducks

Birds of prey

Gamebirds, rails, cranes, bustards

Waders, gulls, terns, auks

Doves, cuckoos, owls, swifts, nightjars, kingfishers and allies, woodpeckers

Songbirds

Signs and Abbreviations

Status: Indicates time of year species can be seen in Britain:

R Resident: remains throughout the year in the breeding area. Although some species – for instance Nuthatch – spend the whole year in their territories, others, such as tits, wander widely.

S Summer visitor: migratory species found only in spring and summer.

(S) Non-breeding visitor, or rare summer visitor.

W Winter visitor: does not breed, but visits in winter.

(W) Rare winter visitor.

M Passage migrant.

P Partial migrant: some birds migrate to winter quarters in the autumn, while others overwinter in the breeding area. May be seen throughout the year, but often in very small numbers in the winter.

V Vagrant: recorded very rarely and irregularly, usually by accident or as a result of mis-oriented migration.

I–XII Roman numerals indicate the months in which the species may be seen in Britain.

♂ Male

♀ Female

ad. Adult

juv. Juvenile

> Larger than

< Smaller than

— About the same size as

O Does not breed in Britain

Red List

Red lists are regional accounts of threatened animals and plants which have been drawn up to identify the level of threat to each species and thus account for their status. Today they are essential in providing the scientific basis for plant and animal conservation. Many European countries publish these lists. The most recent British list, researched and published by the Royal Society for the Protection of Birds (RSPB), defines seven categories. They are as follows:

BI Internationally significant breeder (more than 20% of the western European population breed in Britain).

BR Rare breeder (fewer than 300 pairs breed regularly in Britain).

BD Declining breeder (species whose British breeding numbers have declined by more than 50% since 1960).

BL Vulnerable breeder (species confined to rare and vulnerable habitats, such as reedbeds, and with more than half their population occurring at 10 or fewer of these sites).

WI Internationally significant non-breeder (as BI, but referring to regular passage numbers or, more often, wintering numbers).

WL Vulnerable non-breeder (as BL, but referring to wintering species).

SC Special category (probably meeting one of the above criteria, but evidence uncertain and more research required).

The text of the individual species descriptions contains all the necessary information to identify the species, in a compact and easily understood form.

The most characteristic features or behaviour of the species are given under **distinctive character**. The **features** section describes the appearance of the bird, enlarging on the illustrations, and pointing out any variations according to age, season, sex, and colour variants. Characteristic calls and songs are described under **voice**, and other sections give the major habitat for each species, its **behaviour**, and **food**. Under **breeding habits** there is information about the time of breeding, number of broods each year, as well as the location and appearance of the nest.

The Information Panels

The panels beneath each description give a quick summary of the species: its group (family silhouette), approximate size (compared with a familiar species), status (resident, summer visitor, and so on), period during which it may be seen in Britain, and conservation status.

Bird sizes are not given as lengths in centimetres. This is because it is difficult to visualize such measurements, especially for smaller species, when it is the overall shape which is more important. The Long-tailed Tit and Nuthatch are the same length (14 cm), but the dumpy Nuthatch weighs almost three times as much as the delicate Long-tailed Tit.

Instead of measurements, the size of each species is indicated by comparison with a well-known bird, or 'reference species'. In the case of the reference species themselves, no other bird is referred to, since it is assumed that they are well known. The approximate sizes/weights of the reference species are:

House Sparrow	15 cm/30 g
Blackbird	25 cm/90 g
Feral Pigeon	33 cm/300 g
Black-headed Gull	36 cm/250 g
Carrion Crow	47 cm/500 g
Buzzard	55 cm/800 g
Mallard	58 cm/1,200 g
Herring Gull	60 cm/1,100 g

The following species are also used as (second order) reference species: Great Crested Grebe, White Stork, Grey Heron, Greylag Goose, Mute Swan, Golden Eagle, Kestrel, Grey Partridge, Domestic Hen, Coot, Common Tern, Swift, Great Spotted Woodpecker, Swallow and Starling. In the panels for these species, their relative size is indicated with reference to the first order reference species.

Sometimes it is difficult to judge the size of a bird in the wild, since subjective impressions can be misleading. This partly depends upon the distance between observer and the bird, and partly on the bird's surroundings. For example, a Golden Eagle sitting high on a cliff face can seem small, while a Blackbird on a leafless tree in winter may seem large. Also birds often look bigger than they are in the twilight or through the mist.

How to Identify Birds

Field identification of birds is not always easy: quite often it is difficult to get close enough, or the bird may be constantly on the move, or vegetation may get in the way. And if you do finally get sufficiently near the bird can fly off leaving you none the wiser! In the short time available you have to take in as many details as possible of the bird's appearance and behaviour. Consequently, the more species you know, the easier it is to identify an unknown one correctly. It is therefore worth while studying the guide at home, and familiarizing yourself at least with the above-mentioned reference species. Pay special attention to:

– the bird's size and shape (and flight silhouette)
– size and shape of the bill
– length and shape of the tail
– length of the legs
– feather colouring and contrasts, such as eye-stripes and wing-bars
– special movements and behaviour patterns (in flight, wing-beat frequency)
– calls

- habitat
- season

Fieldmarks can vary in importance. The Cuckoo and Chiffchaff, for example, can be identified mainly by voice, the Kingfisher by its electric-blue upperparts, and the Long-tailed Tit by its shape (small bird with a long tail). If there are no such distinctive fieldmarks, other characteristics can give a positive identification, although often only in combination.

Sample Identification

For quick, easy identification there is a key to families from pages 15 to 22. Each family has at least one typical silhouette, a short piece of explanatory text about its characteristics, and a reference to the appropriate section in the identification guide itself.

Example: November, in a park. A black bird is sighted swimming on a lake. It moves its head like a domestic hen and keeps flicking its tail. As it disappears into the undergrowth at the edge of the lake you notice its short tail has a white underside. Comparison with the silhouette in the family key points to the rail family. Now read the short text to see if this is likely, bearing in mind the observation that the bird was hen-like. Turn to the relevant pages in the identification section and look at the photographs of the different rail species. The choice is narrowed to the two black species, Moorhen and Coot. Check your identification using the species descriptions and panels. From the panels it is clear that both species are found throughout the year, but the choice is narrowed by the size comparison: 'smaller than Partridge' (for the Moorhen) seems more likely than 'smaller than Mallard'. For confirmation check the distinctive character section for the Moorhen, which should match all your observations.

Bird Song

The Importance of Identifying Birds by Song

Calls play an important role in the lives of birds, both within and between species, and it is therefore not surprising that birds have developed such a wide repertoire. Since so many calls are species-specific they can be used in bird identification. Indeed if it were not for their calls we would be unaware of many species, since they often hide deep within thickets or out of sight in the tree-tops.

Certain species are so similar that they are difficult to separate in the field. Fortunately the calls of these 'twin species' tend to be markedly different, so they can be separated by song alone. It is therefore essential to know these songs to establish how many different species inhabit a particular piece of woodland because most birds will be out-of-sight.

Knowledge of bird calls not only helps in bird identification, it also allows estimates to be made of bird densities for particular species, and gives clues about the situation in which a bird finds itself. For instance, a loud clamour may indicate the presence of a cat or weasel; a high-pitched drawn-out *tsee* suggests this time the threat comes from the air (a Sparrow-hawk, for example); repeated full song indicates an unpaired male; and begging calls by nestlings reveal a successful brood.

Learning Bird Song

The best way to learn is either from a competent friend or relation, or by taking part in trips organized by bird-watching societies or other naturalists' groups. You can also learn from bird-song discs or tapes. Begin by concentrating on the calls and songs of a few common species. By starting early in the season you can familiarize yourself with various songs before the huge number of different sounds commence with the arrival of the summer migrants.

Compare an unknown call or song with one that you know and try to describe it verbally, using terms such as fluting, scratchy, monotonous or melancholy. Also note whether the song is divided into phrases, or is more or less continuous. And is it varied, are

sections repeated, or are they made up of repetitions of a single note? As a further aid to identification do try and obtain a sighting of the bird. The more information you have to work from, the better.

Calls and Songs

Bird sounds are divided according to their function into calls and songs. Calls are normally short sounds that are not learned, but which are part of an inherited repertoire. They are usually heard all the year round, although there are also calls that are heard only at particular seasons, such as the so-called 'rainsong' of the Chaffinch (breeding season), or the *tseedit* of the Dunnock (autumn). Various kinds of call are recognized, according to their function, such as contact, warning, threat and begging calls.

With a few exceptions only the male bird sings. Unlike calls, songs are limited to certain times of the year. Most songbirds sing in the spring, although some species also have a distinct autumn song. Singing activity is controlled by hormone levels and can be induced in the laboratory by administering the male hormone testosterone, even in female birds. Songs are normally more complex than calls and consist of smaller elements (syllables) from which larger elements (phrases) are built up.

In some species there is a single phrase type, continually repeated; other species, such as the Chaffinch, have a small repertoire of phrases, with first one phrase repeated several times and then another, and so on. Some very musical species incorporate very many different phrases. For example the Nightingale uses more than 200 and the Woodlark over 100. The function of the song is twofold: it is used to delimit a male's territory so that wandering males are kept away from the occupied area and it attracts a mate. Spotted Flycatchers, for instance, aim their singing almost entirely at the female, and cease singing after successful pairing. However, the males of many species continue to sing after mating, and their song is thought to play a general role in the synchronization of the sexes during and after courtship. Song sometimes helps to keep the pair together, as in the case of the Coal Tit, where both sexes sing throughout the year to maintain contact.

Representation of Bird Song

It is quite difficult to describe a bird song to someone else – unless it is the call of the Cuckoo, or the 'pink' sound of the Chaffinch. Even when bird song used to be represented using musical notation, this could lead to the same song being subjectively interpreted and written down in different ways. The confusion remained.

The current trend is for books (including this one) to represent bird calls in script, for example *tsee-tsee tay* for the song of the Great Tit. However, since this method cannot transmit the tone of the call, descriptions such as fluting and raucous have to be added. An even more exact, scientific method involves bioacoustics. This became possible with the use of tape recorders and sonagraphs. The sonagraph makes a permanent and objective record of bird calls, with

its tracings (sonagrams) being made on special paper. Today it is possible, with the help of the sonagram, to do detailed research into questions of individual song development, acoustic learning behaviour and the development of song dialects.

Structure and Function of the Syrinx

In contrast to other vertebrates, including humans (where sounds are produced in the voice-box), birds have evolved a special organ in the chest, the syrinx. This is sited at the junction of the two bronchii with the trachea (windpipe), and consists of two membranous skin structures stretched between the cartilaginous rings of the trachea. Movement of air in the windpipe causes these to vibrate. The precise structure of these outer and inner syrinx membranes varies from group to group. In the song-birds they can apparently move independently, since these birds can sometimes make different non-harmonic tones at the same time.

The syrinx muscles also vary between bird groups. Songbirds have between four and nine pairs of such muscles, whereas the other passerines have only three pairs. These special muscles enable songbirds to produce their huge variety of calls and songs. As might be expected, virtuoso performers such as the nightingales, thrushes and larks have the best-developed syrinx muscles. However, certain other birds without such highly developed syrinxes are unquestionably more musical than the crows!

Equipment for the Birdwatcher

The single most important piece of equipment for the birdwatcher is a good pair of binoculars. They should not be too heavy, and simple and quick to use. It helps if they have a rubber reinforcement as protection against knocks. A magnification of between 8 and 10 is best, the commonest choices being 8×30, 8×40, 10×40, and 10×50. However, you do not necessarily see more through 10× magnification than through 8× because the image brightness is reduced at higher magnification, and the effect of shaking is increased. Prices for good 8× and 10× binoculars range from £50 to well over £500. When choosing a cheaper pair of binoculars test several different makes because there is often considerable variation in adjustment; for the top end of the price-range such a test is usually superfluous, though still desirable, owing to variation in comfort and handling ability. When watching for birds at a greater distance, for example waterbirds and waders, it is a good idea to use a telescope. The best magnifications are between 25× and 40×, and while there are more powerful (and more expensive) telescopes of 80×, 100×, and even higher power, they are normally used for astronomy. The most important qualities are sharpness and image brightness, so there is not much point in having a 60× magnification if the image is too dark under cloudy conditions. Since memory is notoriously unreliable it is also essential to take a notebook for recording field observations, otherwise they can easily be forgotten after a couple of hours. Record place, habitat, time, and other local factors. If identification is in doubt, record as many of the bird's features as possible, including behaviour and calls, and if possible make a sketch. You can then check these features later on with descriptions and illustrations in books, and hopefully make a positive identification.

Bird Protection

Many people think of feeding birds and providing nest-boxes when they think of bird protection, and great sums of money are spent on these activities. However, these activities are not sufficient, and a species-rich bird life can be maintained only if suitable habitats can be provided for the birds. In other words there is no point in providing tits with a nest-box if there is not enough natural insect food for the young when they hatch.

In order to understand why a particular species declines and to provide help, one needs to know the details of its life-history, its habitat requirements, and behaviour. As an example of how different such requirements can be, consider the Capercaillie and the Chaffinch.

The Capercaillie, a large bird of open coniferous forests, has very particularly requirements. The forest must be near-natural and contain clearings, and the distance between the individual trees must be sufficient for these large birds to fly easily between them; they also require a rich forest-floor vegetation with bilberry, different moss species and other food plants, much dead wood, old trees with strong branches for the tree display of the cock birds, small patches of bog or clearings with wider open spaces where they can gather small stones, and finally ants' nests for feeding the chicks. Clearly, habitat suitable for the Capercaillie is of great ecological value, and the existence of the species is a good guide to forest quality. Wherever Capercaillies are found, the conditions are right for a whole host of other threatened animals and plants.

The Chaffinch, by contrast, is found in every kind of woodland, from monotonous spruce plantations to deciduous and mixed forests, and even in parks and gardens with trees. It has no very stringent requirements, needing only a few tall trees, and therefore has relatively low value as an ecological guide. On the other hand the adaptable Chaffinch is much easier to protect than the fussy Capercaillie.

A great deal of research has been done on the dramatic decline of the Capercaillie across Europe – partly because of its usefulness as an indicator species – and we are now reasonably clear why it is threatened with extinction over much of its range. Using this knowledge it is possible to remedy the situation and give the Capercaillie protection. However, other threatened species have not been so well researched and it is therefore more difficult to set up the right measures to protect them.

Until a few years ago conservationists concentrated their efforts upon species with special habitat requirements, which were therefore particularly threatened, like the Capercaillie. Today, however, populations of recently quite common species have also decreased in a worrying manner. It is not just a few 'specialist' birds that are in danger, but bird life as a whole that is under pressure. Deforestation, for instance, threatens the habitats of many of our bird species including songbirds, woodpeckers, most owls and birds of prey. This problem obviously affects all the other woodland animals too, such as mammals, amphibians, reptiles and insects. Ecological balance – the basis of our survival – can be guaranteed only through the diversity of plant and animal species; the loss of each individual species weakens the whole system.

It is crucial that all those who are involved with landscape planning understand the full implications of the facts. The most important step is to spread basic biological awareness, for the problems described are not always known. The second step is the preparation of scientific data so that the status of animal species and groups is known for each area. Without such scientific reports it is often very difficult to argue with officials and prevent damaging developments going ahead. Even amateur ornithologists can play an important role in bird and nature conservation by publishing their field studies or making their findings accessible to whoever requires them.

There are other practical ways in which amateurs can help, for instance guarding nest sites of rare species, such as Red Kite, Osprey, and the Peregrine, or by creating suitable breeding places for such species as the Kingfisher or Dipper. Organizations can achieve more than private individuals, so every birdwatcher should join a bird club or conservation group (see page 68) where individual initiative can be discussed and best achieved with the help of other members. Well-supported conservation organizations can nowadays prevent damaging developments, or at least help reduce their impact. The more people who join such groups, the more influence they will have politically.

Finally, a word about bird photography. This rewarding, enjoyable hobby demands that bird disturbance is kept to an absolute minimum. Photography at or near the nest should be completely taboo (the few nest photographs in this book are taken from old archive material). The aim of the bird photographer should be to capture the bird in its characteristic habitat, showing its undisturbed natural behaviour. This way, the pictures have a permanent scientific value.

Bittern

Key to Families

Bird families with at least one European species

Divers (Gaviidae): Approximately goose-sized, slim diving birds with pointed bill and webbed feet, well back on the body; lie deep in the water, remain submerged for long periods. In flight appear rather hunched, with neck held low. Juv. uniformly dark.
.... page 72

Grebes (Podicipedidae): Duck-sized diving birds with narrow, pointed bill; lobed feet positioned well back on body. Appear tailless. Fly seldom; dive frequently. Juv. with clearly striped down plumage.. page 74

Storm-petrels (Hydrobatidae): Small ocean birds, with fluttering or bouncing flight low over waves; mostly very dark with white rump. Hooked bill, with tube-shaped nostrils.................... page 78

Petrels and shearwaters (Procellariidae): Birds of the open sea, with long, narrow and usually stiffly held wings; very elegant in flight......:.. page 79

Cormorants (Phalacrocoracidae): Large, dark, water birds; bill with hooked tip. Feed on fish; often sit with wings extended. Resemble divers when swimming.. page 81

Herons (Ardeidae): Medium-sized to large birds with long legs and necks; medium-long pointed bill. Often stand motionless while awaiting prey. Neck held back in S-shape during flight, with head back towards shoulders. Wetlands.
.... page 82

Ibises and spoonbills (Threskiornithidae): Stork-like birds, but with curved or spoon-like flattened bill. Neck held stretched out during flight, like a stork's.. page 89

Storks (Ciconiidae): Large birds with long legs, long neck and long, straight bill. Majestic stride; neck stretched out during flight; glides for long periods. .... page 90

Waterfowl (Anatidae): Small to very large water birds with short legs and webbed feet: Swans (page 92): very large swimming birds with long, graceful neck; in Europe white. Geese (page 95): large water birds with long, thick necks, normally feeding on land; sexes similar. Shelduck (page 101): characteristics of geese and ducks. Dabbling ducks (page 102): most with noticeable wing speculum; dive only exceptionally, dabble in water; take off direct. Diving ducks (page 107): lack noticeable wing speculum; dive frequently for food; patter on water surface at take-off. Sawbills (page 119): narrow bill, hooked at tip and with saw-like teeth at edges; longer and narrower in shape than other ducks.

Swan

Goose

Dabbling Duck

Diving Duck

Sawbill

Osprey (Pandionidae): At least buzzard-sized bird of prey with pale underside and long, narrow, often angled wings; usually seen over lakes and rivers.. page 126

Hawks and eagles (Accipitridae): Small to very large birds of prey which capture and kill their (normally vertebrate) prey using talons; powerful bill, hooked at tip.................................... page 127

Harrier

Buzzard

Sparrowhawk

Falcons (Falconidae): Small to medium-sized birds of prey with long, pointed wings; round head with large, dark eyes; flight rapid and skilful, usually with shallow wing-beats; prey killed with bill.
.... page 142

Grouse (Tetraonidae): Medium-sized to large ground-dwelling birds with feathered feet and legs; tails not particularly long. Many are woodland species. .... page 150

Pheasants (Phasianidae): Small to medium-sized game birds with unfeathered legs; tail either short (partridges, Quail), or very long (Pheasant). Open habitats, mountains.................... page 154

Pheasant

Grey Partridge

Rails (Rallidae): Small to medium-sized hen-like ground birds with laterally compressed bodies and often with long toes; many species are shy birds of marshy habitats and are hardly ever seen. Coot is a less shy water bird. .... page 157

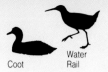

Coot   Water
Rail

Bustards (Otididae): Medium-sized to very large, powerful ground birds, found in steppe or cultivated steppe regions, ♂ usually > than ♀... page 163

Cranes (Gruidae): Very large heron- or stork-like ground birds with long neck and long legs; bill is, however, relatively short. In flight (often V-formation) neck and legs held stretched out. Characteristic loud trumpeting call.
.... page 164

Oystercatchers (Haematopodidae): Medium-sized black and white waders with long red bill. .... page 168

Stone-curlews (Burhinidae): Large, powerful waders with long, stocky legs, powerful bill and large eyes; protectively coloured; mainly crepuscular and nocturnal. .... page 169

Stilts and avocets (Recurvirostridae): Medium-sized, in Europe black and white; waders with long to very long legs and long neck; much slimmer and longer-legged than Oystercatcher.
.... page 170

Plovers (Charadriidae): Rather squat, small to medium-sized waders with large eyes and short, powerful bill; feed mainly by pecking... page 172

Sandpipers (Scolopacidae): Small to large waders, most with long legs and long (sometimes decurved) bill; mostly coastal and wetland birds. Feed mainly by probing. .... page 179

Skuas (Stercorariidae): Large, mostly dark-coloured seabirds, in flight reminiscent of gulls or birds of prey; wings narrow and normally held angled. Juv. without extended tail feathers are difficult to identify.. page 201

Gulls (Laridae): Slim long-winged seabirds (some species also inland) with mainly white or grey plumage; some species with dark upperside, dark facial mask or black wing tips............... page 203

Terns (Sternidae): Slimmer, more graceful and with shorter legs than gulls, many species white with a black cap; bill usually thin and pointed. Often hover and dive steeply when feeding; unlike gulls, swim rarely... page 210

Auks (Alcidae): Short-necked seabirds with feet set well back, short, narrow wings and pointed bill; skilful divers; sit upright when on land. Colonial... page 217

Pigeons and Doves (Columbidae): Small to medium-sized, small-headed birds with rounded appearance. Feed mainly on the ground; flight often rapid. Typical cooing call.................. page 224

Cuckoos (Cuculidae): Slim, long-tailed birds with two forward-pointing and two backward-pointing toes. Flight pattern like the Sparrowhawk. Characteristic call. .... page 229

Typical owls (Strigidae): Mostly twilight and night hunters with large forward-directed eyes; hooked bill; sharp, pointed talons. Feathers on face arranged to form discs. Some species with obvious 'ear' tufts. Silent flight... page 230

Barn owls (Tytonidae): Light-coloured, long-legged owls with heart-shaped facial discs and relatively small, dark eyes; underside of wings very pale in flight. .... page 239

Swifts (Apodidae): Larger than swallows but with similar flight pattern; wings long and sickle-shaped, tail short; blackish plumage. Flight very rapid; rarely seen perched. .... page 240

Nightjars (Caprimulgidae): Crepuscular and nocturnal insect-hunters with long narrow wings and long tail; eyes large and dark, bill short; bark-coloured plumage. By day sit motionless on the ground or lengthways on a branch. .... page 242

Kingfishers (Alcedinidae): Beautifully coloured birds with large head, long powerful beak and short legs. Single European species (sparrow-sized), feeds on fish and breeds in nest holes dug in steep stream banks. .... page 243

Bee-eaters (Meropidae): Slim, attractively coloured aerial feeders with pointed, slightly decurved bill. Flight swallow-like, often gliding on broadly spread wings. One species in Europe.
.... page 244

Rollers (Coraciidae): Brightly coloured birds with Jay-like appearance; powerful bill; hunt a wide range of insects in shrike-like manner. One species in Europe. .... page 245

Hoopoe (Upupidae): Unmistakable. Large, erectile crest; thin decurved bill; striking black and white wings. One species in Europe. .... page 246

Woodpeckers (Picidae): Small to medium-sized tree-living birds with powerful pecking bill and stiff tail feathers used as a prop. Frequently drum on hard branches during breeding season. One species, the Wryneck, is bark-coloured and behaves unlike other woodpeckers. .... page 247

Larks (Alaudidae): Mainly striped, brownish songbirds, living mostly on the ground; sexes normally similar; striking, sometimes beautiful songs. .... page 260

Swallows (Hirundinidae): Slim and rather small songbirds with long, pointed wings; hunt insects in flight; beak and feet small.
.... page 264

Wagtails and pipits (Motacillidae): Mainly ground-living songbirds, adept at walking and running (they do not hop). Wagtails with long or very long tail and long legs. Pipits with average tail length, brown striped plumage with white outer tail feathers; striking song-flights. .... page 268

Wagtail

Pipit

Waxwings (Bombycillidae): Very sociable birds, starling-like in shape and behaviour and brown-grey-looking from a distance; noticeable erectile crest. One European species. .... page 275

Dippers (Cinclidae): Starling-sized songbirds with dumpy, wren-like appearance. Breed near fast-flowing rivers and feed mainly under water; bob frequently. One species in Europe. .... page 276

Wrens (Troglodytidae): Small, brownish, insectivorous songbirds; finely barred tail often held upright; striking calls and song. One species in Europe. .... page 277

Accentors (Prunellidae): Unobtrusive songbirds, strongly reminiscent of sparrows, but with thin, pointed bill. Two species in Europe, one only in high mountains. .... page 278

Thrushes and allies (Muscicapidae): Small to medium-sized songbirds with relatively long legs and thin, insect-eating bill; often with loud, attractive songs; feed mostly on the ground. Includes: robins (page 280), flycatchers (page 284), redstarts (page 288), stonechats (page 290), wheatears (page 292), rock thrushes (page 293), thrushes (page 294).

Thrush   Chat

Flycatcher   Redstart

Warblers (Sylviidae): Small, mostly drab-coloured, insectivorous songbirds with thin bill; many species hard to identify, except by their song. Includes: reed warblers (also Grasshopper Warbler, Savi's Warbler, Cetti's Warbler, Icterine and Melodious Warblers; page 300), scrub warblers (page 307), leaf warblers (page 312).

Leaf warbler

Acrocephalus warbler   *Sylvia* warbler

Goldcrests (Regulidae): Very small, delicate insectivores with olive-green plumage and conspicuous head markings; live mostly in coniferous trees. Two species in Europe................... page 316

Reedlings (Panuridae): Songbirds with long, rounded tails, living in reedbeds or thick scrub; build bowl-shaped nests. Characteristic direct whirring flight and nasal calls. One species in Europe. .... page 318

Long-tailed tits (Aegithalidae): Small, insectivorous songbirds with very long tails and unusually small bill; accomplished acrobats amongst thin twigs; flock outside breeding season. One species in Europe. .... page 319

Tits (Paridae): Small, rotund songbirds with short bills, active and acrobatic feeders amongst foliage; breed in holes. Often in mixed-species flocks during winter. .... page 320

Nuthatches (Sittidae): Small, dumpy songbirds with strong woodpecker-like bill and short tail; climb up and down tree trunks using their powerful feet. One species in northern Europe.
.... page 326

Wallcreeper (Tichodromadidae): Sparrow-sized songbird with long, thin decurved bill; rounded wings with striking red and white markings. Only one species worldwide, found in high mountains.
.... page 327

Treecreepers (Certhiidae): Small songbirds with narrow, curved bills and plumage patterned like tree bark; climb up tree trunks and branches. The two European species are very similar.
.... page 328

Penduline tits (Remizidae): Small tit-like songbirds with pointed bills. Single European species easily identified by its black mask and brown back; builds elaborate nest. .... page 330

Orioles (Oriolidae): Thrush-sized songbirds; ♂ of most species have striking yellow plumage. Live mainly in Africa and southern Asia; one species in Europe. .... page 331

Shrikes (Laniidae): Large songbirds with striking plumage and bills hooked at the tip; behave rather like birds of prey; sit-and-wait predators. Store surplus food by impaling on thorns or wedging on a branch. .... page 332

Crows (Corvidae):   The largest songbirds by far; powerful bill; most with black plumage; raucous calls, no true song, but often well-developed ability to mimic. .. page 336

Crow

Magpie

Starlings (Sturnidae):   Thrush-sized birds with long, pointed bill and short tail; feed on ground; move with a wobbly walk (they do not hop); very sociable, lively and often noisy.................. page 344

Sparrows (Passeridae): Mostly plain-coloured, sturdy songbirds with finch-like bill; often very sociable and noisy. Three species in central and northern Europe, of which one (Snow Finch) is found only in high mountains....................................... page 345

Finches (Fringillidae): Typical seed-eaters with small, finely pointed to large, heavy bills; plumage often brightly coloured, ♀ usually drabber; many different species............................ page 348

Hawfinch

Chaffinch

Buntings (Emberizidae):   Finch-like, rather elongated songbirds with relatively short, thick bills, feeding mainly on seeds. ♂ usually more striking marked than ♀. Habitat often open landscapes with scattered trees and bushes... page 362

Eggs and Clutches

The eggs of birds are closed capsules containing everything required for development up to the stage of the hatching. Unlike the eggs of other animals, birds' eggs are surrounded by a hard shell.

Birds' eggs are not all like the typical hen's egg: owls' eggs for instance are almost spherical, while swifts' eggs are elliptic. The eggs of the Guillemot narrow very sharply towards the tip at one end. These birds nest on open cliff ledges, off which a normally shaped egg would easily roll; their special shape means they tend to roll about their own axis instead. Waders also have sharply tapered eggs. Normally a wader clutch consists of four eggs, arranged with the pointed ends facing the centre of the nest, in a four-leafed clover pattern. It is only in this way that these relatively large eggs can be successfully incubated.

Some bird species, for example Guillemot, Razorbill and Gannet, lay just one egg. Most small birds, however, have clutches of 2–6, tits perhaps 6–10, with game birds having particularly large clutches, partridges claiming the record with as many as 22 eggs.

The number of broods a year also varies and, although the larger species

Previous page: Ringed Plover's clutch is difficult to spot against the sand, as the eggs are well camouflaged.

Complete clutch of Mute Swan (below left) consists of 5–7 eggs, each about 11 cm long. Their colour varies from pale blue-grey to light greenish. At first they are dull, but become shiny towards the end of the incubation period, and the young hatch after about 34–38 days.

The greenish eggs of the Eider (below right) nestle in a cushion of down. The female broods the eggs for 25–26 days. The Kestrel (bottom left) lays 4–6 rounded eggs, with red-brown spots. They are incubated mainly by the female for about 4 weeks.

The Coot (bottom right) lays dark brown spotted eggs, incubated by both sexes for around 3 weeks.

Little Ringed Plovers commonly nest on gravel or sand banks (above left). The eggs of the Lapwing (above right) are equally well camouflaged. In Barn Owls the clutch varies between 3 and 10, reflecting the availability of prey (right). Pied Flycatchers lay 5–7 blue-green eggs (below left). Song Thrush eggs are a beautiful intense light blue (below right). Icterine Warbler clutch (bottom left). Great Tit clutch (bottom right).

Nuthatch eggs are delicately spotted and speckled reddish-brown, especially at the blunt end; they are laid on a layer of thin leaves or pine bark (above left). The 4–6 eggs of the Chaffinch (above right) are a shiny light blue, usually spotted reddish or brownish. Hawfinch eggs (left) have heavy spots and delicate scribbles on a light blue or grey-green background. The markings are often concentrated at the blunt end.

have one brood, smaller birds may breed as many as four times in a season. With each brood the size of the clutch decreases, presumably reflecting the decrease in available food.

Many birds' eggs are white. This is especially true for those that nest in holes, such as woodpeckers and owls, whose eggs need no camouflage protection. However, the eggs of certain species that nest in the open, such as some pigeons and ducks, are also white. The ducks camouflage their eggs by covering them with nest material.

In contrast the eggs of most ground-nesting species with open nests, such as gulls, terns and plovers, are heavily patterned, as are those of ground-nesting song-birds such as larks and pipits. Dunnock and Song Thrush have beautiful bright blue eggs. Both these species hide their nests in thick bushes or young trees, so the eggs are not conspicuous. The Cuckoo has developed a highly unusual way of breeding: it lays its eggs in the nests of other species, where they are brooded by the foster parents (brood parasitism). In many cases the Cuckoo's eggs match those of the host quite closely, although they are usually somewhat larger. There are, however, exceptions – no blue Cuckoo eggs have yet been found in Dunnocks' nests, but in spite of this the eggs are accepted by Dunnocks and the young Cuckoos are successfully reared by them.

Chaffinch

House Sparrow

Linnet

Goldfinch

Greenfinch

Yellowhammer

Skylark

Tree Pipit

Tree Pipit

White Wagtail

Treecreeper

Short-toed
Treecreeper

Nuthatch

Great Tit

Blue Tit

Marsh Tit

Long-tailed Tit

Spotted Flycatcher

Red-backed Shrike

Great Grey Shrike

Icterine Warbler

Goldcrest

Chiffchaff

Willow Warbler

Wood Warbler

Reed Warbler

Marsh Warbler

Blackcap

Lesser Whitethroat

Great Reed Warbler

Nightingale

Wheatear

Redstart

Black Redstart

Whinchat

Robin

Swift

Dipper

Nightjar

Swallow

House Martin

Dunnock

Wren

Song Thrush

Blackbird

Golden Oriole

Jay

Magpie

Jackdaw

Starling

Lapwing

Snipe

Carrion Crow

Little Ringed Plover

Common Sandpiper

Common Tern

Kestrel

Sparrowhawk

Buzzard

Hobby

Honey Buzzard

Moorhen

Black Kite

Grey Partridge

Coot

Pheasant

Herring Gull

Black-headed Gull

Oystercatcher

30

Nests and Nest Holes

Nests protect birds from enemies and from the weather (cold, wet and heat). In some cases they also give the young birds security. Other animals, including some mammals and insects, also make nests, but most nests found in woods or in other vegetation are made by birds. Birds' nests are most often seen in winter when they become visible in the bare trees and bushes. Then they can be inspected and identified, and the species which have nested, for example at the edge of a wood or in a hedge, can be verified.

In spring and summer, when eggs and the young are in the nest, they should not be approached, let alone inspected. This can be extremely disturbing. Nest-robbers, such as Magpies, may even be attracted to a nest by our presence.

Previous Page: The stable nest of the Reed Warbler consists of grass and stalks: the sides are woven on to upright reed stems so that it moves with them in windy conditions, and can even withstand fierce storms.

Top left: *A Kittiwake builds its nest on a narrow cliff ledge.* Top right: A large Coot nest – it is often built on shallow water. Above Left: *Mute Swans building a huge nest, as often on an ornamental lake.* Above right: *The Great Crested Grebe covers its eggs before it leaves the nest.* Left: *Eider nests covered in insulating down.*

The loose nest of a Blackcap (above left), woven on to twigs. Above right: The Marsh Warbler's preference for nesting in nettles. Nest of Hawfinch (right) is usually better hidden than this. Below left: Song Thrush nest. Below right: Blackbirds often build right next to houses. Bottom left: Red-backed Shrike's nest is well hidden in a thorn bush. Bottom right: Chaffinch nest.

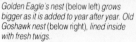

The edges of the Golden Oriole's nest (top left) are slung around the supporting branches. Top right: Swallows build only inside buildings. Above left: Grey herons nest colonially in tall trees. Above right: Nest of Marsh Harrier, in extensive reedbed. The

Golden Eagle's nest (below left) grows bigger as it is added to year after year. Old Goshawk nest (below right), lined inside with fresh twigs.

Black Storks nest only in a few large tracts of forest in central Europe. The large nest (right) is usually sited high in the tree canopy, in a strong fork in the trunk. Like many birds of prey, the nest is added to each year and may eventually become very large.

Rooks also nest high in the trees (centre). They breed in colonies spanning neighbouring trees, in open cultivated country. Both sexes help to build the nest which may be used from year to year and improved each season.

Magpies build their large, roofed nests (below) in tall hedges, avenues, in trees at the woodland edge, or in isolated trees in open country. They are made using large twigs, consolidated in places with earth.

Each bird species builds a particular type of nest, according to its requirements. This variety is a prime example of adaptation to the environment, and nest type certainly cannot be taken as a guide to the close relationship between the individual species concerned. For example, the Swallow and Sand Martin are closely related, yet their nests are quite different. Whereas the Swallow builds a shallow cup-shaped nest inside a building, the Sand Martin digs a burrow up to 1 metre long in a steep bank.

Two aspects of nests that need to be examined are their siting and construction. Many species nest on the ground, in meadows, farmland, fields, on bogs and other wetlands (for instance most ducks, all game birds and waders). Some birds, such as the Nightjar, make no nest at all, laying their eggs directly on the ground, or, in the case of some owls, on the bare wood at the base of a nest hole. Grebes, Coots and Mute Swans construct floating nests on still water.

Most species – for example the smaller birds, crows and birds of prey, and all our pigeon and woodpecker species – breed in bushes and trees. Vulnerable small species rely particularly on concealing their nests to avoid attack by predators.

The survival of the brood depends both upon the site of the nest and its construction. The majority of European birds build cup-shaped nests, varying in depth from species

The Wren makes a spherical, moss nest with thick walls (above left), often nestling amongst the roots of a fallen tree. Both the male and female Dipper build their large, roofed moss nest, almost always sited on the bank of a fast-flowing stream (above right). The oval nest of the Long-tailed Tit is camouflaged on the outside with lichens (left). Penduline Tit's nest hangs freely, woven into the thin outer twigs of a willow tree. The extended entrance tunnel (below right) is characteristic; in the basket stage (below left) it is not yet completed.

to species. Wren, Dipper, leaf warblers, Long-tailed Tit and the Penduline Tit build closed nests with a side entrance. The latter two species are master-builders whose nests really are works of art. Many pigeons raise their young in flat twig nests, while crows and Jays make more stable twig nests, and Goshawks, Golden Eagles and Ospreys nest on large mounds of twigs. Small birds make a new nest for each brood, whereas herons and the larger birds of prey often keep their nests in good repair throughout the year.

Many bird species nest in holes, where they are better protected from predators and the weather. Examples are woodpeckers, tits, Nuthatch and Starling, as well as Stock Dove, Hoopoe, owls and certain ducks. However, only the woodpeckers and the Willow Tit regularly excavate their own holes, thereby providing sites for other species as well. Some birds, such as Tengmalm's Owl and the Pygmy Owl, rely almost entirely on woodpecker holes for nest sites.

Some birds for example House Sparrow, tits, redstarts, Wallcreeper and Swift, also nest in rock crevices, or in cavities in buildings. Kingfishers, Bee-eaters and Sand Martins dig out their own earth tunnels for their nests, which may then be used for many years.

Unlike Swallows, House Martins nest on the outside of buildings (above). They build the mud nest so close under the roof that just a small hole remains as an entrance.

Nuthatches (below) have a clever way of keeping larger hole competitors away from their nests. They make the entrance narrower by applications of mud until the hole is wide enough for themselves alone. Nest-boxes used by Nuthatches are often difficult to open, because the birds tend to stick mud along these joins as well.

Above: *Sand Martins breed in colonies and excavate long tunnels in a steep bank. The entrance holes are oval (below left).*

Kingfishers *nest in vertical banks of streams and rivers, usually 1–4 m above the water surface (below right).*

Young Birds

Most people seem particularly helpless when confronted by a young bird; they do not know what kind it is, still less what to do with it. Young birds from the most important groups are illustrated on the following pages, so that any young bird found can be identified to this extent. It should be possible to tell whether it is a bird of prey, an owl, pigeon, gull, duck, wader, or songbird. However precise species identification of young birds is often a difficult matter, even for the expert.

The photographs in this chapter should on no account encourage disturbance of wild birds, at the nest or of adults feeding young. On no account should birds be captured, with an attempt to rear them at home.

If young birds are alone in the nest this does not mean they have been abandoned, but that their parents are hunting for food for their offspring. Fledglings make characteristic begging or contact calls to alert their parents to their needs. When they can fly properly they follow the adult birds and go to them when they bring food.

If a fledgling is found in the middle of a path or street, carry it carefully to a nearby safe spot, such as the highest branch you can reach of a tree or bush, safe from passers-by and, hopefully, cats. But, if you know where it came from, the young bird should be returned close to the nest where its parents will usually continue to feed it. In rare cases, when the bird

Previous page: *Young Long-eared Owl.*
Below left: *Young Greylag Geese accompanied by both parents, although they can feed themselves from the start.*
Below right: *Shelduck chicks leave their nest burrow straightaway.* Bottom left: *The down of this newly hatched Mallard chick is still wet, but it soon dries and the chick can swim* (bottom right), *being fledged in 7–8 weeks.*

Honey Buzzards often decorate their nests with fresh twigs. The young initially have a pale downy plumage (above left), becoming increasingly dark as the contour feathers grow (above right). The photograph right captures them just before flying. Young falcons have two stages of downy plumage. The young Kestrels in the nest-box (below right) are beginning to show their first true feathers. Below left: A young Kestrel in the second stage.

head and bill colours. Young waders are typical of nidifugous birds. An adult keeps a lookout while a young Oystercatcher feeds (below left). Young Little Ringed Plovers (below right) at 2 days old blend in well with their gravelly background. Newly-hatched Curlews (bottom left), and Snipe a few hours old (bottom right).

These young Hazel Grouse (above left) are just 4 days old. Their mother indicates suitable food by pecking at it. Young rails have black down. Some species, such as the Moorhen (above right), have striking

Kittiwakes (above left) nest high on cliffs, so their young have to stay in the nest until they can fly. However, the young of other gulls and terns leave their nest after a day or two, and hide nearby. This newly hatched Lesser Black-backed Gull (above right) still shows the egg-tooth on its pink bill tip.
Arctic Terns (right) feed their chicks on young fish.

Above left: A nestling Stock Dove.
Young pigeons and doves are nidicolous, like young songbirds. At first they are fed on so-called 'crop-milk' from the adult bird's gullet. On day nine the eyes of these young Tawny Owls (above right) are beginning to open. At about 4 weeks old, usually around the middle of May, they leave the dangers of the nest-hole and clamber on to nearby branches (right); they are still fed by their parents for several weeks.

has really been abandoned, or cannot be returned, it should be given to an expert since rearing fledglings is difficult and often unsuccessful, requiring great effort and skill.

There are two different kinds of nestlings: nidifugous (which leave the nest soon after hatching) and nidicolous (which stay in the nest after hatching). Nidifugous species hatch with their eyes open, are already covered in down, and can walk. Young birds of this type are called precocial. They often leave the nest after one or two days and many of them immediately start feeding for themselves. In some species (such as game birds) the chicks are directed towards particular food by their parents. In some other species, such as gulls, terns and nightjars, the precocial young remain in or near the nest for some days, even though they can walk.

Nidicolous species hatch in a much less developed state and remain in the nest for a longer period. They are incapable of locomotion and are known as altricial. With the

Above left: A Tawny Owl. The young of larger owls only gradually become independent, and depend on their parents for about 2 months after fledging.
Young Barn Owls (above right) already have the characteristic heart-shaped facial disc at an early age.

exception of a few groups whose young can see, most nidicolous young birds are initially blind, and are either naked or have a partial downy covering. They depend entirely on their parents for food and warmth until they are ready to leave the nest. When their parents land on the rim of the nest with food, the young respond to even the slightest vibration by stretching up their necks and holding their beaks high. In all songbirds the nestling's oral cavity and its gape flanges are brightly coloured, and the stretching behaviour, combined with the pattern on the inside of the mouth, is the signal for the parent birds to offer food.

Above left: *Young Yellowhammer, and above right young Woodlarks, each a few days old. The Woodlark nestlings, right, will soon leave the nest.*

Young Skylarks (below left) leave the nest before they are able to fly. Below right: Swallows about to leave the nest. Bottom left: Young Wrens which have just left the nest. Bottom right: Young Robins before they have acquired the red breast.

Juvenile Redstart (top left) *is considerably paler than the juvenile Black Redstart. The nestling that is hungriest and stretches up first gets fed first (top right* is a Song Thrush). Above left: These young Blue Tits *are almost fledged and will soon leave their nest-box. Checking the nest-box now might cause them to flutter out, unmonitored by their parents.* Above right: Young Carrion Crows *beg like all young songbirds; the inside of the mouth is a bright red.* Left: This *young Greenfinch still has traces of nestling down on its head. It has just left the nest, is unable to fly properly, and is still dependent upon its parents.*

Signs

Many birds provide visible clues to their feeding behaviour. By studying these signs we not only gain an insight into their feeding habits, but establish which species are inhabiting certain areas. In a book of this size it is clearly not possible to look at the feeding signs of all species, but the following examples should kindle an interest in this fascinating study. As ever, do take care not to disturb birds when studying them in their natural habitats.

Excavations made by woodpeckers can often be found, particularly in old and rotten wood. Unlike the characteristic circular or oval holes that these birds excavate for their nests, damage caused when they are looking for insect grubs in wood is often extensive and untidy.

One often finds cones that show signs of having been fed on by birds. The Great Spotted Woodpecker has a special technique – it hacks off the cone and carries it in its beak to a cleft in the bark (known as an anvil), where it firmly wedges it in. If the cleft is not big enough the bird widens it with well-directed pecks until the cone just fits. It treats hazel-nuts in the same way. Some woodpeckers leave additional signs: they peck out horizontal lines of holes in the bark and lap up the sap that oozes out. The Great Spotted Woodpecker does this on a wide variety of different species, but the Three-toed Woodpecker usually selects healthy old spruce.

Song Thrushes use certain sites in woods or gardens to smash open snail shells (Song Thrush anvil page 49)

Previous page: Great Spotted Woodpeckers often feed on Spruce seeds in winter. To work the cones they wedge them in a cleft in the bark, often one they have made themselves. The cleft is known as a 'woodpecker anvil'. *Many birds find other eggs a tasty morsel, and crows often plunder other birds' clutches, especially in spring. Below: A Song Thrush's clutch after an attack by a Jay.*

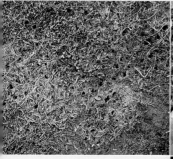

Above left: *Starlings poke their bills in the ground when feeding, leaving tell-tale small holes.* Above right: *Song Thrushes use stones to break open snail shells.* Right: *An anthill opened up by a Green Woodpecker. Red-backed Shrikes impale their prey on thorns or barbed wire – a young bird (below left), a vole (bottom left), and a bumblebee (below right). In this way they can lay down provisions for leaner times.*

Above left: *House Sparrows have shredded and frayed the leaves of this maize cob to get at the corn – droppings are clearly visible. A maize cob which has been stripped by Pheasants (above right). Left: The red berries of this firethorn have been eaten by Bullfinches, which were after the seeds.*
Flocks of House Sparrows often feed on ripe cereals – these ears of wheat (below left) show clear sings of attack. Below right: Dandelion seeds, a favourite of Goldfinches.

Top left: *Nutcrackers split hazel nuts into two.* Top right: *These seeds of Arolla Pine, also opened by Nutcrackers.* Above left: *Crossbills split the individual scales from Spruce cones.* Above right: *One often finds* *several opened nut shells below a Great Spotted Woodpecker's anvil. Black Woodpecker feeding holes* (below left and right) *are mostly low down on the trunk.*

Left: *Black Woodpeckers often dismantle tree stumps to get at ants' nests. In Spring Three-toed Woodpeckers frequently feed on tree sap, pecking horizontal rows of holes in the bark (below right). Great Spotted Woodpeckers peck open scales from cones to get at the seeds underneath (centre left): one often finds many cones underneath an anvil (bottom).*

and one often comes across collections of empty snail shells as evidence.

The feeding habits of shrikes are particularly noteworthy. The Red-backed Shrike, which is extinct as a breeding species in Britain, but can still be found across Europe, impales surplus food on thorns or barbed wire. It stores mice and young birds in this way, as well as its main food, large insects (page 49). The Great Grey Shrike feeds mainly on mice and small birds in winter, and prefers to wedge them in the angle of a branch, rather than to impale them.

Feather Remains

Birds of prey have to pluck their victims, at least partially, before eating them, to remove the indigestible feathers. They therefore carry their prey, if it is light enough, to a particular spot, the plucking site. Most of the large tail and flight feathers are pulled out using the bill, leaving clearly visible marks on the lower part of the feather shaft. The rest of the feathers, are more or less left undamaged. Another sign left by birds of prey is seen on the breastbone. They normally start eating in this area, where there is the most flesh, in the process hacking small pieces off the edge of the bone as they feed, leaving telltale signs behind.

If the feathers look as if they have been cut off with scissors this is usually the work of a fox or marten. They bite off many feathers at once, often even the whole tail. They may also leave behind droppings or in the case of a fox, its unmistakable, pungent smell. Whereas it is relatively easy to decide whether a bird or mammal made the kill, it is by no means so easy to identify which species of bird made the attack on the basis of the remains. For example, female Sparrowhawks and male

Previous page: Sparrowhawks like to pluck their prey at a site in cover in a woodland clearing, at the forest edge, or in a small copse. Here the victim was a Hawfinch.

Three examples of Goshawk kills. Top left: Sparrowhawks occasionally fall victim to Goshawks. Although the picture shows Fox droppings, the ripped out feathers show that a Fox did not make the kill. In some areas pigeons and doves make up as much as 50 per cent of the Goshawk's diet – centre left shows the remains of a Woodpigeon. Besides pigeons and doves, European Goshawks take many Jays – here (right) the head and characteristic blue, black and white wing-covert feathers can be clearly seen.

Peregrines take almost exclusively flying birds. Right: Woodpigeon feathers and the wing of a small bird. Below left: The red mandible and black and white primaries from a Black-headed Gull, probably killed by a Goshawk or Peregrine. Below right: A Hooded Crow apparently killed by a Fox because the feathers have been bitten out several at a time. Remains of a Long-eared Owl (bottom left), probably killed by a bird of prey. Remains of a Lapwing (bottom right), a wader often killed by Goshawks or Peregrines.

Goshawks can catch similar-sized prey, and both use plucking posts.

Most plucking sites do tend to be the work of Sparrowhawks or Goshawks. On the other hand the Hobby plucks its prey in tree branches, so most of the feathers are carried away in the wind. The much rarer Peregrine uses exposed rocky outcrops or sites out in the open.

Top: Members of the crow family often fall victim to Goshawks. These are Magpie feathers – shiny green and black and white. The Goshawk's white droppings can also be seen to the top and the left of the picture. Above: Sparrowhawks first carry their victims into cover to hide them from competitors. These birds of prey have their favourite plucking sites on tree-stumps or similar raised areas close to the nest. The remains of this Great Spotted Woodpecker contain a few red undertail-coverts, as well as the characteristic white-spotted wing feathers.

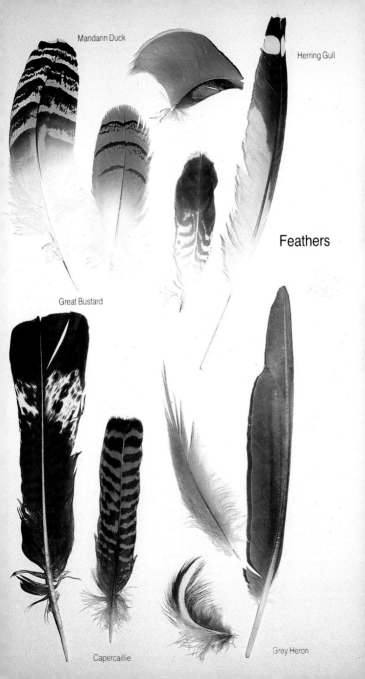

Mandarin Duck

Herring Gull

Feathers

Great Bustard

Capercaillie

Grey Heron

All birds have feathers, which are unique in the animal kingdom. Feathers are the most complicated organs of the skin, and the most varied in function. They have evolved over millions of years from simple reptilian scales in a way that is still not well understood. Feathers are light and yet very strong, elastic and resistant. They protect against cold, wet, heat and injury, help to camouflage the bird, and provide the supporting surfaces for flight. Despite enormous technological progress, no artificial material has yet been produced that can match a feather's different qualities.

Feathers give birds their characteristic body shape and appearance. They carry the colour and patterns which are the basis of communication between individuals of a species, and at the same time they enable the birdwatcher to identify species. However, it is not easy to identify a bird from a single feather and in many cases it is not possible. On the other hand some feather are very characteristic, for example the bright blue patterned wing-coverts of the Jay, the up-curved tail feathers of the drake Mallard, the Blackcock's lyre-shaped outer tail feathers, and the sail-like wing feathers of the drake Mandarin.

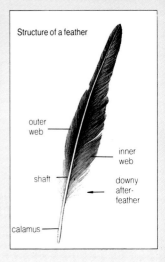

Structure of a feather

outer web

inner web

shaft

downy after-feather

calamus

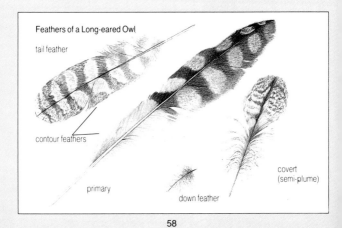

Feathers of a Long-eared Owl

tail feather

contour feathers

primary

down feather

covert (semi-plume)

Cuckoo

Kestrel

Honey Buzzard

Montagu's
Harrier

Buzzard

Goshawk

Sparrowhawk

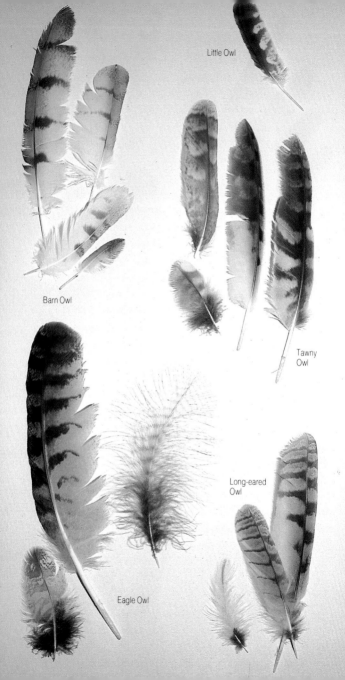

Little Owl

Barn Owl

Tawny Owl

Long-eared Owl

Eagle Owl

Green Woodpecker

Great Spotted
Woodpecker

Jay

Hoopoe

Nutcracker

Wood pigeon

Collared Dove

Lapwing

Greenfinch

Golden Oriole

Redstart

Goldfinch

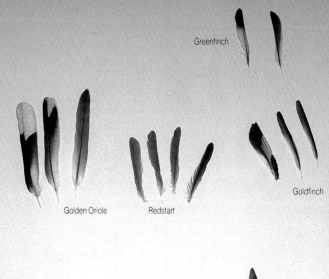

Rock Partridge

Song Thrush

Grey Partridge

Pheasant

Black
Grouse

Ptarmigan

Pellets and Droppings

Pellets

After feeding, many birds regurgitate the indigestible remains of hair, feathers, chitin and bones as pellets. The pellets are coated with mucus to assist their passage through the oesophogus; this covering dries rapidly on exposure to the air.

Whereas most birds' pellets quickly distintegrate, owl pellets and those of certain birds of prey are relatively stable. Since their diet includes rodents, the pellets last much long being held together by the victims' fur. The bones of small animals

and birds are often amazingly well preserved inside owl pellets, and experts are frequently able to identify precisely on which species the owl has been feeding by examining these remnants. Pellet analysis is particularly useful as evidence of the distribution and frequency of particular species of small mammals, and it also gives ornithologists precise information about the feeding ecology of different owl and raptor species.

Previous page: Partridge droppings can be found in open fields. To identify prey animals in pellets. the latter first have to be teased apart. to reveal the bones (below left). The jaw bones of small mammals are of most interest, since the individual species can be identified using a hand-lens or microscope.

Barn Owl pellets (below right) contain jaws and other bones of field mice and shrews. Grey Heron pellets (bottom left) are found mainly beneath the nest trees. White Storks digest the bones as well, so their pellets do not contain bones (bottom right).

Above left: *Buzzard pellet with matted hairs.*
Above right: *Honey Buzzard pellet showing beetle wing-cases.* Right: *Kestrel pellets taper towards one end.* Below left: *Black-headed Gull pellets with chitinous material.* Below right: *A Herring Gull pellet with remains of bivalves.* Bottom left: *Long-eared Owl pellets can often be found underneath their roosts.* Bottom right: *Tawny Owl pellets.*

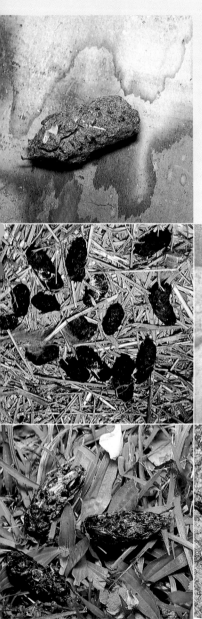

Little Owl pellets (left) are about 3–5 cm long and contain mostly chitin and rodent hair. Barn Owl pellets (below left) are relatively large (up to 8 cm) and bulky, and shiny when fresh. Songbird pellets contain mainly chitin from insects: below right is a Spotted Flycatcher pellet. bottom left are Red-backed Shrike pellets. Great Grey Shrike pellets (bottom right) are quite different. resembling small owl pellets. The teeth and bones of the rodent prey can be clearly seen. The Shrike also feeds on lizards and small birds, as well as large insects and young birds in summer.

Droppings

Bird droppings are normally cylindrical or drop-shaped, and, in species that regurgitate pellets, usually more or less liquid. The urine (uric acid in birds) appears as a white cap at the end of the dropping, or as a film covering the surface.

Heron droppings (right) are usually found below roosts or nests colonies. Below left: Greylag Goose droppings (length 5–8 cm) are a familiar sight on the banks of ornamental lakes. Pheasant droppings (below right) are about 2 cm long. Bottom left: Capercaillie droppings are long (up to 8 cm) and consist almost entirely of pine needles in winter. Bottom right: Wrynecks eat ants and produce well-shaped droppings.

Important Addresses

British Ornithologists' Union (BOU): c/o The British Museum (Natural History), Sub-department of Ornithology, Tring, Hertfordshire HP23 6AP.

British Trust for Ornithology (BTO): The Nunnery, Nunnery Place, Thetford, Norfolk IP26 2PU.

Irish Wildbird Conservancy (IWC): Ruttledge House, 8 Longford Place, Monkstown, Co. Dublin, Ireland.

International Council for Bird Preservation (ICBP): 32 Cambridge Road, Girton, Cambridge CB3 0PJ.

Royal Society for the Protection of Birds (RSPB): The Lodge, Sandy, Bedfordshire SG19 2DL.

Scottish Ornithologists' Club (SOC): 21 Regent Terrace, Edinburgh EH7 5BT, Scotland.

Wildfowl and Wetlands Trust (WWT): Slimbridge, Gloucester GL2 7BT.

There are also numerous county and regional birdwatching clubs and societies throughout Britain. For details, ask at your local library.

In addition, the independent journal *British Birds*, published monthly, covers a wide variety of topics and deals with the whole region of the Western Palaearctic. For details, write to: British Birds, Fountains, Park Lane, Blunham, Bedford MK44 3NJ.

Further Reading

Bruun, B., Delin, H. & Svensson, L. *The Hamlyn Guide to Birds of Britain and Europe* (London, 1987).

Campbell, B. & Ferguson-Lees, I.J. *A Field Guide to Birds' Nests* (London, 1972).

Campbell, B. & Lack, E. *A Dictionary of Birds* (Calton, 1985).

Cramp, S. *et al. The Birds of the Western Palaearctic Volumes 1–5* (6–7 in preparation) (Oxford 1977–).

Delin, H. & Svensson, L. *Photographic Guide to the Birds of Britain and Europe* (London, 1988).

Ferguson-Lees, J., Willis, I. & Sharrock, T. *The Shell Guide to the Birds of Britain and Ireland* (London, 1983).

Gooders, J. *Where to Watch Birds in Britain and Europe* (London, 1988).

Grant, P.J. *Gulls: A Guide to Identification* (2nd edition) (Calton, 1986).

Harris, A., Tucker, L. & Vinicombe, K. *The Macmillan Field Guide to Bird Identification* (London, 1989).

Harrison, C. *An Atlas of the Birds of the Western Palaearctic* (London, 1982).

Harrison, P. *Seabirds: An Identification Guide* (revised edition) (London, 1985).

Hayman, P., Marchant, J. & Prater, T. *Shorebirds: An Identification Guide to the Waders of the World* (London, 1986).

Hollom, P.A.D. *The Popular Handbook of British Birds* (5th revised edition) (London, 1988).

Lack, P. *The Atlas of Wintering Birds in Britain and Ireland* (Calton, 1986).

Madge, S.C. & Burn, H. *Wildfowl: An Identification Guide to the Ducks, Geese and Swans of the World* (London, 1987).

Peterson, R.T., Mountfort, G. & Hollom, P.A.D. *A Field Guide to the Birds of Britain and Europe* (2nd printing of 4th edition) (London, 1985)

Porter, R.F., Willis, I., Christensen, S. & Nielsen, B.P. *Flight Identification of European Raptors* (3rd edition) (Calton, 1981).

Sharrock, J.T.R. *The Atlas of Breeding Birds in Britain and Ireland* (Berkhamsted, 1976).

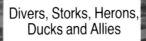
Divers, Storks, Herons,
Ducks and Allies

Divers – Gaviiformes

Divers are strictly aquatic, goose-sized waterbirds. The body is long and streamlined, the neck relatively long. Unlike grebes, divers have fully webbed front toes. The legs are attached so far back on the body that the birds can waddle forwards only with difficulty when on land (for instance when breeding). The nest is usually made on a small island, at most 1 m from the bank.

Divers land breast-first on the water, without using their feet. For take-off they need a long run-up and the larger species cannot take off from land at all. They feed mostly on fish, caught by diving. Sexes are similar and all species have a winter plumage and a summer, breeding plumage, while the juvenile birds are dark with no obvious markings. Divers fly more than grebes. Flight is rapid and direct, with the relatively small, pointed wings beating quickly and regularly. In flight they seem somewhat hump-backed because the neck is held low. All divers have striking calls.

There are five species altogether, four in Europe, of which three are seen regularly in Britain.

Grebes – Podicipediformes

The feet are placed well back on the body, as in the divers, and grebes also specialize in swimming and diving. Their toes are equipped with lobes at the sides (not webbed like divers). Most species have a thin, relatively long neck. The body seems rounded and tail-less.

Plumage is soft and fur-like. In the breeding season many grebe species have decorative tufts and crests on their heads and necks, which are lost in winter plumage when the birds are duller and paler.

The courtship, performed on the water, is often spectacular. Grebes usually build floating nests, anchored to vegetation. The young can swim from the first day, but are often protected in their parents' wing feathers and are fed by them. With their striped heads young grebes look very different from young divers. Five species can be seen in Europe.

Tubenoses – Procellariiformes

Birds of the open sea which come ashore only to breed. The most important feature is the tube-like extension of the external nasal openings. Upper mandible is hooked at the tip. Three front toes are webbed, while the hind toe points backwards or is missing altogether. Wings are long and narrow, and most species are excellent gliders over the waves. Although the smallest species (storm-petrels) are only a little larger than swallows, the largest (albatrosses) can have a 3.5 m wingspan. Only four species breed in north and central Europe.

Pelicans and Relatives (Pelecaniformes)

In addition to the pelicans, this order also contains the cormorant and gannet (booby) families. The most important character of the group is the webbing that unites all four toes.

Cormorants are dark, goose-sized waterbirds. They swim with their backs almost submerged, upright neck, and head and bill tilted upwards. They often sit upright, with wings stretched out to dry. They breed colonially mostly on cliffs or tall trees. In northern Europe there are two species, the Cormorant and the Shag.

The **Gannet** is a large, mainly white seabird, usually only seen far out at sea, and only coming to land to breed in huge colonies. It feeds by diving for fish, often from a great height. The wings are held very flat, unlike gulls. Juveniles are mainly brown and gradually acquire the adult plumage over a 4–5 year period.

Herons, Storks and Relatives – Ciconiiformes

This order contains long-legged birds that stalk their (animal) prey. When disturbed they usually fly.

Herons are distinguished in flight by their habit of tucking their heads into their shoulders, and making the neck appear S-shaped. Some species develop plumes on the head, neck or back during the breeding season.

Storks are large birds with long legs and they hold their necks outstretched in flight. They are accomplished gliders, making good use of thermals. Two species breed in Europe.

Ibises and spoonbills fly like storks with necks extended. The bill is either long and curved, or, in the sole northern European species, flattened and spoon-shaped.

Waterfowl – Anseriformes

This order contains some quite diverse groups of swimming birds, all of which have relatively short legs and webbed feet. The bill is usually covered with soft skin and has a hard, horny plate at its tip.

Swans are very large waterbirds with remarkably long necks. Juv. plumage is brownish or grey (rarely white) in the three European species. Adults pair for life.

Geese are large (usually larger than ducks), powerful swimming birds with long necks. Sexes similar, as in swans. Normally pair for life. Feed (mostly on plant material) almost entirely on land. Eight species in northern and central Europe.

Shelgeese and shelducks share characters of the geese and ducks. In north and central Europe there is a single species. (The Egyptian Goose *Alopochen aegyptiacus* was introduced to Britain in the 18th Century and occurs in Norfolk and elsewhere.)

Dabbling or surface-feeding ducks feed mainly by up-ending; they also feed at the surface and to some extent on land. Many species have a noticeable speculum, a coloured panel on the trailing edge of the wing. They swim high in the water and can take off almost vertically. Eight species in northern and central Europe.

Diving ducks have legs set far back and feed mainly by diving. They swim lower in the water than dabbling ducks and need a long run-up to take off. No obvious speculum. Ten species regularly seen in northern Europe, some only as winter visitors.

Sawbills are elongated diving ducks that feed mainly on fish. Their long, narrow, hooked bills have many saw-like teeth at the rim. Three species in Europe.

Stifftails are small, compact, diving ducks with large bills and long, stiff tails (frequently cocked). One introduced species in north and central Europe.

Black-throated Diver *Gavia arctica*
Family: Divers Gaviidae
F Plongeon arctique
G Prachttauler

Distinctive character: Unlike Red-throated Diver, bill straight and head usually held horizontally.
Features: Longer body and shorter neck than grebes, more compact appearance. In breeding plumage (photo), head and neck rather snake-like, back with striking black and white markings. In winter plumage (drawing), uniformly dark above, pale underneath, with clear border on head and neck; bill black; juv. in winter rather paler with light grey bill.
Voice: Seldom heard in winter; long drawn-out, eerie *ah-oo-ah*, and a mewing call when alarmed.
Occurrence: Breeds on large fish-rich lakes in northern Europe, including Scotland. In winter most often seen at sea near the coast: regular in North Sea and Baltic, more rarely on large inland lakes, usually as individuals.

Black-throated Diver,
winter

Behaviour: Needs long run-up to take off from water surface.
Food: In winter entirely fish.
Breeding habits: April-June, 1 brood; nests on islets at water's edge.

	> Mallard	R. W. M	I–XII	BR,WI

Red-throated Diver *Gavia stellata*
Family: Divers Gaviidae
F Plongeon catmarin
G Sterntaucher

Distinctive character: Slightly up-turned bill; head normally tilted upwards.

Features: Somewhat smaller than Black-throated Diver, with slimmer head, neck and bill. In breeding plumage (photo), with red-brown patch on neck, looking black from a distance. In winter (drawing), very like Black-throated, but back lighter because of sprinkling of fine white spots. Less distinct border between dark and pale colours on head and neck.

Voice: Occasional ringing *ah-oo-ah* in winter, in flight a goose-like *gag-gag-gag*.

Occurrence: Breeds in northern Europe, including Scotland, on small moorland lakes and on tundra; else-where seen mainly in winter, especially on North Sea coasts; rare but regular on inland lakes, reservoirs and larger rivers.

Red-throated Diver, winter

Food: In winter, fish.

Breeding habits: May-July, 1 brood; nests on islets or lakesides.

Great Northern Diver *Gavia immer*, which breeds in Iceland, is an uncommon winter visitor, mainly to North Sea and Channel coasts. Resembles Black-throated, but larger, with more powerful bill and more angular head.

> Mallard	R, W, M	I–XII	BR,WI	

Great Crested Grebe
Podiceps cristatus
Family: Grebes
Podicipedidae
F Grèbe huppé
G Haubentaucher

Distinctive character: Striking head and neck feathers in breeding season.

Features: In winter plumage (drawing), cheeks and front of neck white, dark cap, not reaching the eyes, leaving a clear white stripe above eye. Juv. with striped head and neck. Swims low in water.

Voice: Harsh *gruck-gruck*, hoarse *rah-rah* or trumpeting *air-air*, mostly in spring.

Occurrence: Widespread on larger lakes with reedy margins, sometimes on small lakes or reservoirs, even those with little or no bank vegetation. In winter often in flocks on large lakes, rivers and coasts.

Behaviour: Spring courtship dance on water easy to observe. Partners approach breast to breast with crests spread out, shaking heads. Very slim outline in flight.

Great Crested Grebe, winter

Food: Small fish, crustaceans and aquatic insects, tadpoles and small frogs.

Breeding habits: February–July, 1–2 broods; floating nest of plant material, usually hidden in reeds or rushes.

	– Mallard	R, W	I–XII	

Red-necked Grebe
Podiceps grisegena
Family:
Grebes-Podicipedidae
F Grèbe à joues grises
G Rothalstaucher

Distinctive character: More compact than Great Crested Grebe, with shorter, thicker neck.
Features: In breeding plumage (photo), neck rust-red, cheeks and throat whitish, bill black with yellow base. In winter plumage (drawing), very like Great Crested Grebe, but without white stripe over eye and with grey neck. Juv. paler with blackish stripes on white cheek.
Voice: In breeding display a loud, horse-like whinnying *oeerh* also at night; alarm call *eck eck eck*. Mostly silent in winter.

Occurrence: Breeds on lakes with wide reed fringe, often near Black-headed Gull colony. In winter on coasts and on large lakes. In Britain an uncommon winter visitor, though occasional individuals or pairs summer (may eventually breed).
Food: Aquatic insects, crustaceans,

Red-necked Grebe, winter

water snails, frogs, newts, small fish.
Breeding habits: May-July, 1 brood; nests near bank, usually hidden, but occasionally in the open.

< Great Crested Grebe	W, (S)	I–XII	BR	

Black-necked Grebe
Podiceps nigricollis
Family: Grebes
Podicipedidae
F Grèbe à cou noir
G Schwarzhalstaucher

Distinctive character: High forehead and gently upturned bill.
Features: Markedly smaller than Great Crested Grebe; easily recognized in breeding plumage (photo), by golden feather tufts at side of head. In winter plumage (drawing), similar to Slavonian Grebe, but black cap extends to below eye; Slavonian has straighter bill and flatter forehead.
Voice: Ascending rather wailing *poo-it*; during displays often a Little Grebe-like high snarl.
Occurrence: Breeds on ponds and lakes with thickly overgrown banks and floating vegetation, fish-ponds; often several pairs in small colony, often among breeding Black-headed Gulls. In Britain breeds only very locally in small numbers. Outside breeding season on large lakes and at the coast.

Slavonian Grebe, winter

Black-necked Grebe, winter

Food: Aquatic insects, snails, small crustaceans, tadpoles.
Breeding habits: March–June, 1–2 broods; floating nest near bank.
Slavonian Grebe *Podiceps auritus* breeds on shallow lakes in northern Europe. It is a regular but rare winter visitor.

	< Great Crested Grebe	R, W, M	I–XII	BR,BL

Little Grebe (Dabchick)
Tachybaptus ruficollis
Family: Grebes Podicipedidae
F Grèbe castagneux
G Zwergtaucher

Distinctive character: Smallest European grebe.
Features: Dumpy and short-necked. In breeding plumage (photo), head and sides of neck chestnut-brown, obvious bright spot at base of bill. In winter (drawing), uniform grey-brown, flanks somewhat lighter.
Voice: Long, vibrating trill, mainly in spring, often as a duet between sexes; also a high-pitched *bi-ib*.
Occurrence: Breeds on ponds and small lakes, in overgrown lake margins and on slow rivers. In winter often in small flocks on rivers and lakes, even on urban ponds, also estuaries.
Behaviour: Often difficult to spot in summer, amongst the water plants. In winter more approachable, often with

Little Grebe, winter

feathers fluffed up to give distinct high 'stern'.
Food: Insects and their larvae, small crustaceans, snails, tadpoles, in winter small fish.
Breeding habits: April–August, 1–3 broods; floating nest near bank.

< Coot	R, W	I–XII		

British Storm-petrel
Hydrobates pelagicus
Family: Storm-petrels Hydrobatidae
F Pétrel tempête
G Sturmschwalbe

Distinctive character: Very small, dark seabird with white rump and bat-like flight.
Features: Dark sooty-brown; prominent white rump; underwing has a variable white band, sometimes conspicuous; upperwing may show hint of pale narrow bar. Juv. also shows indistinct bar on upperwing.
Voice: At nesting colonies a continuous cacophony of noises, including a long purring sound ending with an abrupt hiccup.
Occurrence: Breeds on rocky or grassy offshore islands and headlands on W. coasts of British Isles, and also in Iceland, north Norway and Mediter-ranean. Oceanic outside breeding season.
Behaviour: When feeding, patters feet on surface of sea and makes short fluttering flights with brief glides; sometimes follows ships. Comes ashore to colonies only at night.
Food: Plankton, occasionally small fish, also offal.
Breeding habits: June–October, 1 brood; nests colonially in burrows or under boulders.
Leach's Storm-petrel *Oceanodroma leucorrhoa* is slightly > than British Storm-petrel. Longer wings and a forked tail. More obvious pale bar on upperwings and a more U-shaped white rump; it lacks white on underwings. Breeds on offshore islands in extreme N. Scotland, N. Norway and Iceland. At sea outside the breeding season. Large numbers occasionally driven inshore, and even inland, by severe storms in autumn/winter.

	– Swallow	S, M	mainly IV–X	BI, BL

Manx Shearwater *Puffinus puffinus*
Family: Shearwaters Procellariidae
F Puffin des Anglais
G Schwarzschnabel-Sturmtaucher

Distinctive character: Medium-sized black and white seabird with long wings; glides and banks low over waves with periodic rapid wingbeats.
Features: Upperparts entirely black or brownish-black, underparts all white. In flight shows dark rear border to underwing. In Mediterranean browner above and greyer or brown-tinged below (probably a separate species).
Voice: At nesting colonies screams and cawing sounds; silent at sea.
Occurrence: Breeds on grassy offshore islands and headlands on west coasts of Britain, Ireland, and in Mediterranean. Outside breeding season lives out at sea, but birds from the Mediterranean occur regularly around English Channel coasts and more rarely in North Sea.
Behaviour: Comes ashore to breeding colonies at night. Usually seen in flocks offshore, wheeling around or resting on water; plunges for food.
Food: Fish, crustaceans, cephalopods, offal.
Breeding habits: May–September, 1 brood; colonial breeder, making sparse nest at end of a burrow.
The **Sooty Shearwater** *Puffinus griseus* is a regular visitor from the southern hemisphere to Atlantic coasts and North Sea area, mainly from July–October. Larger than Manx, and dark sooty-brown all over apart from a broad pale band on the underwing (but looks entirely dark at distance); flight is more direct, with wings more backswept.

– Black-headed Gull	S, M mainly II–X	BI, BL		

Fulmar *Fulmarus glacialis*
Family: Petrels Procellariidae
F Pétrel glacial G Eissturmvogel

Distinctive character: Glides over the waves and around cliffs on stiffly held wings with occasional wingbeats.
Features: Resembles large gull, but plumper, with thicker head and neck. Bill short and thick.
Voice: Cackling, whining and grunting calls such as *airr*, *keh-keh* or *ahr gock-gock*. In flight often *ku*.
Occurrence: Breeds in colonies on rocky coasts and islands. At sea outside breeding season, often far from coasts. Breeds on most coasts of British Isles where suitable cliffs exist, also locally inland on crags.
Behaviour: Often follows ships.
Food: Dead fish, squid, small crustaceans, offal. Blubber of dead sea mammals.
Breeding habits: May–August, 1 brood; nests mainly on rocky cliffs.

Gannet

The goose-sized **Gannet** *Sula bassana* (drawing) can be seen at sea in small numbers outside breeding season. It dives for fish from up to 40 m vertically into the sea. Breeds in huge colonies on rocky islands and cliffs of north and west Britain.

	< Herring Gull	R, S	I–XII	

Cormorant *Phalacrocorax carbo*
Family: Cormorants Phalacrocoracidae
F Grand cormoran
G Kormoran

Distinctive character: Black water-bird with white chin and cheeks, bill hooked at tip.
Features: White patch on thigh in breeding season. Juv. brownish with whitish underside.
Voice: Usually heard only on breeding ground: grating, gurgling and crowing sounds such as *kra*, *kor kor*, or *rair rair*.
Occurrence: Breeds in colonies on rocky coasts; on Continent also inland in tall trees by large lakes,

often with herons nearby. Breeds in British Isles, Holland, northern East Germany and Poland, reduced to a few colonies in West Germany. Regular on larger lakes in winter.
Behaviour: Swims low in water, like divers.
Food: Mainly fish.
Breeding habits: March–August; 1 brood; nests on trees or cliffs.

The rather smaller and slimmer-necked **Shag** *Phalacrocorax aristotelis* has black plumage with a greenish tinge; upturned crest in breeding season. Breeds in colonies on rocky coasts, in Britain in north and west; more widespread on coasts in winter. Feeds on fish like Cormorant.

< Greylag Goose	R	I–XII	▽2	

Bittern *Botaurus stellaris*
Family: Herons Ardeidae
F Butor étoilé G Rohrdommel

Distinctive character: When disturbed, stands motionless with head erect, often for long periods.
Features: Much more squat than Grey Heron, and with shorter neck. Reed-coloured plumage, legs and feet green (camouflage). Owl-like in flight. Head stretched out in short flights, tucked in for longer flights.
Voice: During breeding season a foghorn-like booming, audible over a long distance; flight call a harsh *aark*.
Occurrence: Breeds in large reed-

beds near lakes, marshes and bogs. Rare and decreasing. Very local in Britain.
Behaviour: Shy and only rarely seen; very well camouflaged. Clambers about slowly amongst reeds, rocks slightly in upright position in rhythm of swaying reeds to increase effect of camouflage, or moves away in slow motion. Threat posture similar to that of Eagle Owl, with wings spread, feathers fluffed out, and bill held slightly open.
Food: Fish, frogs, newts, leeches, worms, aquatic insects.
Breeding habits: April–July, 1 brood; nest in reeds, mostly in shallow water.

| | < Heron | R, W | I–XII | BR, BD, BL |

Little Bittern *Ixobrychus minutus*
Family: Herons Ardeidae
F Butor blongios
G Zwergdommel

Distinctive character: Europe's smallest heron.
Features: ♂ (on right in photo), with dark cap and upperparts, ♀ with less contrasting plumage, streaked on neck, breast and flanks. Pale wings obvious in flight, especially in ♂.
Voice: Flight call a short, harsh *kehr*. ♂ gives low bark-like *wu* about every two seconds in breeding season.
Occurrence: Breeds in thick reedbeds on lakes, in damp riverside willow scrub, in marshes and flood-plain woods; common in same habitat as Great Reed Warbler. Range and numbers now reduced by habitat destruction and recreational disturbance. Rare summer visitor to Britain (has bred).
Behaviour: Clambers well in the reeds, using its very long toes with which it can grasp several stems at a time; freezes like Bittern when danger threatens, or creeps slowly away. When disturbed it flies low over reeds with rapid wing beats, quickly diving down again into fresh cover.
Food: Fish, frogs, aquatic insects, tadpoles, leeches, worms, young birds.
Breeding habits: May–July, 1 brood; nests in reeds or in thick, swampy scrub, often above water.

Feral pigeon	(S), (M)	IV–X	BR	

Grey Heron *Ardea cinerea*
Family: Herons Ardeidae
F Héron cendré G Graureiher

Distinctive character: Europe's largest and commonest heron.
Features: Long neck and legs; long, pointed yellowish bill. Plumage mainly grey; black stripe above eye, continued as two long drooping feathers. Young birds lack eye-stripe and these decorative feathers. Flies with slow, heavy wing beats, neck always held in an S-shape, and legs outstretched behind. Looks very large in flight.
Voice: Flight call a harsh *kaarnk*.
Occurrence: Breeds in colonies in tall deciduous and coniferous trees, occasionally in reedbeds. Feeds in shallow water, including on coast, marshes, and from low banks of rivers, ponds and lakes, or (when hunting voles) in damp fields. Widespread.
Behaviour: Often stands motionless at the water's edge or strides slowly through shallow water with neck stretched forward when fishing. Catches fish by a rapid stab of the bill. In some areas feeds increasingly at fish-farms, owing to destruction of natural wetlands and water-meadows.
Food: Mainly fish, also small mammals, frogs, worms.
Breeding habits: February–August, 1–2 broods; large nest usually high in a tree.

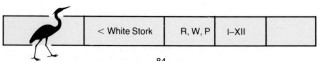

| | < White Stork | R, W, P | I–XII | |

Purple Heron *Ardea purpurea*
Family: Herons Ardeidae
F Héron pourpré G Purpurreiher

Distinctive character: Often holds thin neck in snake-like way.
Features: Slimmer and longer-necked than Grey Heron; plumage very dark, especially in flight. Juv. paler, lacking black head and neck markings, easily confused with Grey Heron from a distance. In flight large feet noticeable and the low-slung neck appears angular.
Voice: Flight call *kra* or *kreg*, rather higher-pitched than Grey Heron. Alarm call *kwar*. Rather silent outside breeding season.

Occurrence: Breeds in extensive reedbeds, and in marshy areas with thick willow with alder scrub. Local and often irregular breeding bird, in small colonies; larger colonies at Neusiedlersee (Austria) and in Holland. Regular but rare summer visitor to Britain, mainly in southern half.
Behaviour: Rarely sits in trees, preferring the reeds; freezes like bitterns when disturbed and is then very difficult to spot. Hunts by lurking near small patches of open water in thick reedbeds.
Food: Small fish, frogs, insects.
Breeding habits: April–July, 1 brood; nest usually above water in the reeds.

< Grey Heron	(S), (M)	IV–IX	O	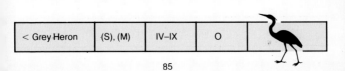

Great White Egret *Egretta alba*
Family: Herons Ardeidae
F Grande aigrette
G Silberreiher

Distinctive character: Snow-white plumage, with (breeding season) long plumes on the wings.

Features: Markedly slimmer than Grey Heron, with very long, thin neck. Bill black with yellow base in breeding season, in winter more or less completely yellow. Legs and feet green-black, upper leg yellow in breeding plumage.

Voice: Normally silent; occasional raucous *krah*; rattling and barking calls at nest.

Occurrence: Breeds in extensive reedbeds on lakes and wide deltas in south-west Europe, also in open swamps with bushes and low trees; regular breeder on Neusiedlersee (Austria and Hungary).

Behaviour: Wades slowly through shallow water when feeding. Often waits motionless in the water for suitable prey. It is therefore easier to see than Purple Herons, with which it shares habitat.

Food: Fish, frogs, aquatic insects.

Breeding habits: April–June, 1 brood; nest usually in reeds; colonial.

| | – Grey Heron | (S), V | III–X | O |

Little Egret *Egretta garzetta*
Family: Herons Ardeidae
F Aigrette garzette G Seidenreiher

Distinctive character: Smaller, snow-white egret with black bill, black legs and yellow feet.
Features: Long plumes on head and shoulders in breeding season, raised during displays. In flight, distinguished from Great White Egret by smaller size, faster wing beat, and more rounded wings. Yellow feet also best seen in flight (drawing).
Voice: Various gurgling, snoring and raucous noises at nest.
Occurrence: Breeds in colonies in large wetlands with bushes and trees, but also (increasingly) in rice fields, as in Hungary. Mainly a southern species, but small numbers regular in summer further north. Annual visitor to Britain (where has been recorded in all months).
Behaviour: Hunts by darting rapidly

Little Egret, in flight

in shallow water, stabbing to left and right.
Food: Small fish, frogs, aquatic insects.
Breeding habits: April–June, 1 brood; nest usually in trees or bushes, rarely in tall reeds. Colonial.

< Grey Heron	(S), M	I–XII	O	

Night Heron *Nycticorax nycticorax*
Family: Herons Ardeidae
F Héron bihoreau
G Nachtreiher

Distinctive character: Mainly crepuscular; roosts by day in trees, often with head tucked in.
Features: Squat and short-necked with a single long white feather hanging over neck; wings broad and rounded; flight owl-like with soft wing strokes. Juv. (drawing), with Bittern-like striped plumage, and pale spots.
Voice: Harsh *ark* alarm call, usually in twilight or at night; various guttural and raucous sounds.
Occurrence: Breeds in thickly overgrown swamps with trees and bushes, and in river valleys with ox-bow lakes and rich, jungle-like vegetation. Very rare in northern and central Europe, with a few small colonies in Holland and southern Germany; in Hungary and Czechoslovakia, slightly commoner. Annual but rare in Britain (has been recorded in all months).

Night Heron,
juvenile

Food: Frogs, fish, tadpoles, insects, leeches.
Breeding habits: April–July, 1 brood; nests in trees or bushes; colonial.

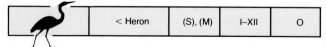

	< Heron	(S), (M)	I–XII	O

88

Spoonbill *Platalea leucorodia*
Family: Ibises and spoonbills
Threskiornithidae F Spatule blanche G Löffler

Distinctive character: The long spoon-shaped bill with yellow tip.
Features: White plumage with yellow-ochre chin; in breeding season yellowish crest and yellow breast-band. Juv. lack crest, yellow chin spot and breast-band, and wings have dark tips. In flight head and neck held outstretched with neck slightly sagging.
Voice: Nasal grunting and wailing sounds at nest, otherwise mostly silent.
Occurrence: Breeds in wide, open marshy areas, with reedbeds and shallow water, in willow and alder scrub near open water; breeds in colonies. Feeds in open water; often at coasts outside breeding season. Rare breeding bird in Holland, at Neusiedlersee (Austria) and in Hungary. Scarce visitor to southern and eastern Britain (mostly summer, but recorded in all months).
Behaviour: When feeding, stands in water and sieves small animals from water and mud by swishing bill from side to side. Flocks often fly in long lines or in V-formation.
Food: Fish, aquatic insects, molluscs, snails, tadpoles, crustaceans.
Breeding habits: April–June, 1 brood; nest commonly on broken reed stems, over water. Colonial.

< White Stork	(S), (M)	I–XII	O	

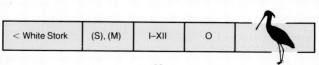

White Stork *Ciconia ciconia*
Family: Storks Ciconiidae
F Cigogne blanche G Weißstorch

Distinctive character: The long, red bill and long, red legs.

Features: Very large white bird with black flight feathers, easily identified. In Juv. bill and legs much paler. Often soars, with neck outstretched (drawing), unlike herons

Voice: More or less silent, except for bill-clappering during breeding displays. Occasional hissing sounds when disturbed.

Occurrence: Feeds on damp meadows and cultivated fields in open lowland; breeds mainly on buildings and chimneys, often on a wheel positioned specially for the birds. A few pairs breed in trees in river-valley woodlands in Austria. In western Europe has been decreasing markedly for decades, mainly because of habitat destruction, collisions with power lines, and shooting in

White Stork
in flight

winter quarters. Rare visitor to Britain, mostly in summer, but has been recorded in all months.

Food: Mice, frogs, worms, insects.

Breeding habits: April–June, 1 brood; large nest, usually high on building.

	> Grey Heron	(S), (M)	I–IX	O

90

Black Stork *Ciconia nigra*
Family: Storks Ciconiidae
F Cigogne noire G Schwarzstorch

Distinctive character: Found in woodland.

Features: Easy to distinguish from similar-sized White Stork by mainly black plumage, with greenish and purple sheen, only belly and undertail-coverts white. Juv. grey-brown, with bill and legs greenish. Often soars for long periods at a great height.

Voice: Rich vocal repertoire, unlike White Stork. A melodious *fee* when soaring; threat call, *feeeh*; on the nest, a subdued *chichu*.

Occurrence: Eastern species; breeds in large, old and undisturbed mixed forests with pools, rivers and scattered wet meadows. Feeds at shallow water. Severely reduced by habitat destruction and afforestation, but slowly increasing again. Rare visitor to Britain.

Black Stork
in flight

Food: Aquatic insects, newts, frogs, fish, occasionally small mammals.

Breeding habits: April–July, 1 brood; large stick nest in old pine or oak, sometimes uses old raptor nest.

– White Stork	(S), V	III–XI	O	

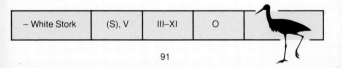

Mute Swan *Cygnus olor*
Family: Ducks and relatives Anatidae
F Cygne tuberculé G Höckerschwan

Distinctive character: Largest and heaviest waterbird.

Features: Pure white plumage, bill reddish with black base; obvious knob on bill, more developed in ♂, especially in spring. Juv. grey-brown; bill grey, without knob.

Voice: Fairly silent; explosive *heear*, and a loud hissing in defence.

Occurrence: Found on many lakes and ornamental ponds, even in urban areas. In winter often in large numbers on lakes and rivers. Breeds at lakes with rich vegetation cover and reedy banks; also banks of slow rivers and on the coast.

Behaviour: Swims with S-shaped neck (unlike following swan species) and downward-pointing bill, often with wings raised like shield. Flies with powerful wingbeats, with neck stretched out. Wings make distinct throbbing sound.

Food: Water and marsh plants, also grazes on land.

Breeding habits: March–June, 1 brood; large nest of old reeds and other plant material, usually well hidden on bank.

	> Greylag Goose	R	I–XIII	

Whooper Swan *Cygnus cygnus*
Family: Ducks and relatives Anatidae
F Cygne sauvage
G Singschwan

Distinctive character: Best told from Mute Swan by yellow base to bill and lack of knob.
Features: Neck less curved when swimming and head usually more horizontal. Juv. greyer than young Mute, bill flesh-coloured with dark tip.
Voice: Calls frequently; swimming flocks have goose-like nasal calls; loud trumpeting *ang-her* in flight.
Occurrence: Breeds in bogs and tundra lakes in northern Europe. In winter regular flocks in North Sea and southern Baltic coasts, as well as on lakes, flooded rivers, and even in smaller numbers on the larger lakes as far south as Alpine foothills.
Behaviour: Threat display with wings spread to the sides and neck held upright, whereas Mute Swan raises wings and arches neck. Much less awkward on land. In flight wings make only slight swishing sound, but calls frequently; flocks often fly in oblique line.
Food: Mainly water plants and their roots, grasses and other plants on land.
Breeding habits: May–June, 1 brood; large nest, usually on a small island close to water.

– Mute Swan	W	X–IV	BR, WI	

Bewick's Swan *Cygnus columbianus*
Family: Ducks and relatives Anatidae
F Cygne de Bewick G Zwergschwan

Distinctive character: More goose-like than two previous species, especially in flight.

Features: Head and bill shorter than in Whooper, neck somewhat shorter and thicker, nearly always held straight. Yellow on bill much less extensive, with a more rounded border than in Whooper (in which it tapers forwards to a point). Less often flies in formation.

Voice: Deeper and clearer than Whooper. Melodious trumpeting *Kuhk* or *gluglu*, calls of more distant flocks mixing to produce a pleasant chorus.

Occurrence: Breeds on small lakes and ponds in the tundra of north-east Europe. Regular winter visitor to coastal lakes in southern North Sea, also flooded grasslands inland. Winter flocks also graze on fields and

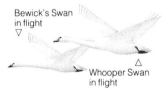

Bewick's Swan
in flight
▽

△
Whooper Swan
in flight

meadows well away from water.

Food: Water plants and their roots, grass and young crops.

Breeding habits: June–July, 1 brood; large nest of plant material, usually on a small island.

	< Mute Swan	W	X–IV	WI, WL

94

Pink-footed Goose
Anser brachyrhynchus
Family: Ducks and relatives Anatidae
F Oie à bec court G Kurzschnabelgans

Distinctive character: Back and wing-coverts are pale and 'frosted' and contrast with the dark head and neck.

Features: Compact, with relatively small black and pink bill and flesh-coloured legs. Head and neck are dark brown, occasionally with a little white at the base of the bill (though never so much as on White-fronted Goose); back and upperwing-coverts pinkish-grey with pale barring, underparts pinky brown with darker barring on belly and flanks, and a white vent. In flight the pale ash-grey forewings and white uppertail are prominent. Young birds are somewhat darker and less clearly barred pale above.

Voice: A short *ang-ank* and a higher-pitched, yelping *wink wink*.

Occurrence: A winter visitor in large flocks from the Arctic to northern Britain and, in much smaller numbers, to southern shores of the North Sea. Grazes by day on stubble, crop fields, pastures and saltmarshes; roosts on lakes and sheltered estuaries.

Food: Cereals, grain, potatoes, grass.

The **Bean Goose** *Anser fabalis* breeds in the taiga and tundra regions of N. Europe. In winter large numbers visit central Europe, with very small numbers also in Britain (in S.W. Scotland and E. Anglia). Bigger than the Pink-footeds, longer neck, clearly darker upperparts; legs orange (not pink). Bill larger and stronger than Pink-footeds: orange with black tip and rather narrow (taiga race *A. f. fabalis*), or black with a narrow orange band and very deep (tundra race *A. f. rossicus*). Intermediate forms and races hard to separate.

< Greylag Goose	W	IX–V	WI	

Greylag Goose *Anser anser*
Family: Ducks and relatives Anatidae
F Oie cendrée G Graugans

Distinctive character: In flight by the clear silver-grey leading edge to the wings.

Features: Large, powerful pale grey goose, ancestor of farmyard goose; bill orange-yellow (western race) or flesh-coloured (eastern race), with intermediates; legs flesh-pink, grey in juv.

Voice: Rather vocal; often a nasal *ga-ga-ga*, *ahng-ahng*, *angangan-gang*, or similar, like farmyard goose.

Ocurrence: Breeds on large inland lakes with thick fringing vegetation such as reeds, rushes or swampy thickets, or in bogs. Rare breeding bird, in north. In south the breeding birds are not of wild origin. It is a Winter visitor to northern and eastern Britain.

Behaviour: In some places resident as feral park bird, often with Canada Geese.

Greylag Goose in flight

Food: Grasses, herbs, shoots, roots, berries, seeds, cereals, crops, potatoes.

Breeding habits: April–June, 1 brood; large, loose nest of plant material, usually near water in thick vegetation.

	> Mallard	R, W	I–XII	WI

White-fronted Goose *Anser albifrons*
Family: Ducks and relatives Anatidae
F Oie rieuse
G Bläßgans

Distinctive character: White fore-head and black barring on belly.
Features: Bill long and pink; yellow in Greenland race. Juv. lacks black belly markings and white forehead patch; bill with darker tip.
Voice: Higher-pitched, more rapid voice than previous species: *kwi kwi kwi, klikli* or *keowlyow*.
Ocurrence: Breeds on tundra in northern Russia and Greenland, mostly near water; in winter in large flocks to British Isles, North Sea coasts of Holland and Germany. Rare inland and in Hungary. Feeds on coastal meadows, wet grassland and saltmarshes by day, spending the night on the water.
Food: Grasses and their seeds, also marsh plants in winter.

The very similar **Lesser White-fronted Goose** *Anser erythropus* is smaller and shorter-necked, with rounder head and shorter bill. The white patch extends above eye, which has a characteristic yellow eye-ring. Flight very agile. This species is relatively common as a migrant in Poland and Hungary, in mild seasons overwintering in the Hungarian plain; one or two visit Britain every winter. Call a high-pitched *kyee-yee*.

< Greylag Goose	W	X–V	WI, WL	

Canada Goose *Branta canadensis*
Family: Ducks and relatives Anatidae
F Bernache du Canada
G Kanadagans

Distinctive character: Very large goose with long, black neck.
Features: Head black and white, tail, bill and legs black. Hybridizes occasionally with Greylag. Flocks often fly in V-formation.
Voice: In flight a nasal trumpeting, *a-honk*, rising on the second syllable and audible form a distance. Flocks make penetrating calls when alarmed.
Occurrence: Introduced from North America; originally bred on marshy lakes and river banks, right up into tundra region. In Europe it has been established as a resident for many decades. Feral birds have established themselves on reservoirs, lakes, fishponds and above all on ornamental lakes in parks. Breeds mainly in British Isles and Scandinavia; mostly winter visitor to Germany and Holland; rare elsewhere. Swedish population winters on southern North Sea coast.
Food: Grasses, herbs, clover, roots, seeds, crop seedlings, water plants, algae.
Breeding habits: March–June, 1 brood; large nest of vegetation, usually on bank or small island.

	> Greylag	R, (W)	I–XII	

Barnacle Goose *Branta leucopsis*
Family: Ducks and relatives Anatidae
F Bernache nonnette R
Nonnengans

Distinctive character: White face, contrasting with black neck.
Features: Medium-sized goose with small, black bill; from distance, looks black above and white below. Juv. and first-winters have grey-white face and dark brown neck.
Voice: Flight call a soft *gek gek gek*, large distant flocks sounding rather like small dogs yapping.
Occurrence: Breeds mainly on inaccessible cliffs and rocky outcrops high above river valleys or fjords in Greenland, Svalbard and Novaya Zemlya (USSR). Nest sites are safe from Arctic Foxes and can be reached by the geese only by flying. Small colony established off southeast Sweden. Regular winter visitor to coastal meadows in Scotland, Ireland, and to Wattenmeer area in North Sea.
Behaviour: Very sociable, small flocks often join other geese but large flocks tend to be single species. Flocks usually unstructured in flight.
Food: Grasses, eelgrass, samphire, herbs, algae, also seedling crops.

< Greylag	W	X–IV	WI, WL	

Brent Goose *Branta bernicla*
Family: Ducks and relatives Anatidae
F Bernache cravant
G Ringelgans

Distinctive character: Deep guttural calls.
Features: Small, very dark, rather duck-like goose with black bill and legs; white 'stern'; long white patch on side of neck, lacking in juv. Two races, a pale-bellied and a (commoner) dark-bellied form; sometimes both races in mixed flock.
Voice: Deep nasal *rrott rrott rrott* or guttural *rronk* when disturbed, in flight short hard *ack* with quieter, higher sounds.
Occurrence: Breeds in colonies near lakes in coastal Arctic tundra, light-bellied form often on small coastal islands. In winter on mudflats with eelgrass and samphire, and on adjoining farmland. Rare further inland. Numbers have increased greatly in recent decades following reduction in hunting in wintering areas.
Behaviour: Very sociable, usually in large flocks; flight rapid and flocks usually fly in lines or unstructured.
Food: Eelgrass, samphire, green algae, grass and seedling crops.

	< Greylag	W	IX–V	WI, WL

Shelduck *Tadorna tadorna*
Family: Ducks and relatives Anatidae
F Tadorne de Belon G Brandgans

Distinctive character: Contrasting colours and knob on bill (♂).
Features: Large duck, looking black and white. Goose-like with distinctive plumage. Colours paler outside breeding season. ♂ has knob at base of bill, lacking in ♀ (drawing). Juv. mostly grey-brown above, whitish below, bill and legs light grey.
Voice: ♂ has high piping *tyutyu-tyutyu*, often followed by a trill; ♀ calls much deeper and harder *ak-ak-ak, ga-ga-ga-ga* or *ahk.*
Occurrence: Common breeding bird on coasts; occurs locally inland in Britain.
Behaviour: Flies with relatively slow wing-beats, often in lines or wedge formation. Young of several broods gather in large flocks (crêches).
Food: Mussels, snails, worms, small

Shelduck, ♀

crustaceans, insects.
Breeding habits: April–July, 1 brood; nests in old rabbit burrows, underneath bushes or in holes specially constructed for them.

> Mallard	R, W	I–XII	WI, WL	

Wigeon *Anas penelope*
Family: Ducks and relatives Anatidae
F Canard siffleur G Pfeifente

Distinctive character: Outside breeding season often in large, dense flocks.
Features: Medium-sized duck with high forehead and short bill. ♂ very colourful and easy to identify; ♀ similar to Mallard ♀, but more delicate, with more rounded head and shorter bill, rust-brown plumage and more pointed tail. In flight the long wings are noticeable, as is the sharply defined white belly; ♂ in flight told by large white patches towards front of wings (lacking in first-winter birds).
Voice: has a whistling *whee-oo*, accentuated on first syllable, occasionally *arr*. ♀ a rattling *rrarr*, *verr* or *krr-krr*.
Occurrence: Breeds on lakes, bogs and river deltas in northern Europe (rarely in Britain), occasionally in Holland, northern East Germany and Poland. Regular and widespread winter visitor to muddy shores and freshwater lakes, often in large numbers.
Behaviour: Very sociable, often mixed with Brent Geese. Often feeds on land.
Food: Eelgrass, grasses, herbs, green algae.
Breeding habits: May–June, 1 brood; flat down-filled nest near to water, under low shrubs or hidden in grass.

	< Mallard	R, W, M	I–XII	WI, WL

Gadwall *Anas strepera*
Family: Ducks and relatives Anatidae
F Canard chipeau G Schnatterente

Distinctive character: White speculum visible in all plumages, especially in flight.
Features: Somewhat more delicate than Mallard and with steeper forehead. ♂ relatively drab, distinguished from afar by black 'stern', in flight by white belly and contrasting black tail coverts; in eclipse resembles ♀ but has red-brown wing coverts. ♀ mainly by bill (yellow-orange with black culmen).
Voice: ♂ has display call, a deep *treb* or *errp*, accompanied by *fyee*; ♀ Mallard-like quack *kaak kaak kak kak kak* in diminuendo.

Occurrence: Breeds in lowland in eutrophic freshwater lákes with rich vegetation, and on slow rivers. Scat-

Gadwall,
♀

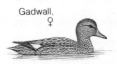

tered distribution and often absent entirely. In winter on lakes, reservoirs, gravel pits.
Food: Mainly water plants, occasionally small animals.
Breeding habits: April–June, 1 brood; nest usually close to water in thick vegetation.

< Mallard	R, W	I–XII	WI, WL	

Teal *Anas crecca*
Family: Ducks and relatives Anatidae
F Sarcelle d'hiver G Krickente

Distinctive character: Very small duck with green speculum.

Features: ♂ in breeding plumage beautifully coloured; yellow triangle with black borders at side of tail. ♀ with yellow-bown spots, white line on tail sides and dark grey bill. Very nimble in flight, often keeping low in dense flocks; flight reminiscent of waders.

Voice: ♂ has low repeated melodious *krick*, often given in flight. ♀ has a high-pitched quack, and a rattling *trrr* on take-off.

Occurrence: Breeds on lakes with thick bankside vegetation, on bogs and in forest lakes, in upland as well as lowland, occasionally on damp meadows with reeds. Widespread but not common, rare in south. Very common outside breeding season, especially on flooded meadows and on muddy banks.

Behaviour: Feeds by dabbling in open water or loose mud.

Food: Water plants and small seeds (winter), molluscs and insect larvae (summer).

Breeding habits: April–June, 1 brood; nest well hidden in thick vegetation, close to water.

	< Mallard	P, W	I–XII	WI

Garganey *Anas querquedula*
Family: Ducks and relatives Anatidae
F Sarcelle d'été G Knäkente

Distinctive character: Broad white supercilium of ♂, reaching to back of head.
Features: Only slightly larger than Teal, somewhat slimmer in body and neck. ♂ in eclipse like ♀, but with blue-grey front of wing. In eclipse both sexes have a more marked supercilium and eyestripe than Teal, and a paler face; ♀ in flight distinguished by less obvious speculum and paler forewing. When swimming the front of body is more submerged, wings more pointed and prominent.

Voice: During courtship and when excited ♂ has a crackling, wooden-sounding *klerrrek*, and a short *yek*; ♀ a high nasal quack, like Teal.
Occurrence: Scarce breeder on eutrophic shallow water with rich, floating vegetation; outside breeding season found on large and small lakes, flooded meadows, marshes, also small damp sites.
Behaviour: Flight not as rapid as Teal.
Food: Water plants, seeds of pond-weeds, small crustaceans, insect larvae, soft-bodied small animals.
Breeding habits: April–June, 1 brood; nests close to water in thick vegetation.

< Mallard	S	III–X	BR	

Shoveler *Anas clypeata*
Family: Ducks and relatives Anatidae
F Canard souchet G Löffelente

Distinctive character: Long broad bill, often visible from afar.
Features: Squatter than Mallard, with more pointed wings. ♂ in flight has dark head, white breast and chestnut belly and flanks. Both ♂ and ♀ (drawing) have pale blue forewing. Eclipse ♂ similar to ♀ but with a hint of pink on the flanks.
Voice: Usually rather silent. ♂ has a deep, hoarse *took-took* or *klak*.
Occurrence: Breeds on eutrophic shallow lowland lakes, bordered by

rushes, sedges or reeds, and in marshy areas with open water. Outside breeding season also at coast and on all kinds of shallow water. Rare

Shoveler,
♀

breeder in Britain, much commoner in winter.
Food: Takes very small food items (seeds, small crustaceans, insects) filtered from water surface.
Breeding habits: April–June, 1 brood; nest well hidden on bank.

	< Mallard	P, W, M	I–XII	WL

Pintail *Anas acuta*
Family: Ducks and relatives Anatidae
F Canard pilet G Spießente

Distinctive character: Head and neck colouring and long pointed tail of ♂.
Features: Slimmer and more graceful than Mallard; ♀ (drawing) similar to Mallard ♀, but has more pointed tail and smaller, grey bill. Eclipse ♂ very similar to ♀, but darker above. In flight long pointed wings, slim body, long neck and white edged speculum noticeable. Flies rapidly with swishing wings.
Voice: Breeding call of ♂ *kreek* or *pyeep*, similar to ♂ Teal; ♀ quack is slightly longer and more grating than Mallard.

Occurrence: Breeds mainly on shallow lakes in upland moors in northern coniferous forest or tundra regions, in Britain also rarely on lowland marshes

Pintail,
♀

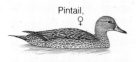

and fens. Outside breeding season mainly on sheltered estuaries and floodlands.
Food: Mainly water plants and seeds, small animals.
Breeding habits: April–June, 1 brood; nests near water, well hidden.

< Mallard	S, W	I–XII	BR, WI, WL	

Mallard *Anas platyrhynchos*
Family: Ducks and relatives Anatidae
F Canard colvert G Stockente

Distinctive character: Largest and best known of the dabbling ducks ('wild duck'); ancestor of many different domestic duck breeds.

Features: Body decidedly plump. ♂ in breeding plumage (X–VI) easily identified by shiny bottle-green head with yellow bill, reddish-brown breast and curled black central tail feathers. Eclipse ♂ similar to ♀ but rather darker, and with uniform green-yellow bill. ♀ has brown camouflaged plumage and a dark culmen on bill. Flies rapidly, with long neck and black-and-white-tipped blue speculum prominent.

Voice: Displaying ♂ have a low *raib*, often repeated, and a thin, high-pitched whistle. ♀ a descending quack, *waak-wak-wak-wak-wak*.

Occurrence: Breeds on nearly all types of still or slow-flowing water. Common as feral bird in parks.

Food: Very varied: water plants, seeds, worms, snails, small crustaceans, insects, bread.

Breeding habits: March–July, 1 brood; nest usually well camouflaged close to water; rarely in tree holes.

	Well-known	R, W, M	I–XII	

Red-crested Pochard *Netta rufina*
Family: Ducks and relatives
Anatidae
F Nette rousse G Kolbenente

Distinctive character: Large, compact, thick-headed diving duck. Sits relatively high in the water.
Features: ♂ in breeding plumage has chestnut head (crown paler) and red bill. ♀ uniform grey-brown with sharply delineated pale grey cheeks, reminiscent of ♀ Common Scoter.
Voice: Breeding ♂ has loud, short *bait* or slow, nasal *geng*; ♀ a mechanical *urr* or *trr-trr*, in flight *wu-wu-wu*.
Occurrence: Breeds on eutrophic lakes with reedy margins, in steppe and semi-desert regions. Breeds in only a few places in Europe, mainly in south but also in Netherlands and Denmark. Escapes also occur.
Behaviour: Looks like a dabbling duck and, unlike other diving ducks, needs only a short run before take-off.
Food: Mainly water plants such as pondweeds and algae, more rarely small animals.
Breeding habits: May–June, 1 brood. Nest well hidden at water margin.

< Mallard	(M), (W)	IX–III	O	

Pochard *Aythya ferina*
Family: Ducks and relatives Anatidae
F Fuligule milouin G Tafelente

Distinctive character: Plump duck with long, tall head and steep forehead. Wings whistle in flight.
Features: ♂ easy to tell by contrasting silver-grey, black and chestnut-brown plumage. ♀ dark brown, bill blackish with narrow, paler markings, best told by head profile.
Voice: Quiet; breeding ♂ has low wheezy *wiviyerr*; ♀ a harsh, *cherr cherr*.
Occurrence: Breeds on rich freshwater lakes with large open areas and well-developed reed zone. Widespread breeding bird, but not common, and distribution patchy. Outside breeding season on large lakes, reservoirs, fish ponds and slow-flowing rivers. often in large flocks.

Pochard,
♀

Sometimes tame in parks and lakes.
Food: Water plants, worms, snails, insect larvae; in winter crops as well.
Breeding habits: April–June, 1 brood; nest hidden in bankside vegetation, or on small island.

	< Mallard	P, W, M	I–XII	BR, WI

Ruddy Duck *Oxyura jamaicensis*
Family: Ducks Anatidae
F Erismature roux
G Schwarzkopf-Ruderente

Distinctive character: Large bluish bill, and long tail often held cocked.
Features: ♂ has a chestnut body with a white belly, and a distinctive head pattern of black forehead, crown and rear of head and white cheeks; the bill is bright blue-grey and very broad. ♀, winter ♂ and juv. are much duller and browner and have lightly barred underparts. Swims high in the water.
Voice: During display the ♂ makes quiet grunting and belching noises; ♀ has a high-pitched squeak, a low hiss and makes rattling sounds with the bill.
Occurrence: Breeds on lakes with reedy margins, dispersing more to open reservoirs in winter. Introduced to England from North America .earlier this century, and now breeds locally at a number of lakes in the western Midlands and in the southwest, wandering short distances outside the breeding season.
Behaviour: Sociable. When displaying the ♂ cocks its tail, exposing the white undertail-coverts, stretches up its neck and raises its crown feathers, and slaps its bill against its breast. Walks on land only with difficulty and spends virtually all its time on the water.
Food: Insect larvae, also seeds of aquatic plants.
Breeding habits: April–September, 1 brood; nest is a platform of aquatic vegetation built in low rushes or reeds.

< Mallard	R	I–XII		

Tufted Duck *Aythya fuligula*
Family: Ducks and relatives Anatidae
F Fuligule morillon G Reiherente

Distinctive character: ♂ black and white with long drooping crest on back of head.
Features: Small, compact diving duck; ♂ dark brown, head crest very short or absent, and sometimes with whitish patch at base of bill. In flight white wing bar clearly visible.
Voice: Breeding ♂ has guttural *gee-gee-gee* or *bik-bik*; ♀ a hard grating *kreck-kreck*.
Occurrence: Breeds on lakes and reservoirs (not too shallow) with plenty of open water, both inland and coastal. Relatively common breeding bird, occasionally in urban areas too.

Often in large flocks outside breeding season, on lakes, reservoirs and slow rivers, where they are usually the commonest waterfowl after Mallard

Tufted Duck, ♀

and Coot. In winter may be tame enough to feed in park lakes.
Food: Snails, insect larvae, seeds of water plants.
Breeding habits: May–July, 1 brood; nests close to water, more or less well hidden.

	< Mallard	R, W, M	I–XII	

Scaup *Aythya marila*
Family: Ducks and relatives Anatidae
F Fuligule milouinan G Bergente

Distinctive character: Somewhat larger than Tufted, without crest. Head larger and more rounded, bill wider.
Features: ♂ has green-black head, pale grey speckled back and white flanks; in eclipse less contrasty with brown head and greyish-white flanks. ♀ (drawing) very similar to Tufted but always has broad white area at base of bill; in breeding season with white spot near ear as well.
Voice: Seldom heard. Breeding ♂ has whistling *pik pik peoo* or *vigh-ar*; ♀ deep, growling *karr*, somewhat deeper than Tufted.
Occurrence: Breeds in northern Europe by clear upland pools and lakes in the birch and willow region, and on coasts; sporadic breeder in Britain. Regular winter visitor in large flocks to northern coasts and coastal

Scaup, ♀

lakes, rarely as individuals further inland. Rarer in south.
Food: Insects, small crustaceans, snails, seeds.
Breeding habits: May–June, 1 brood; nests close to water, often underneath shrubs.

< Mallard	W, (S)	IX–IV	BR, WL	

Eider *Somateria mollissima*
Family: Ducks and relatives Anatidae
F Eider à duvet G Eiderente

Distinctive character: Large size and extended head profile.
Features: Heavier than Mallard, looks more compact and shorter-necked. Breeding plumage ♂ black and white, first-year ♂ dark with partially white feathers, giving dappled pattern. ♀ (drawing) brownish with darker barring.
Voice: Breeding ♂ has loud *ohuuo* or *hu-huo*; ♀ a deep and rumbling *goggoggog* or *korr*.
Occurrence: Breeds on coast and nearby islands; common in north Britain. Outside breeding season in shallow bays and estuaries, also at sea.

Behaviour: Very sociable; often flies low over water in long straggling flocks.
Food: Molluscs, crustaceans, worms

Eider,
♀

hardly any plants.
Breeding habits: April–July, brood; well-camouflaged nest is a hollow with vegetation and down (eiderdown).

	> Mallard	R, W	I–XII	

Long-tailed Duck *Clangula hyemalis*
Family: Ducks and relatives Anatidae
F Harelde de Miquelon
G Eisente

Distinctive character: Long tail feathers of ♂.
Features: About the size of Tufted, short-billed. Plumage highly dependent on the season, but ♂ nearly always with long tail. In winter plumage (photo), mainly white with brown patch on head, dark brown breast and wings. Winter ♀ (drawing), pale with dark forehead and ear patch. In breeding plumage (summer) ♂ has dark upperparts and conspicuous white area around eye.
Voice: In breeding season ♂ have a melodious call, *owa-owlik*, which is

audible from a distance; ♀ *ark ark ark*.
Occurrence: Breeds on small lakes and slow rivers in birch and willow region of Scandinavian tundra, and at coast. Common winter visitor to

Long-tailed Duck,
♀

winter

Baltic, less so to North Sea, usually well out to sea; occasional individuals on all coastsand, rarely, inland lakes.
Food: On breeding grounds midge larvae and snails; in winter molluscs, small crustaceans and worms.

< Mallard	W	X–IV	WL	

Common Scoter *Melanitta nigra*
Family: Ducks and relatives Anatidae
F Macreuse noire
G Trauerente

Distinctive character: Breeding plumage ♂ uniform black, black bill with orange-yellow spot.

Features: Squat and short-necked; eclipse ♂ brown-black, ♀ (drawing) dark brown with paler head and sides of neck.

Voice: ♂ has short fluting call in courtship – *piie* or *pipiu*; ♀ *how how how* or a loud grating *knarr*.

Occurrence: Breeds on lakes (even small ones) in Scandinavian mountains, from upper coniferous forest region to willow zone, also tundra

lakes; rare breeder in northern Britain. Outside breeding season mainly at sea, often far from coast.

Behaviour: They fly quickly in irregular strings or groups, the drakes

Common Scoter, ♀

making a whistling sound with their wings.

Food: Molluscs, snails, crustaceans, insects.

Breeding habits: May–July, 1 brood; nest, containing dark brown down, placed near to water.

	< Mallard	(S), W, M	I–XII	BR, WL

Velvet Scoter *Melanitta fusca*
Family: Ducks and relatives Anatidae
F Macreuse brune G Samtente

Distinctive character: From smaller Common Scoter by the white wing patches. However, these are often hidden when swimming.

Features: ♂ black with white patch below eye. ♀ dark brown with pale patches at side of head (sometimes absent), forehead less steep.

Voice: In breeding season, ♀ has a nasal rolling *arr-har* or *braa braa*, and a whistling wing noise. ♂ a piping *kyu* or *kyuerr*.

Occurrence: Breeds on Baltic coast of Scandinavia and on clear lakes in Scandinavian mountains, especially in upper coniferous forest and lower birch forest zones. Outside breeding season common on North Sea and Baltic coasts as passage bird and winter visitor.

Behaviour: On breeding site the pair often make morning and evening flights around the territory. Sometimes seen in flocks of Common Scoters in winter.

Food: Snails and other molluscs, crustaceans, some plant material.

Breeding habits: May–June, 1 brood; nests often under tree or bush, may be far from water.

– Mallard	M, W	X–V	WL	

Goldeneye *Bucephala clangula*
Family: Ducks and relatives Anatidae
F Garrot à oeil d'or G Schellente

Distinctive character: Fast flight with rapid wingbeats and loud whistling wing noises (especially in adult ♂).
Features: Very squat duck with large, tall head and yellow eye. ♂ black and white, with oval white patch between eye and bill. ♀ (drawing) mainly grey with brown head and yellow-tipped bill. Juv. ♂ similar to ♀, but with darker head, hint of white head patch and uniformly black bill.
Voice: ♂ has nasal *wee wee* in courtship display; ♀ in flight a rasping *krerr*.
Occurrence: Breeds on lakes and fast-flowing rivers in the coniferous forest zone of northern Europe; rare breeder further south, including Scotland. Outside breeding season common passage migrant and winter

Goldeneye.
♀

visitor on lakes, reservoirs and larger rivers, especially by the coast.
Food: Snails, small crustaceans, insect larvae, fish.
Breeding habits: May–June, 1 brood; nests in tree-holes (especially old Black Woodpecker holes) and special nestboxes, near to water.

	< Mallard	W, (S)	I–XII	BR

Smew *Mergus albellus*
Family: Ducks and relatives Anatidae
F Harle piette G Zwergsäger

Distinctive character: ♂ very beautifully marked; pure white, with black lines, black around eye and on back.
Features: Smallest sawbill; steep forehead, relatively short bill. ♀ (drawing) inconspicuous, with red-brown cap, and white neck and cheeks. Eclipse ♂ like ♀ but with larger amounts of white on wings. Immature ♂ has brownish-white wing patches. Looks relatively dark in flight, wings black and white.
Voice: Fairly silent. ♂ has rasping *kairrr* as alarm call, or in courtship. ♀ a *grek*, or quacking *gagaga*.

Occurrence: Similar to Goldeneye in requirements; breeds on fertile lakes surrounded by woodland in northern Europe. In winter regular on

Smew,
♀

southern North Sea and Baltic coasts. Occasional on shallow inland lakes, reservoirs and rivers.
Behaviour: Often with Goldeneye in winter; dives frequently; flies rapidly.
Food: Mostly fish, crustaceans and insect larvae.

< Mallard	W	XI–IV		

Red-breasted Merganser
Mergus serrator
Family: Ducks and relatives Anatidae
F Harle huppé G Mittelsäger

Distinctive character: Double crest at back of head.
Features: Slimmer than Mallard and with long, narrow bill. ♀ (drawing) similar to Goosander ♀ but has thinner, less tapered bill and less clear boundary between head and neck colouration. Eclipse ♂ resembles ♀, but with more white on wings, darker back and red eyes.
Voice: Breeding ♂ has nasal *kwee kwee eeh* or hoarse *gweng*. ♀ a grating flight call, *aark aark aark*.

Occurrence: Breeds on clear lakes and rivers of northern Europe, and on shallow sandy or stony coasts, often on small grassy islets. Outside breeding season mainly at coasts.

Red-breasted Merganser, ♀

less often on inland lakes.
Food: Fish, crustaceans.
Breeding habits: May–July, 1 brood; nest in thick ground vegetation, often between stones near to water.

	– Mallard	R, W	I–XII	

Goosander *Mergus merganser*
Family: Ducks and relatives Anatidae
F Harle bièvre G Gänsesager

Distinctive character: Largest and commonest European sawbill.
Features: Long, narrow, hook-tipped red bill. ♂ mostly white, with salmon-pink flush underneath, head greenish-black, back black. ♀ (drawing) mainly grey, with head and upper neck brown, sharply delineated from body colouring. Eclipse ♂ resembles ♀, but has darker back and more white on wings.
Voice: Breeding ♂ has a high-pitched crane-like *ree-ro*, and a quiet *week*. Breeding ♀ has a series of hard *skrrak* sounds.
Occurrence: Breeds on clear fish-rich lakes and rivers in forested areas, right up into the tundra, more rarely on the coast. Common in some parts of northern Britain. In winter on large open lakes and reservoirs, less

Goosander,
♀

commonly on rivers and at coast.
Food: Mainly fish, sometimes crustaceans too.
Breeding habits: April–June, 1 brood; nests in holes in trees or nest-boxes near to shore, sometimes in holes in rocks or walls.

> Mallard	R, W	I–XII		

Mandarin *Aix galericulata*
Family: Ducks and relatives Anatidae
F Canard mandarin G Mandarinente

Distinctive character: Very ornate (♂).
Features: Small, neat duck with large head. ♂ has orange 'sails' on wings, especially prominent during display, and a red bill. ♀ (drawing) is an inconspicuous grey-brown, with a white eye-ring and stripe behind the eye and at base of bill. Eclipse ♂ resembles ♀ but with pink bill and more metallic back.
Voice: Flight call of ♂ a whistling *vrrick*, in display, a *pfruip*. ♀ has coot-like *kett* or *eck*.
Ocurrence: Introduced from East Asia. Breeds at still or moving water with trees and cover at edges. Mainly on ornamental lakes and in parks, but now also established as feral breeder on certain lakes and rivers, especially in southern England.

Mandarin, ♀

Food: Seeds, fruit, plant material, small worms.
Breeding habits: April–June, 1 brood; nests in holes in trees close to water, more rarely on the ground between stones or amongst thick vegetation.

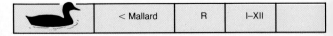

	< Mallard	R	I–XII	

Birds of Prey – Accipitriformes

Birds of prey vary enormously in size but all have powerful, hooked bills with which they tear up the flesh of their prey. Their feet (talons) usually have sharp, curved claws. Most kill their prey by striking them with their powerful talons (but see falcons). Some have long legs with long, slender talons (to catch flying birds, for instance) or shorter legs with short, heavy talons (to hold and kill mammals or reptiles on the ground). There are many intermediates between these two extremes, and most species are not so dependent on one particular prey type. Females are mostly noticeably larger than the males, especially the Sparrowhawk and Goshawk. Incidentally, when the young are in the nest the male usually feeds both them and the female.

Most birds of prey hunt vertebrates, but some species mainly eat insects, and others take carrion or refuse. Most species build large nests which they may use for several years.

The **Osprey** is not very closely related to the eagles, and is listed in a family of its own. Its flight is reminiscent of that of large gulls and the long, narrow wings are often held at an angle. Since the Osprey commonly hovers over water its legs are frequently wet and therefore are sparsely feathered; the toes have a rough underside to facilitate grasping slippery prey. There is only a single species worldwide.

Most European birds of prey belong to the hawk family, which can be conveniently divided into the following groups:

Goshawks and sparrowhawks have long tails and relatively short, rounded wings. They are woodland birds, attacking by surprise, and can weave in and out of the trees as they hunt. They prey mostly upon birds, the Goshawk also taking mammals. There are two northern European species.

Harriers are medium-sized birds with rather long wings and tail. They often fly low and slowly in the open. Adult males are easily identified by their striking plumage. The nest is always sited on the ground. They feed mostly on small mammals and birds. There are three species in northern Europe.

Kites are buzzard-sized but have longer wings and a more or less forked tail. They feed mainly on carrion and refuse, often searching lakes for dead or dying fish. There are two northern European species.

Buzzards are often seen soaring, often more than one at a time (unlike hawks). The broad wings and relatively short tail are characteristic. The talons are not as powerful as those of the eagles, and they feed mainly on small mammals. There are two true buzzards in northern and central Europe. The Honey Buzzard is not closely related.

Eagles vary from being slightly to very much larger than buzzards, with very strong talons and normally powerful bills. Their wings are long and broad, the tail relatively short and the plumage usually rather dark. Eagles are usually seen as individuals, often soaring in thermals. The White-tailed Eagle is not closely related to the other eagles (three species in north and central Europe). The Short-toed Eagle,

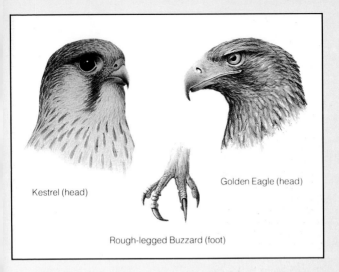

Kestrel (head)

Golden Eagle (head)

Rough-legged Buzzard (foot)

also not a true eagle, can be confused with the buzzards.

Vultures are accomplished in gliding and soaring flight and are some of the largest of all birds of prey. They feed mostly on carrion, the Lammergeier specializing on hollow bones. They occur mostly in southern Europe and are therefore not included in this book.

Falcons are small to medium-sized birds of prey with large, rounded heads, large, dark eyes and relatively weak talons. Many species have a dark 'moustache', the prominence of which is important in identification. The upper mandible is equipped with a tooth-like projection which is used to help kill the prey with a bite to the neck. Most falcons have narrow, pointed wings, and are adept at catching birds in flight. They fly fast, some reaching top speeds of over 200 km/h (125 mph). Falcons do not build nests but lay their eggs in holes, on ledges, or take over old nests of other species. In north and central Europe six species can be seen, although two are very rare.

Osprey *Pandion haliaetus*
Family: Osprey Pandionidae
F Balbuzard fluviatile G Fischadler

Distinctive character: Very pale beneath in flight; long, narrow angled wings. Somewhat reminiscent of large gull.

Features: Upperparts dark brown, mostly white underneath. Brownish breast band especially in ♀ and young birds. In juv. the upperparts have pale feather edges.

Voice: Usually heard only near nest. Loud, melodious *cheep-cheep-cheep*, *tyipp-tyipp-tyipp*, or *kyu kyu kyu* varying in tone and tempo.

Occurrence: Breeds in forested areas near to clear, fish-rich lakes, slow-flowing rivers and by the coast. Stable but small population in Scotland, frequent in Scandinavia, but breeding only in a few sites in northern central Europe. Regular migrant in spring and autumn, to lakes and rivers.

Behaviour: Flies with shallow, graceful wingbeats, hovering frequently over water. Dives almost vertically with wings half closed, thrusting talons forward shortly before hitting the surface. Often submerges completely for a short time.

Food: Medium-sized fish.

Breeding habits: April–June, 1 brood; large nest often in the branches of high, old pine.

	> Buzzard	(S), M	IV–X	BR

Distinctive character: In flight very broad, parallel-sided wings (not angled when soaring), head well extended, tail short and wedge-shaped.

Features: Very large, sturdy bird of prey with powerful yellow bill and short white tail. Immatures (1–4 years) dark, even on head, tail and bill. Flies with slow, powerful and rather stiff wing strokes.

Voice: During courtship (from January) very vocal, with a loud raucous *kyowkyowkyow*, somewhat reminis- cent of Black Woodpecker; ♂ has higher-pitched call. At nest, *kli-kli-kli*.

Occurrence: Breeds near large lakes and rivers, surrounded by forest, even a few kilometres from water, at coast and in the tundra. Mostly extinct in central Europe, with relict populations in northern East Germany and Poland; good popula- tion on coast of Norway. Reintro- duced in west of Scotland. Regular on certain large lakes (such as north- eastern France, and foothills of the Alps) outside breeding season.

Food: In summer mostly fish, but also young birds to the size of heron and mammals to size of Roe Deer. In winter mainly waterbirds and carrion.

Breeding habits: February-June, 1 brood; very large nest in tall tree.

> Golden Eagle	R, (W)	I–XII	BR	

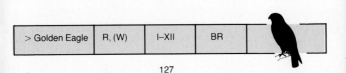

Black Kite *Milvus migrans*
Family: Hawks and relatives Accipitridae
F Milan noir G Schwarzmilan

Distinctive character: In flight long, relatively broad wings, and long sometimes slightly forked but always angular-looking tail.

Features: Slimmer than Buzzard. Plumage very dark. Juv. have paler markings above and below, but never so much white in wings as in Red Kite. Elegant in flight, circling with wings held horizontal.

Voice: Frequent whinnying and wailing *heeiirr* or *veehihihihi* often cut short.

Occurrence: Normally breeds near to water; in river-valley forests, at woodland margins, also on cliffs. Often hunts over water, but also over land. Outside breeding season mainly on rivers and lakes. Widespread but patchy in central, southern and eastern Europe; rare visitor to Britain (non-breeding).

Behaviour: Often flies slowly over water and along the banks in search of dead fish, sometimes along roads on the look-out for animals killed by traffic. Also harries other birds of prey and herons for their food. Very sociable outside breeding season.

Food: Very varied, but mainly dead fish. Also young birds, smaller mammals, mainly dead or injured animals.

Breeding habits: April–June, 1 brood; nest, often lined with mud, built in tall tree.

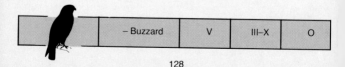

| | – Buzzard | V | III–X | O |

Red Kite *Milvus milvus*
Family: Hawks and relatives Accipitridae
F Milan royal G Rotmilan

Distinctive character: Long wings and long, deeply forked tail.
Features: Much longer-winged than Buzzard; contrasting plumage – light grey head and red-brown body, large white patch on outer wing. Underside and upperwing-coverts of juv. paler, back more red-brown, head browner, and chest heavily streaked. Often soars with slightly raised wings; uses tail to steer, with deep, relatively slow wingbeats; often twists tail when on hunting flight.
Voice: Drawn-out, plaintive whistling *weeoo-weewee wee wee-weeoo*,

often heard in spring; also single *deeair* or *yeee* calls.
Occurrence: Less dependent upon water than Black Kite; breeds in heterogeneous, preferably hilly, wooded landscape, with open areas such as small bogs, wetlands and clearings, but also in dry, flat areas with small pockets of woodland. Widespread but scattered in central, southern and eastern Europe, with outlying populations in southern Scandinavia and Wales.
Food: Fewer fish than Black Kite, tends to kill its own prey more. Mainly small mammals, birds, sick larger animals, carrion, refuse.
Breeding habits: April–June, 1 brood; nest (which often contains incorporated litter) in tall tree.

> Buzzard	R, (M)	I–XII	BR	

Short-toed Eagle
Circaetus gallicus
Family: Hawks and relatives Accipitridae
F Circaète Jean-le-Blanc
G Schlangenadler

Distinctive character: Large, broad head and yellow eye.
Features: Underside more or less strongly patterned. In flight pale underside sharply contrasting with dark upper chest. The large head (held well forward), long narrow, square-ended tail, and long, broad wings, held horizontal when soaring, are all characteristic. Wings sharply angled and held forward when gliding.
Voice: Quite vocal, especially during courtship. ♂ whistle somewhat reminiscent of Golden Oriole; ♀ less tuneful.
Occurrence: Breeds in open, varied landscapes with rich reptile fauna. Likes wet areas, interspersed with heath, woodland and cultivated land. In the south in bare and rocky areas with isolated tall trees for nesting. Rare breeder in Hungary, Czechoslovakia and east Poland. Not recorded in Britain.
Food: Mainly snakes, especially Grass Snakes, but also adders, slow-worms, lizards, and more rarely small mammals and birds.
Breeding habits: April–July, 1 brood; small nest in crown of tree or cliff.

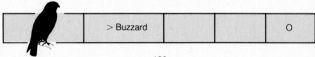

> Buzzard

O

Marsh Harrier *Circus aeruginosus*
Family: Hawks and relatives Accipitridae
F Busard des roseaux
G Rohrweihe

Distinctive character: Slow and frequent flight in search of prey, with soft wing strokes, interspersed with buoyant gliding, wings held up in a V-shape.
Features: Slimmer and more narrow-winged than Buzzard and with longer tail. ♂ relatively colourful, with pale grey tail and flight feathers, contrasting with black wing tips and otherwise dark plumage. ♀ (photo), and juv. dark with cream-coloured head and shoulders.
Voice: Displaying ♂ has shrill *keeay*; ♂ and ♀ alarm call is *kike-kike-kike* . . . .
Occurrence: Breeds in dense and extensive reedbeds on lowland lakes and rivers. Hunts over reeds, water meadows and nearby fields and open country. Even on migration mainly in wetlands, but also in open cultivated areas. Rare breeding bird in Britain.
Food: Small mammals to size of rats, birds to size of Teal, also fish, amphibians, insects, eggs and young of waterbirds.
Breeding habits: May–August, 1 brood; nests in thickest and tallest part of reedbed, rarely on dry land.

< Buzzard	(S), (W), (M)	I–XII	BR	

Hen Harrier *Circus cyaneus*
Family: Hawks and relatives Accipitridae
F Busard Saint-Martin
G Kornweihe

Distinctive character: Slim and light in flight.
Features: ♂ easily distinguished by ash-grey plumage, contrasting black-tipped wings and white rump. ♀ (photo) dark brown above, pale yellow-brown beneath, barred wings and tail, clear white rump.
Voice: ♂ has a plaintive high-pitched *piu piu* in courtship flight, or a bleating *kekeke-keke*; ♀ a hoarser *pih-e*. Woodpecker-like alarm call *chek-ek-ek-ek'*.

Occurrence: Breeds in open land-scapes – in boggy areas, heather moor, dunes, marshes and damp meadows, occasionally in young plantations or open country. Uncommon breeder in Britain, mainly in north. In winter regular in open wet areas and cultivated land.
Behaviour: Soars and glides with V-shaped wings, often 'floats' low over open country.
Food: Small mammals to size of rats, especially voles; birds, especially small species and young waders, ducks and game birds.
Breeding habits: May–July, 1 brood; nests on ground in thick vegetation.

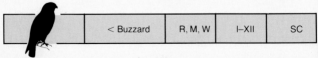

	< Buzzard	R, M, W	I–XII	SC

Montagu's Harrier *Circus pygargus*
Family: Hawks and relatives Accipitridae
F Busard cendré
G Wiesenweihe

Distinctive character: Very slim and graceful in flight, somewhat gawky, yet still elegant. Reminiscent of gull or tern.

Features: ♂ (photo and drawing), similar to Hen Harrier but with narrower, more gull-like wings and with longer tail, and black band on wings and rufous streaking on belly and flanks. ♀ almost identical to ♀ Hen Harrier, but wings narrower and white rump less marked. Juv. resembles ♀, but with plain red-brown underside.

Voice: Courting ♂ has shrill *kyekyek-yek . . .*, ♀ a soft *pee-i*.

Occurrence: Breeds in low vegetation near water, but also in damp heath, especially on fens, increasingly also in young plantations and

Montagu's Harrier, ♂ in flight

open fields. Hunts mainly over wetlands with low cover, and in cultivated fields. Rare breeder.

Food: Small mammals, insects, small birds, birds' eggs.

Breeding habits: May–August, 1 brood; skimpy nest in tall vegetation.

< Buzzard	(S), (M)	IV–X	BR	

Goshawk *Accipiter gentilis*
Family: Hawks and relatives Accipitridae
F Autour des palombes
G Habicht

Distinctive character: Large size (♀), long tail and relatively short and rounded wings; surprise hunter.

Features: ♂ smaller and lighter in weight than ♀ (photo); upperparts of ♂ grey-brown to slate-grey, ♀ brown. Underside whitish with dense barring; in juv. yellowish to rust-coloured with heavy dark brown drop-shaped spots. ♂ easily confused with ♀ Sparrowhawk, but appears heavier with more powerful chest and slower wingbeats.

Voice: During courtship (from March) a large range of urgent *gek-gek-gek* calls, especially when disturbed by nest; also a Buzzard-like *hee-ay*, accented on the first syllable. Fledged young have hoarse, high-pitched, wild-sounding contact call, *peee-eh*.

Occurrence: Breeds in well-varied wooded areas, particularly in tall conifer forests, sometimes even quite near human habitations. Widespread in Europe but usually rarer than Buzzard.

Food: Very varied diet, depending on opportunity. Birds to size of domestic hens and mammals to young Hares, commonly birds of crow family, doves, partridges, Rabbits, squirrels.

Breeding habits: March–July, 1 brood; well-hidden nest, usually high in conifer.

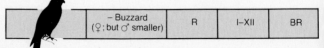

	– Buzzard (♀; but ♂ smaller)	R	I–XII	BR

Sparrowhawk *Accipiter nisus*
Family: Hawks and relatives Accipitridae
F Épervier d'Europe
G Sperber

Distinctive character: Surprise hunter, skilful in use of cover.
Features: ♂ about size of Collared Dove, ♀ markedly larger. Shape and colouring similar to Goshawk, but tail seems longer, narrower and squarer-ended. Underparts narrowly barred, rust-brown in ♂ (photo). Upperparts of ♀ browny-grey, ♂ blue-grey. Juv. dark brown above, heavily barred below.
Voice: Usually heard only in spring. Alarm call in area of nest a high, fast kyikyikyi, higher-pitched in ♂ than ♀. Calls of fledgling birds, *yee yee*, resemble contact calls of young Long-eared Owls.
Occurrence: Mainly in coniferous and mixed woodland, interspersed with open areas (cultivated, bog, heather-moor), hedges and copses. In winter also hunts in villages and towns. Widespread but local.
Behaviour: Often shakes tail after landing and often sits upright with head retracted.
Food: Mainly birds from Goldcrest up to size of Woodpigeon (♂ to thrush size); rarely small mammals.
Breeding habits: April–July, 1 brood; flat nest well hidden, usually in 20–50 year-old-spruce or pine.

| > Thrush (♂)
< Carrion Crow (♀) | R, W, M | I–XII | | | 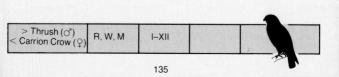 |

Buzzard *Buteo buteo*
Family: Hawks and relatives Accipitridae
F Buse variable G Mäusebussard

Distinctive character: Commonest larger bird of prey.
Features: Medium-sized rather plump bird of prey with short neck and large, rounded head; wings broad; tail rounded when spread. Very variable in plumage, from almost white to uniform dark brown, usually brownish with paler breast-band. Eye dark brown to yellow. Rather compact in flight with wings held somewhat stiffly. Wingtips noticeably upturned when soaring.
Voice: Characteristic mewing *pee-yay* at all times of year, but especially in spring.

Occurrence: Breeds in well-varied wooded regions with fields, bogs, hedges and copses. Hunts over open country and moorland, and nests mostly at woodland edge. In Britain mainly in north and west.
Behaviour: Often soars for lengthy periods over open country, especially in spring. Often sits patiently on a post, waiting for small mammal prey. In winter frequently looks for run-over animals along roads.
Food: Mainly voles and other small mammals such as mice, other rodents and young rabbits; worms, reptiles, insects; only rarely birds.
Breeding habits: March–July, 1 brood; nests high in deciduous or coniferous tree, also on cliffs.

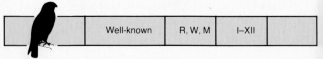

| | Well-known | R, W, M | I–XII | |

Rough-legged Buzzard *Buteo lagopus*
Family: Hawks and relatives Accipitridae
F Buse pattue
G Rauhfußbussard

Distinctive character: Tail white with wide dark band at tip; hovers much more frequently than Buzzard.
Features: Plumage nearly as variable as Buzzard's, but usually paler, especially on the head, and heavier contrast. Legs feathered to toes. In flight distinguished from Buzzard by longer wings and tail, and by black belly, contrasting with pale undersides of the wings.
Voice: Similar to Buzzard, but somewhat mournful – *pee-ee-ee*. Usually silent in winter.

Occurrence: Breeds in mountains of northern Europe, mostly above tree-line, and in the tundra. Like Buzzard, highly dependent upon supply of small mammals, and it is numerous only after rodent population explosions. In some winters it migrates south in large numbers. In winter found on moorland and heaths, river flood-plains and open cultivated areas. Overwinters in larger numbers in eastern Europe, much rarer in west.
Behaviour: Often flies low when hunting; frequently sits on hummocks or low shrubs. Often hovers.
Food: At breeding grounds, voles and lemmings, young hares and game birds. In winter as Buzzard; often eats dead animals.

– Buzzard	(W), (M)	X–IV	O	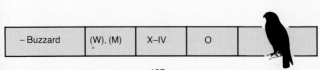

Honey Buzzard *Pernis apivorus*
Family: Hawks and relatives Accipitridae
F Bondrée apivore
G Wespenbussard

Distinctive character: In flight identified by pigeon-like protruding head, by relatively narrow wings, and long, narrow tail with one or two clear bands and a black tip.

Features: Size of Buzzard, but slimmer and longer-winged and with longer tail. Plumage likewise very variable – upperside usually dark brown; underside pale with heavy brown markings, but can be almost white or uniform brown. Head dove-grey, eye always yellow. Wingbeats deeper, softer and less stiff than Buzzard.

Juv. have less narrow wings, more like Buzzard. Hovers rarely.

Voice: On breeding ground often a high-pitched, melodius *deeh-dlee-lew*.

Occurrence: Well-structured, often hilly areas, with mixed woodland interspersed with clearings, pasture or fields. Usually nests at woodland edge and hunts in open areas. Widespread in Europe, very rare breeder in Britain.

Food: Mainly larvae and pupae of wasps and bees, more rarely of bumblebees. Also adult insects, frogs, lizards and young birds. Rarely small mammals.

Breeding habits: May–August, 1 brood; nest, usually lined with fresh leaves, in tall tree.

	– Buzzard	(S), (M)	IV–IX	BR

Golden Eagle *Aquila chrysaetos*
Family: Hawks and relatives Accipitridae
F Aigle royal G Steinadler

Distinctive character: Large, dark eagle, size often underestimated.
Features: Very powerfully built, with large bill and strong talons. Top of head and neck golden-brown, wings long and relatively narrow, unlike broad vulture-like wings of White-tailed Eagle. Tail quite long and broad. Juv. very dark with large white patches on wings and white tail with broad black tip.
Voice: Only rarely heard. Musical *kloöi* or *kiyeh* during courtship, but also yapping *klikliklikli* or *gergergergerger*.
Occurrence: Originally in diverse forest and mountainous country, but today almost entirely restricted to remote mountain areas in Scandinavia, northern Britain and Iberia; rare breeding bird in Alps and Carpathians. Young birds wander long distances.
Food: Medium-sized mammals up to size of Roe Deer, birds such as grouse; in Alps in summer mainly Marmots, in winter carrion.
Breeding habits: February-June, 1 brood; large nest on cliff, more rarely in large old tree. **Imperial Eagle** *Aquila heliaca* is somewhat smaller and less powerful. There are now only a few pairs breeding in Hungary and Czechoslovakia, and (a different race) in Iberia. In soaring adults, the front and rear edges of wings are almost parallel.

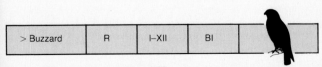

> Buzzard	R	I–XII	BI	

Booted Eagle *Hieraaetus pennatus*
Family: Hawks and relatives Accipitridae
F Aigle botté G Zwergadler

Distinctive character: Long series of calls at breeding site.
Features: Reminiscent of Buzzard, but only from a distance. In flight has much longer, usually square-cut tail, narrower wings (with primaries more spread) and with head more prominent. Two colour forms, a rarer dark phase (photo), and a commoner pale phase (drawing).
Voice: Often heard at breeding site. Calls somewhat reminiscent of waders: plover-like *yeeip*, a high-pitched *kyikyikyi* or Buzzard-like *peee-ay*.
Occurrence: Breeds mainly in hilly areas, in light deciduous and mixed forest with bushy and open areas;

often nests in warm, dry oak woodland. Occurs mainly in south west and south east Europe; very rare breeder in central Europe, a few pairs

Booted Eagle   in flight

in Hungary, Poland, and Czechoslovakia. Threatened by habitat destruction, pesticides and hunting. Not recorded in Britain.
Food: Reptiles, mammals and birds, also insects.
Breeding habits: April–July, 1 brood; nests mainly in abandoned nests of herons, storks or other birds of prey.

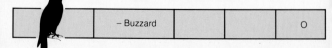

| | – Buzzard | | | O |

140

Lesser Spotted Eagle *Aquila pomarina*
Family: Hawks and relatives Accipitridae
F Aigle pomarin
G Schreiadler

Distinctive character: When soaring the long wings are of similar width from the base to the tip, and often held flat.
Features: Medium-sized well-proportioned eagle. Flies with primaries well spread (like White-tailed); tail rounded. Plumage brown; from below flight feathers darker than red-brown wing-coverts (other way round in Spotted Eagle). Juv. have one or two rows of white spots on wings.
Voice: A loud melodious *yew yew* at breeding site.
Occurrence: Undisturbed mixed forests with scattered wetland and clearings. Rare in central Europe, now breeding only in eastern part (East Germany, Hungary, Czechoslovakia, Poland). Not recorded in Britain.
Food: Voles and other small mammals, frogs, young birds, large insects, carrion.

Lesser Spotted Eagle in flight

Breeding habits: April–July, 1 brood; large nest high in deciduous tree.
Spotted Eagle *Aquila clanga* is very similar but darker. A few pairs breed in east Poland.

> Buzzard			O		

141

Kestrel *Falco tinnunculus*
Family: Falcons Falconidae
F Faucon crécerelle G Turmfalke

Distinctive character: Commonest small bird of prey, often seen by main roads; hovers frequently.
Features: Small falcon with long tail, long pointed wings and brown upperparts. ♂ has weakly speckled red-brown back, grey head, and grey tail with broad black terminal band. ♀ has uniformly red-brown, barred upperparts. Juv. resembles ♀, but more heavily streaked. (Photo is of juv ♂.)
Voice: Calls frequently, especially in breeding season. High-pitched rapid *kikikiki . . .* or *kyikyikyi . . .* , ♀ often a vibrating *vrreeh vrreeh*.
Occurrence: Often hunts in open countryside, breeds in trees in fields and at woodland edges; also in quarries, villages and cities, and mountains. Outside breeding season in open country, often in cultivated

juvenile ♂
hovering

Kestrel

fields; often beside motorways and main roads.
Food: Mainly field mice, but also other small mammals, reptiles, insects, young birds.
Breeding habits: April–June, 1 brood; nests in old crow nests, in holes in trees, on ledges of tall buildings, amongst rocks, and in nest boxes.

	< Carrion Crow	R, W, M	I–XII	

Red-footed Falcon *Falco vespertinus*
Family: Falcons Falconidae
F Faucon kobez
G Rotfußfalke

Distinctive character: Small falcon, rather Hobby-like in flight. Rare visitor.
Features: ♂ (drawing), dark slate-grey with red thighs and undertail-coverts ('trousers'). ♀ (photo), has yellow-brown underside, light grey, barred back and tail, and a short moustache. Juv. very like young Hobbies, but with longer, more narrowly barred tail and less heavily patterned underside. Hovers like Kestrel.
Voice: In breeding colony very vocal; otherwise silent. Calls reminiscent of Wryneck – such as *kyay kyay kyay* and, when alarmed, *kikiki* . . . or *tsrriitsrrii* . . . .
Occurrence: Lowland open steppe-like country with bushes and scattered groups oftrees or light river-valley woodland. Breeds in Hungary and Czechoslovakia, and sporadically

Red-footed Falcon, ♂

in Austria. In summer in small numbers to northern Europe, including Britain, mainly over insect-rich bogs and heaths, and at lake margins.
Food: Large insects such as beetles, dragonflies, crickets, ants; lizards, small mammals, young birds.
Breeding habits: May–September, 1 brood; nests colonially (up to several hundred pairs) in old Rook and Magpie nests.

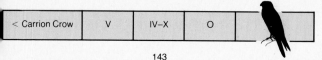

< Carrion Crow	V	IV–X	O	

Hobby *Falco subbuteo*
Family: Falcons Falconidae
F Faucon hobereau G Baumfalke

Distinctive character: Resembles a large swift in flight.

Features: About size of Kestrel but much shorter tail and long, sickle-shaped wings. Upperparts blue-grey, head with conspicuous moustache; leg feathers ('trousers') and undertail-coverts rust-red. Juv. with yellowish 'trousers', brownish upperparts and cream-coloured, heavily streaked underside.

Voice: Calls frequently in breeding season, even after young have flown. Usual call is a penetrating rapid *kew-kew-kew*, rather like Wryneck's song. Also a Kestrel-like *kikiki . . .* and extended *kyee kyee*.

Occurrence: Wooded country with bogs, heath, damp meadows and vegetated lake margins. Breeds in light woodland, at forest edges and in trees in fields. Unlike Kestrel rarely in built-up areas or cultivated fields. Widespread, but not common.

Food: Small birds such as swallows, larks, sparrows, finches, even swifts; dragonflies, beetles, butterflies, crickets.

Breeding habits: May–August, 1 brood; usually nests in old crow nests, or those of Magpie, pigeons or other birds of prey.

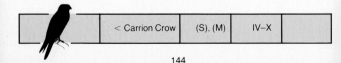

| | | < Carrion Crow | (S), (M) | IV–X | |

Peregrine *Falco peregrinus*
Family: Falcons Falconidae
F Faucon pèlerin
G Wanderfalke

Distinctive character: Crow-sized, powerful and swift falcon.
Features: Long pointed wings, broad at the base; short, tapering tail; broad dark moustache; underparts pale with dark barring. ♂ > ♀. Juv. dark brown above, yellow-brown with heavy dark streaking below. Normal flight relatively slow with powerful, shallow wingstrokes, interspersed with variable periods of gliding.
Voice: Plaintive *kyay kyay kyay* . . . or *keeay-ee* when disturbed near nest.
Occurrence: Hilly and mountainous areas, and at coast. Needs steep rocks or cliffs for nest-site. Often hunts over water in winter. Beginning to increase after marked decline due to pesticide poisoning.
Food: Birds to size of heron; mainly pigeons, birds of crow family, thrushes, starlings, larks, gulls and waders.
Breeding habits: April–July, 1 brood; nests on rock ledges, in some areas in trees old nests of other birds of prey.

The larger, longer-tailed and paler **Saker** *Falco cherrug* breeds in Hungary and Czechoslovakia, and is a regular visitor to steppe region of east Austria (Burgenland). In Europe the Saker specializes on ground squirrels (souslik), but it also catches other small mammals and birds.

> Kestrel	R, W	I–XII	BI	

Merlin *Falco columbarius*
Family: Falcons Falconidae
F Faucon émerillon G Merlin

Distinctive character: Very small, compact falcon with pointed wings; often flies low and fast.
Features: ♂ (photo right) is grey above with delicate streaks, the hint of a moustache, and rusty-yellow below with dark streaking. ♀ has heavier streaks below, and is dark brown above with a barred tail. Juv. very like ♀. In flight sometimes confused with Sparrowhawk, but latter has much longer tail and more rounded wings, usually with spread primaries.
Voice: Usually heard only near nest.

Very rapid *keke-keke* . . . or *kikiki* . . . .
Occurrence: Breeds in upland birch woodland, on tree-less heather moors and in boggy areas of northern Europe; uncommon breeder in Britain. In winter regular at coast as individuals and, more rarely, further inland, hunting over open country.
Behaviour: Surprise hunter, chasing birds in low, rapid flight, and overpowering them in the air. Also sits on rocks and posts.
Food: Small birds to size of thrushes, rarely small mammals; mainly pipits, larks, buntings, thrushes and plovers.
Breeding habits: May–August, 1 brood; often nests in old crow nests, also in crevice in rocks or on the ground.

	< Carrion Crow	R, W, M	I–XII	SC

Gamebirds, Rails, Cranes, Bustards

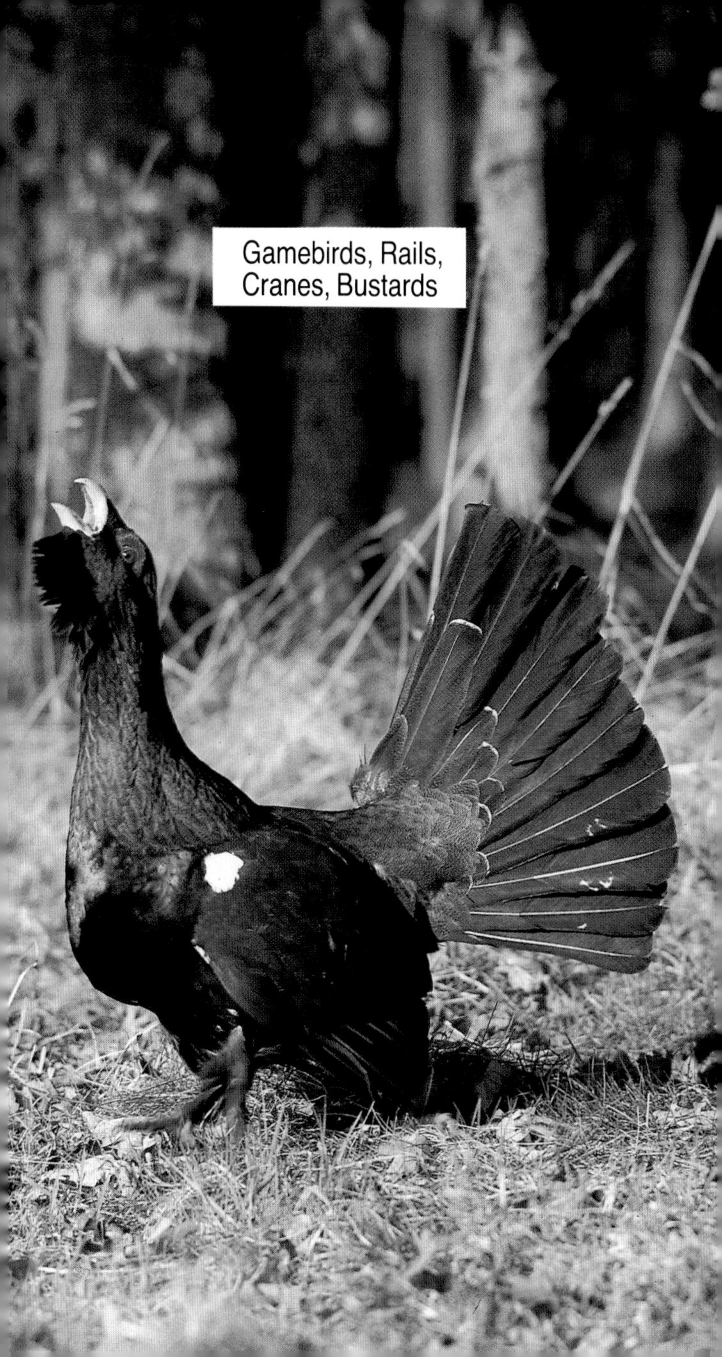

Gamebirds – Galliformes

All gamebirds are well adapted to ground living, with powerful feet and usually long toes. The bill is short, strong, and slightly decurved. The food is mainly plant matter, although the chicks begin with a diet of insects. With the exception of the Quail, a true migratory bird, gamebirds are either resident or partial migrants. In many species the sexes are markedly different; cock birds are usually considerably larger and more colourful than the hens, which normally have camouflaged plumage. The young are nidifugous, can walk soon after hatching, and develop the ability to fly long before they are fully grown. There are two families in Europe:

Grouse have more or less thickly feathered legs and feet. This characteristic, and the rows of horny pads on their toes (which act rather like snow-shoes) are both adaptations to cold, snowy winters. Red patches of bare skin above the eyes (wattles) are also a characteristic. Grouse are above all ground birds, often flying up explosively only at the last moment. They fly with rapid wingbeats, often interspersed with gliding. They tend to be rather sedentary. Some have elaborate breeding displays in the spring. The nest is a simple scrape in the ground; brooding and rearing of the young is carried out entirely by the well-camouflaged hens. Grouse are very sensitive to disturbance and avoid close proximity to humans. In Europe there are five species, of which one (the Ptarmigan) is found only in high mountains; the Hazel Hen *Bonasa bonasia* is a little-known species, occurring locally in damp dense conifer forests in parts of central and eastern Europe and Scandinavia, and is not included here.

Pheasants and relatives live mostly in open country, never in closed extensive forest. Their legs and feet are bare. Partridges and quails are short-tailed, dumpy birds whereas the pheasants have very long tails. Pheasants live in open country with bushes and trees, in wet areas, and even in light forest. Partridges and quails are birds of open fields, but since they are often hidden in the vegetation, are often best identified by their

Great Bustard ♂ displaying

Black Grouse (foot)

Migrating Cranes

calls. There are four species in central and northern Europe. The Pheasant is an introduced species and its populations are often viable only because they are artificially reared and fed.

Rails and Cranes – Gruiformes

This order contains dissimilar swamp and steppe birds. Most are long-legged and long-necked. The young are nidifugous, but not as independent at first as game bird chicks or ducklings. The European species belong to three families:

Rails are small to medium-sized dumpy ground birds with powerful feet and long front toes. They are somewhat reminiscent of gamebirds with their short tails and a habit of nodding their heads. Most species have laterally compressed bodies which helps them move skilfully through dense vegetation. Most of the seven central and northern European rails live in reed or sedge beds. The Corncrake, however, is primarily a bird of hay meadows, while the Coot is a true waterbird. With the exception of Coot and Moorhen, rails are difficult to see because they keep themselves hidden in thick ground cover. Knowledge of their calls is often the only way to identify them.

Bustards by contrast inhabit dry, steppe-like country. They have very powerful running legs with three thick toes, and a long neck. In flight the broad wings with contrasting black and white markings are distinctive. Sexes are quite different in size: cock birds can be more than twice the weight of hens. Two species were found originally in central Europe, but the Little Bustard is now extinct in this region. Male Great Bustards, weighing up to 12 kg, are amongst the heaviest of all flying birds.

Cranes are somewhat reminiscent of storks in appearance, and also fly with outstretched necks; however, their bills are shorter. They have distinctive far-carrying trumpeting calls, produced in a greatly extended windpipe. Cranes often migrate in large flocks in classic v-formation. They live in extensive wetlands, nesting on the ground in inaccessible sites. There is only one species in Europe.

Red Grouse *Lagopus lagopus*
Family: Grouse Tetraonidae
F Lagopède des saules
G Moorschneehuhn

Distinctive character: Typical bird of moorlands in Britain and Ireland.

Features: Plump and short-winged, with dark rufous plumage barred with black and with blackish wings and tail. ♂ has a fairly obvious red 'comb' above each eye (photo), these being less distinct on the ♀. From a distance the birds appear all dark.

Voice: When flushed gives a fast loud cackle, *kokokokokok* (like laughter); also a loud *go-bek go-bek* and when displaying a series of crowing notes ends in a short rattle, *raa ra re rekekekeke rrr*.

Occurrence: Breeds on dry heather moors and peat-bog areas in Ireland and north and western Britain; in winter, when the moors are often covered by snow, many come down to lower levels and can then be seen on stubble fields. About 15 other races occur in a circumpolar distribution from southern Norway across north Asia and northern North America.

Behaviour: Shy; spends most of its time on the ground, concealed by the heather, but sometimes perches on posts or in trees. When startled or flushed, Red Grouse fly up abruptly from ground and move rapidly away, rocking low over the heather with fast, loud whirring wingbeats and long glides, cackling as they go.

Food: Heather shoots, insects and berries.

Breeding habits: April–June, 1 brood; nest is a scrape in the ground among heather or rough grass, sometimes with a little, sparse lining.

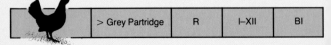

| | > Grey Partridge | R | I–XII | BI |

Ptarmigan
Lagopus mutus
Family: Grouse Tetraonidae
F Lagopède des Alpes
G Alpenschneehuhn

Distinctive character: In flight by wings, which are white at all seasons. Characteristic crackling, grating call.
Features: Only slightly larger than Grey Partridge. Breeding ♂ (photo) marbled dark brown-grey on upperside and breast, otherwise white; small red wattle above eye. ♀ yellow-brown with darker crescent-shaped markings and only faint wattles. In winter snow-white, except for jet-black tail, ♂ with wattles and black stripe from bill to behind eye (drawing is of ♀).
Voice: Breeding ♂ has hollow grating *kwarrr kwarr krrr ak ak ak*. ♂ and ♀ flight call *arr* or *krrr*. ♀ also a sonorous *kick*.
Occurrence: Above tree-line in richly structured rocky sites. At lower levels in winter. Widespread in northern Scotland and in Alps, but not common.

Ptarmigan

♀
winter

Food: Berries, shoots and buds of shrub sand herbs. Chicks insectivorous.
Breeding habits: May–August, 1 brood; nests in small hollow amongst rocks or under shrub, usually well camouflaged.

– Grey Partridge	R	I–XII		

Black Grouse *Tetrao tetrix*
Family: Grouse Tetraonidae
F Tétras lyre
G Birkhuhn

Distinctive character: In flight white underwing-coverts conspicuous.
Features: ♂ (Blackcock) has shiny blue-black plumage and lyre-shaped tail feathers, fluffed out during court-ship to reveal white undertail-coverts (photo). ♀ (Greyhen) (drawing), noticeably smaller with camouflaged brown plumage; in flight note slightly forked tail. Flight rapid and often high. Rapid wingbeats interspersed with periods of gliding. Often perches in trees, particularly in winter.
Voice: ♂'s song at communal dis-play ground (or 'lek') a bubbling *coo*, interspersed with hissing or sneezing *tshooissh*.
Occurrence: Heather moor and bog, open wooded areas; dwarf shrub heath near tree-line. Rare and declining, in Britain confined to north and west.

Black Grouse.
(Greyhen) ♀

Food: Buds, shoots and berries of dwarf shrubs, trees and herbs. Insects.
Breeding habits: May–July, 1 brood; nest on ground, hidden in dense vegetation.

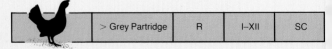

| | > Grey Partridge | R | I–XII | SC |

Capercaillie *Tetrao urogallus*
Family: Grouse Tetraonidae
F Grand tétras
G Auerhuhn

Distinctive character: Crashing take-off especially of ♂, often alarming.
Features: ♂ almost as large as Turkey. Long tail, fanned in display (photo). ♀ (drawing) smaller with orange-brown breastband and rust-red tail with black bands. Flight after noisy take-off is rapid with powerful wingbeats and long stretches of gliding.
Voice: Courting ♂ has strange clicking, grinding, explosive, gurgling song; each phrase lasts about seven seconds.
Occurrence: Well-structured, undisturbed coniferous and mixed forests, with small clearings, Bilberry bushes and ant nests. Scandinavia, Scotland, central and south-eastern Europe. Declined owing to destruction of natural forests, and through disturbance. Restricted to above 1,000 m in the Alps.

Capercaillie,
♀

Food: Buds and shoots of trees, leaves and berries of Bilberry and Cowberry; in winter almost entirely pine needles.
Breeding habits: April–June, 1 brood; nests on ground, often underneath twigs.

> Domestic fowl	R	I–XII	BL	

153

Grey Partridge *Perdix perdix*
Family: Pheasants Phasianidae
F Ferdrix grise G Rebhuhn

Distinctive character: When flushed, fly low and rapidly close to ground, with loud wing noise and calling.
Features: Small, dumpy, with short tail; rust-brown stripes on flank, dark, horseshoe-shaped patch on breast (not always conspicuous). ♂'s and ♀ can be distinguished only by pattern of feathers on shoulders and upperwing-coverts. ♀ occasionally lacks dark breast patch. Flies with rapid wingbeats alternating with glides with wings turned downwards.
Voice: Alarm call a loud *kerripriprip*

. . . . Territorial ♂ a hoarse, penetrating repeated *kirreck*, mainly heard in morning and evening.
Occurrence: Dry, varied, lowland cultivated country, with agricultural fields, hedges and overgrown field margins; heaths, wasteland. Widespread but decreasing owing to more intensive cultivation and corresponding decrease in food and cover.
Food: Seeds and green parts of wild plants, crops, clover; chicks eat insects and spiders.
Breeding habits: April–July, 1 brood; very well-camouflaged nest sited on ground, is a hollow, lined with plants, often beneath shrubs a field margin.

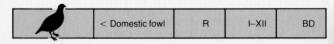

	< Domestic fowl	R	I–XII	BD

Quail *Coturnix coturnix*
Family: Pheasants Phasianidae
F Caille des blés G Wachtel

Distinctive character: The call; bird seldom seen.
Features: Smallest European member of this family. Dumpy and almost tail-less, with camouflaged plumage. ♂ with black markings on head and throat, ♀ has heavily speckled breast.
Voice: ♂ territorial song a characteristic repeated *pik-ve-vik* (accented on first syllable), heard particularly at dusk. When flushed, *rek rek* or *krvi krvi*.
Occurrence: Mixed fields with rough margins, hedges. Likes to breed in winter wheat, clover and lucerne crops, as well as in tall hay-meadows. Widespread in lowlands; numbers vary widely from year to year, but generally decreasing. Main reasons for decline are change from small plots to monocultures in large fields and use of chemical pesticides, thus reducing both food and cover.
Behaviour: Quails spend most of their lives hidden from view in thick vegetation, and nearly always run away rather than fly. Rarely seen skimming low over ground with rapid shallow wingbeats.
Food: Seeds of many plants, cereals, green plants, insects, spiders.
Breeding habits: May–August, 1–2 broods; nests on ground in thick cover.

– Blackbird	(S)	V–X	BR	

Pheasant *Phasianus colchicus*
Family: Pheasants Phasianidae
F Faisan de chasse G Fasan

Distinctive character: ♂ has striking, colourful plumage.
Features: Very long, pointed tail; ♀ yellowish-brown with dark speckles, tail shorter than ♂.
Voice: ♂ has explosive loud *ker-kock*, often followed by bout of loud wing flapping. In flight often a hard, hoarse *ech* or (when flushed) *kukuk*.
Occurrence: Native of southern Asia; introduced to Europe (several races) for sport. Found in cultivated areas, at edges of light woods and in not too wet swampy sites. Widespread and common.
Food: Seeds, grain, fruit, berries, green plants, worms, snails, insects.
Breeding habits: April–July, 1 brood; nest usually well hidden on ground.

The **Red-legged Partridge**, *Alectoris rufa* was introduced to Britain from south-west Europe in the 18th century.

Red-legged
Partridge

Larger than Grey Partridge and with more upright posture, it is easily identified by its conspicuous white throat and black 'necklace' and heavily barred flanks; legs bright red. It inhabits farmland and stony or shingly areas.

	– Domestic fowl	R	I–XII	

156

Water Rail *Rallus aquaticus*
Family: Rails Rallidae
F Râle d'eau G Wasserralle

Distinctive character: Calls sound rather like squealing pig.
Features: Long, slightly decurved red bill and black-and-white-striped flanks distinctive. Upperparts dark brown with black streaking; sides of head, neck and breast slate-grey; undertail-coverts whitish. In breeding plumage ♂ bill bright red in winter; ♀ bill paler and browner. Juv. pale brown below, with delicate barring on neck and breast, and flanks less clearly striped.
Voice: Calls sound like squealing pigs – *kriek krruee krruee* . . . ; in spring territorial ♂ have a repeated sharp *chik-chik-chik* call, often ending with a drawn-out, throaty *chueer*; ♀ a trilling *tip-kuiiir*.
Occurrence: Breeds in thick reed and sedge beds, especially at river or lake margins. In winter can occasionally be seen in the open at the edge of a ditch or bank. Widespread and not uncommon, particularly in winter.
Behaviour: Climbs very skilfully in dense tangled vegetation. Flees intruders by running rather than flying. Very secretive.
Food: Worms, snails, aquatic insects, small crustaceans, tadpoles, sometimes small fish, small mammals and young birds.
Breeding habits: April–July, 1–2 broods; nests made of plant material, well hidden in thick vegetation.

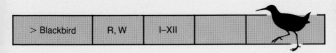

> Blackbird	R, W	I–XII		

Spotted Crake
Porzana porzana
Family: Rails Rallidae
F Marouette ponctuée
G Tüpfelsumpfhuhn

Distinctive character: Very rarely seen; lives in thick vegetation. ♂'s remarkable spring song is characteristic.
Features: Scarcely as big as Blackbird, with dark plumage, speckled with dense and fine white markings; flanks with white bars; undertail-coverts yellowish. Bill much shorter than Water Rail's. Juv. with whiter chin and paler underside.
Voice: Courtship song of ♂ tends to be heard mainly at dusk and at night – a short, monotonously repeated *hwitt*, like a whiplash. ♀ has softer and less sharp call. Other sounds include *kek* or growling *brurr*.
Occurrence: Breeds at thickly vegetated edges of rivers and lakes, particularly where reeds give way to sedges; also in tall wet meadows and thickly overgrown ditch margins. A vital requirement is a low and, if possible, stable water level. Rare and decreasing breeding bird, absent over large areas.
Food: Insects, spiders, snails, and worms, occasionally soft plant material.
Breeding habits: May–July, 1–2 broods; nest constructed of old stems and leaves, usually over shallow (few cm) water.

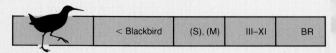

	< Blackbird	(S), (M)	III–XI	BR

Little Crake *Porzana parva*
Family: Rails Rallidae
F Marouette poussin
G Kleines Sumpfhuhn

Distinctive character: Extremely secretive, very rarely seen. Call important in identification.

Features: Bill yellow-green with red at base. Upperparts olive-brown with lighter and darker longitudinal stripes and rows of indistinct white spots. Underside slate-grey, undertail-coverts clearly barred, flanks weakly barred. ♀ cream-coloured below and with whitish throat.

Voice: In spring the ♀ has a rapid, descending trill – *pep perrr*. Alarm call of both sexes a sharp *tvook*. ♂ song, usually heard at dusk, consists of individual elements, running together as it accelerates – *put put put purrr*.

Occurrence: Breeds in thick reed and sedge beds in shallow water. Breeds in only a few places in central Europe, such as the Neusiedlersee. Irregular further west; exact distribution still unknown. Rare vagrant in Britain.

Food: Mainly insects.

Breeding habits: May–August, 1–2 broods; deep nest constructed on bent stems or on a sedge clump, protected from above by overhanging stems.

The very similar **Baillon's Crake** *Porzana pusilla* is equally rare. ♂ has more contrasting plumage, with more marked barring on flanks and uniformly green bill.

| < Blackbird | V | III–XI | O | 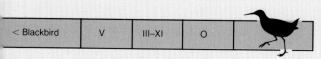 |

Corncrake *Crex crex*
Family: Rails Rallidae
F Râles de genêts
G Wachtelkönig, Wiesenralle

Distinctive character: Rarely seen as remains hidden in vegetation. Usually identified by characteristic voice.

Features: Slimly built; upperparts light grey-brown, black with dark brown streaks. Ungainly fluttering flight, when dangling legs and chestnut wings conspicuous.

Voice: ♂ has monotonous hollow, rasping *rrerrp rrerrp*, often continuing for hours, by night as well as in the daytime, audible from afar.

Occurrence: Breeds in moist grassland, extensively cultivated tail hay meadows; also in dry crops such as cereals, lucerne and clover; and in some places even in potato and root crops. Populations in decline following changes in agricultural practices; now very rare in Britain, with most in western Scotland, and uncommon in Ireland.

Behaviour: Not very sociable; flies seldom and usually for short distance; calls mainly in twilight, in early morning and at night.

Food: Mainly insects, worms, snails, small frogs, seeds, green parts of plants.

Breeding habits: May–July, 1–2 broods; nests in hollow in the ground beneath thick vegetation.

	< Grey Partridge	(S), (M)	IV–X	BD

Moorhen *Gallinula chloropus*
Family: Rails Rallidae
F Poule d'eau G Teichhuhn

Distinctive character: Moves like small hen; nods head whlie swimming and walking; repeatedly jerks tail.

Features: Smaller and slimmer than Coot; bill red with yellow tip and red frontal shield; legs and very long toes green. Snow-white undertail-coverts displayed rhythmically as tail bobbed. Juv. brownish with pale throat area, bill and shield olive-green. Trails legs in flight.

Voice: Alarm call a frequently heard harsh, guttural, yet pleasant *kirrrk*; when danger threatens a penetrating *kirreck*, or sharp *dik dik*; in flight often a repeated *kek-kek*.

Occurrence: Breeds at overgrown margins of still and slow-flowing water, and in ditches and small almost overgrown ponds. Common on streams and in ponds in villages and urban parks. Feeds on adjoining grassland and fields. Widespread and common.

Food: Seeds, shoots and fruits of marsh and water plants, snails, worms, tadpoles, insects.

Breeding habits: March–August, 1–2, sometimes as many as 3 broods; deep nest usually well hidden close to water, occasionally nests in open.

< Grey Partridge	R, W	I–XII		

Coot *Fulica atra*
Family: Rails Rallidae
F Foulque macroule G Bläßuhn

Distinctive character: Black, rotund waterbird, very common on larger rivers and lakes.
Features: A rail that has become a waterfowl. Toes equipped with lobes; bright white frontal shield.
Voice: Calls often. ♂ a voiceless *tsk* or *tsi*, often a *tp* sound, like a popping champagne cork. ♀ a loud, barking *kowk*. Alarm call a sharp *pitts*.
Occurrence: Breeds on nutrient-rich lakes, reservoirs, ponds, and slow-flowing river with well-developed fringing vegetation. Also on small gravel pits and on lakes in urban parks. In winter often gather in large flocks on ice-free lakes, and often become tame where regularly fed, for example at jetties or in parks. Widespread and common.
Behaviour: Swims high in the water, constantly jerking head. Dives with a small forward leap. Patters across water surface, beating wings, for a considerable distance before take-off.
Food: Reed shoots, water plants, grass, leaves, snails and other molluscs, worms, insects, duck food, bread, refuse.
Breeding habits: March–July, 2–3 broods; large nest made of plant material, usually over shallow water.

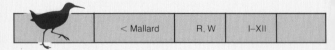

| | < Mallard | R, W | I–XII | |

Great Bustard *Otis tarda*
Family: Bustards Otididae
F Outarde barbue G Großtrappe

Distinctive character: Huge struts with head held high, with dignified steps; impressive courtship display.
Features: Very large and heavy bird. ♂ has thick neck, whitish beard of bristles on chin and brownish breastband. ♀ much smaller with thinner neck, no beard or breastband. Flies with slow, powerful, regular wingbeats. Very shy.
Voice: Virtually silent. In conflicts groaning *uh* or *eh* sounds. Juv. have a high melodious trill – *eerrr*; when danger threatens a whining *jeee* . . . .
Occurrence: Originally a bird of the open steppes. Today found in Europe in open cultivated fields and pastures, now breeding only in East Germany, Poland, Czechoslovakia and Hungary eastwards, Spain and Portugal, with remnant populations in eastern Austria. Decline follows intensification of agriculture, use of pesticides and fragmentation of breeding areas by road building.
Food: Green parts and seeds of steppe and meadow plants; in cultivated areas often clover, lucrene, rape; also insects, earthworms, lizards, mice and young birds.
Breeding habits: April–July, 1 brood; nest is a shallow hollow lined with a little plant material, usually sited in a field with low vegetation.

– Farmyard Goose	V	XII–V	O	

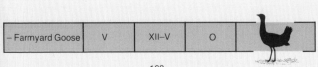

163

Crane *Grus grus*
Family: Cranes Gruidae
F Grue cendrée G Kranich

Distinctive character: Very shy bird, with distinctive loud, trumpeting call.
Features: Very elegant, long-legged bird with relatively short bill. In flight (drawing), has long, out-stretched neck and legs protruding well beyond tail; migrating flocks often fly in wedge formation.
Voice: Very characteristic loud bellowing or trumpeting call such as *kroo* or *krooi-kruh*, often heard in early morning, in flight and during migration.
Occurrence: Breeds in extensive wetlands, marshy lake margins, light swampy woodland in boggy areas

and on isolated forest lakes. In Europe breeds mainly in Scandinavia, East Germany and Poland. On migration also found in cultivated

Crane,
in flight

fields; often spends the night on shallow water, for safety.
Food: Pulses, grain, potatoes and other crops, berries, acorns, earthworms, snails, insects, mice, frogs.
Breeding habits: April–June, 1 brood; large nest made of plant material, often sited on small islets in marsh.

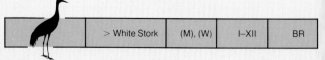

| | > White Stork | (M), (W) | I–XII | BR |

Waders, Gulls,
Terns, Auks

Waders, Gulls, Terns, Auks – Charadriiformes

This order comprises a varied collection of small to large, often long-legged birds, which tend to be associated with wetlands; some are even birds of the open sea. Only a few live in dry areas. In north and central Europe there are nine families represented:

Oystercatchers are sturdy shorebirds, with brightly coloured bill and legs. The feed mainly on bivalves, gastropods and crustaceans, opening their shells and hard carapaces using special techniques. One species is a common breeding bird of European coasts. Often to be seen in large flocks outside breeding season.

Stone-curlews have rather bustard-like short bills and powerful-legs, but are much smaller. They also share the same habitat – dry, steppe-like country. They are most active in twilight and at night, and have unusually large eyes. Their camouflaged plumage lets them blend well into their stony background. Knowledge of their calls makes them easier to find. The single European species has become increasingly scarce.

Avocets and stilts have long legs and thin bills, upturned in avocets. The two European species are medium-sized, elegant birds and easily identified by their black and white plumage.

Plovers are short-legged and short-billed compared with other waders. The bill, which is slightly thickened at the tip, is adapted for picking food items from the surface, rather than for probing. Body is usually compact, the head rounded, and the eyes large. There are two groups in Europe – lapwings (one species), and the true plovers (six species), which have pointed wings and fly rapidly.

Sandpipers and snipes are typical waders, with long legs and bills, although some are small, with short neck and legs. They feed by probing in soft ground, using the highly sensitive tips of their bills. Live mainly in wetlands and at coasts; with few exceptions ground nesters, the clutch normally consisting of four well-camouflaged eggs. In Europe more than 25 diverse species can be seen.

Skuas are medium-sized to large gull-like seabirds, mostly dark in plumage. The central tail feathers are protracted, bill hooked at tip. The different species, especially juveniles, are often hard to separate. Skuas are skilful fliers and are often parasitic, chasing other seabirds, forcing them to give up their food. They also hunt small animals for themselves. Four species in Europe, mostly seen at coasts, or at sea.

Gulls are medium-sized to large seabirds with long wings and mainly white or grey plumage, often with dark wingtips. Some of the smaller species have a dark head in the breeding season. Gulls live at the coast and on inland waters, but only a few are true ocean birds. Unlike terns they rarely dive but mostly take their food from the water surface. The smaller species attain adult plumage at two years old, but the larger species not until they are four. Gulls are mainly ground nesters and the young leave the nest after a few days, to hide nearby. Ten species can be seen regularly in northern Europe, with a few others as rare visitors.

Oystercatcher

Avocet

Stone-curlew

Snipe

Ringed
Plover,
feigning
injury

Black-headed
Gull

Long-tailed
Skua

Guillemot

Common Tern

Terns are mostly smaller and slimmer than gulls, with narrow, pointed wings, and short legs with which they can walk only clumsily. The tail is often forked. They feed mainly by diving steeply into the water, although the Black Tern normally takes insects from the water surface. They swim rarely, unlike gulls. Terns are strongly migratory, with one species, the Arctic Tern, making the longest migratory round-trip of any bird. Six species are regularly seen in Britain.

Auks are compact, small to medium-sized seabirds with small wings. They fly rapidly with whirring wingbeats. Their legs are set far back on their bodies and on land they stand more or less upright. They are expert divers, using both wings and feet, and feed mainly on fish. They breed in colonies on cliffs and slopes near to the sea. Most lay a single rather large egg. Four species breed on British coasts.

Oystercatcher
Haematopus ostralegus
Family: Oystercatchers Haematopodidae
F Huîtrier pie
G Austernfischer

Distinctive character: Unmistakable appearance and call; common on most coasts.
Features: Large, bulky shorebird with long, red, slightly laterally flattened bill and red legs. Plumage striking black and white. Non-breeding birds with white band across throat. Juv. with pale throat markings and dark bill tip. In flight broad white wingbar and white rump conspicuous.

Voice: Very loud and far-carrying; a penetrating *keleep* or *beek-a-beek*, often repeated. On breeding grounds an attractive, repeated *telee* or *tliee*.
Occurrence: Breeds on different types of coast, above all on sandy and shingle beaches, in some areas (Scotland) often on inland lakes and rivers. Outside breeding season often found in large flocks on mudflats, and coastal pastures and meadows. Common on British coasts.
Food: Bivalves, gastropods, small crustaceans, worms, insects.
Breeding habits: April–July, 1 brood; nest is a shallow hollow on sparsely vegetated terrain, often on beach.

| | > Feral Pigeon | R, W, M | I–XII | WI,WL |

Stone-curlew *Burhinus oedicnemus*
Family: Stone-curlews Burhinidae
F Oedicnème criard
G Triel

Distinctive character: Mainly crepuscular and nocturnal, often crouches on
ground by day, flying away at last
moment.
Features: Large, strong wader with
short bill, large yellow eyes and long,
relatively thick, yellow legs. In flight
shows double white wingbars and
mainly black and white primaries.
Voice: Calls frequently at dusk:
Curlew-like *kroor-ee* or pure fluting
koo-lee, often as duet. Flight call *gigi-
gigigi*.
Occurrence: Breeds in dry, open
areas with sparse plant cover and
sandy or stony soil, in steppe areas,
wide alluvial plains and fields with low
vegetation. Occasional at coast during migration. Western, eastern and
southern Europe, but absent from
most of northern and central Europe.
Rare breeder in Poland, Czechoslovakia and Hungary, a few pairs in
Austria; in Britain, very scarce
breeder in south-east in suitable
habitats.
Food: Earthworms, snails, insects
(especially grasshoppers), spiders,
frogs, lizards, snakes, mice and
young birds.
Breeding habits: April–August, 1–2
broods; nest in shallow depression in
sparse vegetation on dry soil.

> Feral Pigeon	S	III–X	BR, BD, BL	

Avocet
Recurvirostra avosetta
Family: Avocets and stilts Recurvirostridae
F Avocette
G Säbelschnäbler

Distinctive character: Long, upturned bill and bluish legs.
Features: Very elegant black and white wader. Juv. has brownish cap and back maskings. In flight the legs extend well beyond tail.
Voice: Calls frequently: musical *pleet* or *ploo-it*, rapidly repeated when alarmed.
Occurrence: Breeds on saltmarshes and shores, on shallow lagoons, estuaries and shallow inland lakes. Breeds on North Sea coast (sometimes overwinters), parts of southern Baltic, Mediterranean, and in steppe region of Austria and Hungary. Many

British breeders winter in south-west
Behaviour: Feeds in shallow water with sideways swishing of bill. Very sociable outside breeding season. Occasionally swims in deep water, especially at high tide when feeding

Avocets, in flight

grounds covered.
Food: Worms, insects and their larvae, small crustaceans, small fish.
Breeding habits: April–July, 1 brood; nests on ground, a simple hollow near to water; often in colonies.

	– Feral Pigeon	R, S, M	I–XII	BR, BL, WL

Black-winged Stilt
Himantopus himantopus
Family: Avocets and stilts
Recurvirostridae
F Échasse blanche
G Stelzenläufer

Distinctive character: Gawky appearance due to extremely long legs.
Features: Unmistakable with unusually long, red legs. Bill thin, straight and black, somewhat longer than head. Breeding ♂ often has black cap and back of neck; ♀ normally a white cap. Both sexes have grey head and neck in winter. Juv. have brownish upperparts. In flight easily identified by contrasting black and white plumage, and by legs extending far beyond tip of tail.
Voice: Calls frequently when alarmed: *kyepp* or *kyivip*, also *gek* or a nasal, bleating *kwit kwit*.
Occurrence: Breeds near shallow water in estuaries, on shallow lagoons and salinas. Sensitive to changes in water level. Very local in central Europe, where it breeds regularly only in Hungary. Rare summer visitor to Britain, where has bred a few times.
Food: Water insects, tadpoles, small crustaceans, small fish, more rarely terrestrial insects.
Breeding habits: April–July, 1 brood; nests on ground near water, often well hidden on slight hillock.

< Feral Pigeon	S	IV–IX	BR	

Little Ringed Plover
Charadrius dubius
Family: Plovers
Charadriidae
F Petit gravelot
G Flußregenpfeifer

Distinctive character: Loud, some-what melancholy voice.

Features: Small rather rotund wader with dull pink or muddy-yellow legs and bright yellow eye-ring. Outside breeding season lacking the black head markings and with brownish chestband. Juv. lacks white mark behind eye and have plain head and neck. In flight distinguished from Ringed Plover by lack of wing-bar.

Voice: Alarm call a sharp *piu* or *pitt pitt*. Territorial song of a hoarse *krik-rikri . . .* or *krikrikrikriakri-akri-a . . .*, often during bat-like song flight.

Occurrence: Original breeding grounds sparsely vegetated gravelly and sandy river banks and islands; today mainly at gravel and sand pits, wasteland, abandoned fishponds and quarries. Widespread inland but not common. On migration mainly on rivers and mud. Declined owing to regulation of rivers.

Food: Insects, mainly small beetles, small crustaceans, small snails and worms.

Breeding habits: April–August, 1–2 broods; clutch laid in a scrape on gravel and very hard to spot.

| | > House Sparrow | S | III–X | |

Ringed Plover
Charadrius hiaticula
Family: Plovers Charadriidae
F Grand gravelot
G Sandregenpfeifer

Distinctive character: Small plump wader with sandy brown upperparts. Runs rapidly over sand, often stopping abruptly.
Features: Slightly larger than Little Ringed Plover, and with more powerful bill, yellow, tipped with black. Outside breeding plumage bill is black with orange mark at base. Legs orange-yellow; yellowish in winter. Juv. resemble adults in winter, but upperparts show pale feather edges. In flight always distinguished from Little Ringed Plover by white wingbar. Flocks fly rapidly, turning often.
Voice: Alarm call a soft *tee-ip* or *dooi*, and a rapid *kip-kivip*. Song is a rapid hoarse *too-widee too-widee too-widee* uttered during low, wavering song flight.
Occurrence: Breeds on sand and shingle at the coast, and locally on gravel pits and heaths. On migration regularly seen on inland sand or mud banks. Winters mainly on coastal mud.
Food: Insects, especially beetles and flies, small molluscs and snails, worms, spiders, small crustaceans.
Breeding habits: April–August, 2–3 broods; nest is a shallow scrape in sand.

> House Sparrow	R, W, M	I–XII	WI, WL	

Kentish Plover
Charadrius alexandrinus
Family: Plovers
Charadriidae
F Gravelot à collier interrompu
G Seeregenpfeifer

Distinctive character: Most coastal of the small plovers, usually seen near to tidal zone.
Features: Longer-legged than the two ringed plovers, and with less contrasting head markings. Bill and legs dark, breast band only faintly indicated. Breeding ♂ has chestnut crown and black bar on forehead (photo). In winter resembles ♀ but retains blackish forehead bar. ♀ has paler less contrasting plumage. In flight shows white wing-bar and white at sides of tail.
Voice: Alarm call *brirr irrr*; flight call

often a short *pit*. Song is a trill, often given in flight.
Occurrence: Breeds on sandy coasts, mainly in Mediterranean, Atlantic and southern North Sea. Also breeds inland in Hungary and eastern Austria. Very scarce migrant in Britain (formerly bred).

Kentish Plover,

♀

Food: Worms, small snails and other molluscs, small crustaceans, insects.
Breeding habits: April–August, 1 brood; nest is a small scrape made by ♀ in the sand.

	> House Sparrow	M	III-IX	BR

174

Dotterel *Charadrius morinellus*
Family: Plovers Charadriidae
F Pluvier guignard
G Mornell

Distinctive character: Breeding ♂ often very tame and approachable.
Features: Prominent white stripe above eye, meeting behind head to form V-shape. ♀ slightly larger than ♂ (photo), and more brightly coloured. In winter much paler with yellowish grey upperparts, white belly and less clearly marked breast band and supercilium. Dumpy and short-tailed in flight, with no wing-bar. Black belly patch noticeable in the breeding plumage.

Voice: Flight call *kirr* or *dirr*, *britt* or *plitt*. ♀ song, a rhythmically repeated *pit-pit-pit* . . . given in flight.
Occurrence: Breeds on bare tundra of northern Europe, on bare, stony mountains in north Britain, and in a few places on the Alps (Steiermark) and Appennines; also, since 1961, on the Netherlands coast (where summer non-breeders are also regular). On migration seen in small flocks on dry, rocky areas, short pasture and on river banks, often at traditional sites.
Food: Mainly insects and their larvae, also small snails.
Breeding habits: May–July, 1 brood; nests in low vegetation; the brooding male is well camouflaged.

– Blackbird	S, M	IV–X	SC	

Golden Plover
Pluvialis apricaria
Family: Plovers Charadriidae
F Pluvier doré
G Goldregenpfeifer

Distinctive character: Plaintive call in open moorland habitat.
Features: In breeding plumage possibly confusable with Grey Plover. However, latter seen only on migration and in winter, mainly on mudflats and rarely inland. Amount of black on underside is very variable and lacking completely in winter, when upperside is still yellow-gold (drawing).
Voice: Frequent soft, liquid *dui*, alarm call a sharp *tlie*, on breeding ground a plaintive, musical *tlooi-wee*. Song, often given in flight, consists of high whistled, running in to rapid rolls and trills.

Occurrence: Breeds on damp mountain tundra, upland bogs and moorland in northern Europe, including Britain (mainly Scotland). Common in large flocks on migration and

Golden Plover, winter

in winter, in meadows, pasture and fields.
Food: Mainly insects, worms, snails.
Breeding habits: April–August, 1 brood; nests on dry ground.

	> Blackbird	P, W, M	I–XII	WI, SC

176

Grey Plover
Pluvialis squatarola
Family: Plovers Charadriidae
F Pluvier argenté
G Kiebitzregenpfeifer

Distinctive character: Characteristic call, audible over long distance.
Features: Slightly larger and stouter then Golden Plover, with heavier bill. Upperparts greyer in winter plumage. Underside in breeding plumage (seen on migration) richly contrasting black and white. In flight, distinguished from Golden Plover at all seasons by black axillaries and white rump (drawings). Often seen singly. At rest looks somewhat 'dejected' because of retracted neck.
Voice: Flight call *tlee-u-ee*, with middle syllable lowest. Song of ♂ some

what reminiscent of call of Curlew.
Occurrence: Breeds in Arctic lichen tundra. Regular, and in places common, migrant and winter visitor around British coasts, mainly as individuals or small flocks scattered on

Winter

Grey Plover, in flight

mudflats; more rarely on mud inland.
Food: Worms, small molluscs, snails and crustaceans.

> Blackbird	W, M	VII–V	WI,WL	

Lapwing *Vanellus vanellus*
Family: Plovers Charadriidae
F Vanneau huppé
G Kiebitz

Distinctive character: Tumbling spring courtship flight is characteristic (drawing).

Features: Striking black and white plumage, visible from distance; long pointed crest on head. ♀ has shorter crest and white spotting on throat. Both sexes have white throat in winter. Juv. as winter adult but with feather edges and short crest.

Voice: Vocal. Call a rather whining hoarse *peewee* or *keer-vit*; in tumbling, erratic courtship flight a repeated *kchair-owee-a-vip a-vip*, wings producing droning, throbbing noise.

Occurrence: Breeds in open, flat lowland habitats with low vegetation: damp meadows, bogs, coastal pasture, heath, fields and farmland, waste land and gravel areas. Widespread; large flocks in the autumn and winter.

Food: Insects such as beetles,

Lapwing, display flight

craneflies, and flies and their larvae; earthworms, seeds and fruits.

Breeding habits: March–July, 1 brood; nest with small amount of dry plant material placed in slightly raised position on dry ground.

	– Feral Pigeon	P, M, W	I–XII	

Knot *Calidris canutus*
Family: Sandpipers Scolopacidae
F Bécasseau maubèche G Knutt

Distinctive character: Forms densely packed, cloud-like flocks, extended in shape when close to ground, more oval-shaped when higher up.
Features: Large, squat, short-legged wader with short, straight bill. In breeding (photo), rust-brown, with upperparts coarsely patterned pale and blackish. In winter (drawing) plain with pale grey upperparts, whitish below. Juv. have upperparts fringed black and white and underparts tinged buff-pink. In flight long, narrow wings with pale bar, and pale rump.
Voice: Rather muted *chutt*, in flight *vit-it vit-it* or *wit wit*. Song, given in circling flight, rather Curlew-like.

Occurrence: Breeds in moss and lichen tundra in Greenland. Common on coasts on migration and in winter, with huge flocks in favoured localities (The Wash). A few non-breeders summer on British coasts.

Knot,
winter

Food: On migration and in winter mainly small molluscs and crustaceans.

– Blackbird	W, M, (S)	I–XII	WI,WL	

Sanderling *Calidris alba*
Family: Sandpipers Scolopacidae
F Bécasseau sanderling
G Sanderling

Distinctive character: Often runs very rapidly along the water's edge on shoreline, dashing back to avoid waves.

Features: Small wader with straight black bill and black legs. Very pale in winter plumage. In breeding plumage back, neck and upper breast rust-red with darker spots, otherwise pure white. In winter (most often seen) pale grey upperside with dark 'shoulder patch'. Juv. (photo), forehead and upper breast white, crown streaked blackish and sides of breast buff with darker streaking. In flight looks silver-grey, with broad white wing-bar noticeable.

Voice: Vocal. Short *plitt*, *tyick* or *tivick*, often repeated in flight. Has trilling flight song.

Occurrence: Breeds on bare lichen tundra. Outside breeding season at coast, mostly close to strandline. Common passage migrant and winter visitor to favoured coasts, especially sandy ones.

Food: On migration and in winter insects, small crustaceans, worms, small molluscs.

Breeding habits: June–July, 1 brood; nest placed on ground between lichens, *Dryas*, or dwarf willows.

	< Blackbird	M, W	I–XII	WI,WL

Little Stint *Calidris minuta*
Family: Sandpipers Scolopacidae
F Bécasseau minute
G Zwergstrandläufer

Distinctive character: Patters hectically to and fro when searching for food.

Features: Tiny wader with short black bill and black legs; in breeding plumage with rufous and black pattern on upperside and indistinct white V on back. In winter more grey above, with greyish tinge to sides of breast. In juv. white V is clearer.

Voice: Quiet twittering *tirrtirrtirrit* when flushed. In flight *tit*. Song a soft, tinkling trill, varying in pitch and usually given in butterfly-like song flight.

Occurrence: Breeds in damp tundra in far north. On migration fairly common at coast and inland, singly or in small flocks. Usually keeps to open mud, often together with Dunlin.

Food: Insects, small worms, snails, seeds.

Breeding habits: June–July, 1 brood.

The very similar **Temminck's Stint** *Calidris temminckii* is more elongated and shorter-legged. Legs paler, plumage greyer above. Breeds on rivers and lake margins in willow and birch zones of northern Europe. Scarce on migration, on muddy areas at lakes and marshes with a little vegetation; unsociable.

< House Sparrow	M, W	IV–V, VII–X	O	

Curlew Sandpiper
Calidris ferruginea
Family: Sandpipers Scolopacidae
F Bécasseau cocorli
G Sichelstrandläufer

Distinctive character: Often feeds in water up to its belly.
Features: Dunlin-sized but appears larger and less dumpy, with longer legs, bill and neck. Bill gently decurved. Easily identified in breeding plumage (photo); in winter (drawing), paler than Dunlin and with clear white stripe above eye. Juv. have pale feather edging above and buff tinge to sides of breast. In flight shows white wing-bar and rump. Probes in shallow water more often than Dunlin.
Voice: Flight call a trilling *krirrip* or *tirrip*, softer and less nasal than Dunlin's. ♂ has a trilling, purring song.
Occurrence: Breeds in arctic coastal tundra. On migration mostly on mudflats, more rarely on inland muddy sites and lakes. Regular on coasts,

winter

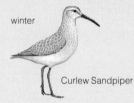

Curlew Sandpiper

especially North Sea. Often associates with Dunlin.
Food: Worms, small snails and other molluscs, small crustaceans, insects.

| | < Blackbird | M | IV–X | O |

Dunlin *Calidris alpina*
Family: Sandpipers Scolopacidae
F Bécasseau variable
G Alpenstrandläufer

Distinctive character: Commonest European wader.
Features: Bill relatively long, slightly decurved at tip. Large black patch on belly in breeding plumage (photo). In winter (drawing) mostly grey-brown, without black belly patch. Juv. dark brown above, with pale feather edges. In flight forms large flocks which wheel about, often changing shape.
Voice: Flight call a nasal *trirr* or *krri*. The song starts with *treer treerr*, followed by purring trill and ending with *krri-ree-ree*.
Occurrence: Breeds in tundra, on marshes and boggy areas above the tree-line, in open coastal grassland, and on upland moors of northern Europe including Britain. Gathers in sometimes huge flocks on mudflats outside breeding season, in smaller

winter

Dunlin

flocks inland.
Food: Insects, worms, small molluscs, small crustaceans.
Breeding habits: May–July, 1 brood; nest hidden in ground vegetation.

< Blackbird	P, W, M	I–XII	WI,WL	

Purple Sandpiper
Calidris maritima
Family: Sandpipers Scolopacidae
F Bécasseau violet
G Meerstrandläufer

Distinctive character: Relatively tame; camouflaged plumage makes it look like a mobile dark rock.

Features: Larger and shorter-legged than Dunlin; dumpy, with rather duck-like rounded breast; bill as long as head, slightly decurved, dark with yellow base; legs grey-green. In breeding plumage back blackish with rufous and pale markings. In winter (photo) mainly dark brown-grey, pale belly, legs orange. Also appears very dark in flight and shows narrow white wing-bar and white base to outer tail feathers.

Voice: Often silent in winter; flight call a short *weet* or *witweet*. Song fluting, somewhat reminiscent of Green Woodpecker's laugh, given from ground or in whirring song-flight.

Occurrence: Breeds on bare, stony plateaux mainly in Iceland and in Scandinavian mountains (has bred in Scotland), usually far from coast. Outside breeding season in small flocks on stony and rocky coasts and around breakwaters, often in surf zone.

Food: Insects, seeds and green parts of plants; in winter small marine molluscs and crustaceans.

Breeding habits: May–July, 1 brood; nest is a hollow on dry soil, lined with plant material.

	< Blackbird	W, M, (S)	VII–V	BR,BL

Ruff (♀ Reeve)
Philomachus pugnax
Family: Sandpipers Scolopacidae
F Chevalier combattant
G Kampfläufer

Distinctive character: Impressive lek display by ♂ in spring.
Features: Breeding ♂ (photo.) has remarkable ruff and head tufts, very variable in colour; face naked and covered with skin papillae. ♀ (drawing) and non-breeding plumage unobtrusive; scaly-patterned upperside. In flight narrow wing-bar, white sides to rump and tail base noticeable.
Voice: Usually silent. A hoarse *gri* during nocturnal migration.
Occurrence: Breeds on open bogs, damp meadows and on wet heaths; favours extensively grazed damp meadows with ditches and ponds, especially near to coast. Outside breeding season often in flocks at muddy lakes, marshes, fields; in spring more on meadows with damp hollows. Rare breeding bird in water-meadows and marshes outside north-

Reeve
♀

eastern European stronghold. Declined in some areas owing to drainage and general habitat destruction.
Food: Aquatic insects, small molluscs, worms, seeds, green plants.
Breeding habits: May–July, 1 brood; nest usually well hidden, in dry site.

♀ – Blackbird ♂ larger	(S), W, M	I–XII	BR, BL	

Distinctive character: Characteristic flight call.

Features: A little larger than Redshank, with longer bill and legs. In breeding plumage (least frequently seen) mainly blackish with fine white spots on back; legs dark red. In winter resembles Redshank, but paler and greyer. Juv. (photo) have dark vermiculated barring below. Lacks wing-bar.

Voice: Flight call a sharp *tchuit*. When disturbed at breeding ground a penetrating *tjicktjicktjicktjick . . . .* Song a melodious purring, somewhat droning, *krrru-i-krrru-i . . .* , often in flight.

Occurrence: Breeds on mires surrounded by forest in northern Scandinavia, Finland and Soviet Union. Outside breeding season in singles or small flocks at margins of shallow water and in tidal channels and brackish areas on shallow coasts.

Behaviour: Often wades in water up to belly, occasionally swims.

Food: Aquatic insects and their larvae, small crustaceans, worms, tadpoles, small fish.

Marsh Sandpiper *Tringa stagnatilis* is a rare visitor, mainly to eastern Europe. Very delicate, with long, thin legs and very thin bill, twice as long as head. Mainly seen on migration at inland marshes or bodies of water.

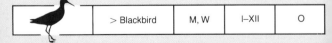

	> Blackbird	M, W	I–XII	O

Redshank *Tringa totanus*
Family: Sandpipers Scolopacidae
F Chevalier gambette G Rotschenkel

Distinctive character: Bright red legs and, in flight, white lower back and broad white trailing edge to wings (drawing).
Features: Inconspicuous except for red legs. Breeding plumage (photo) upperparts brownish with darker streaks and speckles; at other times paler grey-brown above, less speckled. Juv. lack red base to bill, have yellower legs, and are more reddish-brown above.
Voice: When flushed and in flight a loud, fluting *tleu-hu* or *tleu-hu-hu*; at breeding site persistent scolding *tjikt-jiktjik*. Song a yodelling *toolee-a toolee-a toolee-a*, often given in flight.

Occurrence: Breeds in open marshes and wet meadows with short vegetation, especially near coasts. Outside breeding season on shallow

Redshank,
in flight

coasts, often in large flocks on mud-flats, in smaller groups in damp habitats inland. Often feeds in shallow muddy water.
Food: Insects, worms, small crustaceans, small molluscs.
Breeding habits: April–June, 1 brood; ground nest hidden in vegetation.

> Blackbird	R, W, M	I–XII	WI, WL	

Greenshank *Tringa nebularia*
Family: Sandpipers Scolopacidae
F Chevalier aboyeur
G Grünschenkel

Distinctive character: Large size, pale plumage and loud fluting call.
Features: Stately pale wader with long, slightly upturned bill and long, greenish legs. Juv. and birds outside breeding season paler and greyer above, almost pure white beneath. In flight legs extend beyond tail.
Voice: Flight call a loud fluting *tew-tew-tew*, recalling Green Woodpecker. On breeding ground, when disturbed, a hard *kyukyukyu* . . . . Song a fluting *tew-i tew-i tew-i* . . . ,
often from a vantage point or performed in song-flight over territory.
Occurrence: Breeds in northern Europe, including Scotland, on open moorland or on heath with bushes or isolated trees close to water; also in willow region of Scandinavian mountains, and in tundra. Outside breeding season in small groups or as individual birds on flat coasts, or gravelly or sandy river and lake margins and on flooded meadows.
Behaviour: Often feeds in shallow water, running after small fish with bill half open or catching small prey at water surface.
Food: Aquatic insects, worms, small crustaceans, tadpoles, small fish and frogs.

	> Blackbird	P, M, W	I–XII	SC

Wood Sandpiper
Tringa glareola
Family: Sandpipers Scolopacidae
F Chevalier sylvain
G Bruchwasserläufer

Distinctive character: Fast-flying, slim, noisy brown and white wader.
Features: Small, delicate, somewhat unobtrusive, resembling Green Sandpiper. Upperparts more heavily spotted with white; less clearly marked in winter plumage. Juv. with regular yellowish-buff spotting. Legs clearly visible beyond tail in flight. Otherwise distinguished from Green Sandpiper by pale underwing and less contrasting whitish rump and tail.

Voice: Flight call a pleasant *jiff jiff jiff*. Song incorporates *tleea-tleea-tleea* . . . delivered in high song-flight over territory; intruders greeted by a hard persistent *tjip tjip tjip*.
Occurrence: Breeds near water on mires with individual trees, in swampy woodland and in the tundra. On migration in small, loose flocks on open mud, flooded meadows, and lakes and gravel pits, also commonly at coast. Very rare breeder in Scotland; more widespread in small numbers on migration, mainly in autumn.
Food: Insects, small molluscs.
Breeding habits: May–July, 1 brood; nest carefully hidden in thick ground vegetation; occasionally in thrush nests.

< Blackbird	(S), M	IV–X	BR,BL	

Green Sandpiper
Tringa ochropus
Family: Sandpipers Scolopacidae
F Chevalier cul-blanc
G Waldwasserläufer

Distinctive character: When flushed, strong contrast between dark upperparts and snow-white base of tail. Characteristic flight call.
Features: More compact than Wood Sandpiper and with darker, less heavily spotted plumage. Tail white with 3–4 brownish bars. Juv. have yellowish spots above. Head and neck darker than Wood Sandpiper.
Voice: Vocal. Flight call a sharp, ringing *tluee-weet-weet*, especially when flushed. Alarm call at breeding ground an incessant *tick-tick-tick . . . .* Song, given in circling flight, is *keklee-lueet keklee-lueet*.
Occurrence: Breeds on lightly wooded mires, in damp swampy woodland and wooded lake margins. On migration common inland, on lakes, often hidden from view alongside banks, in similar places to Common Sandpiper. Also on small ponds, ditches, marshes, sewage farms and streams. Not on open muddy areas like Wood Sandpiper. Breeds in north-eastern Europe.
Food: Insects and their larvae, spiders, worms, small fish fry.
Breeding habits: April–June, 1 brood; mostly in year-old nests of thrushes, but also in old crow and pigeon nests, and old squirrels' dreys.

| | – Blackbird | M, W | I–XII | O |

190

Common Sandpiper
Actitis hypoleucos
Family: Sandpipers Scolopacidae
F Chevalier guignette
G Flußuferläufer

Distinctive character: Almost constantly bobs tail. Flies low over water with stiff flicking wing-beats interspersed with gliding on down-curved wings.
Features: Small, dumpy, short-legged with straight bill and dark rump. Outside breeding season head and neck markings somewhat paler, upperparts with fine wavy markings. White wing-bar is clearly visible in flight.

Voice: When flushed, a shrill penetrating *hee-di-di-hee-di-di* . . . . Alarm call a sharp *hiehp*. Song, given mostly in bat-like song-flight with quivering wings, is a long phrase – *heedee-tititi-weedee-tititiweedee* . . . .
Occurrence: Breeds at margins of rivers and lakes and on islands with relatively sparse vegetation. Also on rocky shores with open tree stands. In Britain breeds mainly in north. Outside breeding season on gravelly or stony ponds, lakes and rivers, and at sewage farms and estuaries.
Food: Small insects.
Breeding habits: May–July, 1 brood; nest is a hollow lined with plants sited on dry ground close to shore, hidden in vegetation or flotsam.

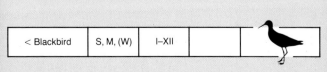

| < Blackbird | S, M, (W) | I–XII | | |

Turnstone *Arenaria interpres*
Family: Sandpipers Scolopacidae
F Tourne-pierre interprète
G Steinwälzer

Distinctive character: Turns over stones and seaweed while searching for food.

Features: Short-legged and squat. Breeding plumage very colourful; in winter (drawing) upperparts brownish-black with pale feather edges, chin and throat white. Juv. similar, but with pale rust-brown feather edgings above. Broad white wing-bar visible in flight, as are the white tail with black band near tip and white rump with black V.

Voice: Flight call a rapid *tritritri* or *tuk-a-tuk*. Song a nasal *kiwee kiwee-tititi*, given from song-post or in flight.

Occurrence: Breeds in northern Europe on rocky or pebbly coasts, relatively bare islands with trees, and in moss and lichen tundra. Winters in small flocks on rocky or sandy coasts, also on coastal mudflats.

Turnstone, winter

Food: On migration and in winter small molluscs, crustaceans, worms, refuse.

Breeding habits: May–June, 1 brood; nests on ground, between stones.

	−Blackbird	W, M, (S)	I–XII	O

192

Distinctive character: Swims when feeding, spinning round like a toy.

Features: Small, delicate wader with very fine bill barely as long as head. In breeding plumage ♀ (drawing) has white chin and bright rust-brown band at sides of neck and breast. ♂ much duller. In winter very pale grey above, white below, with dark patch behind eye. In flight white wing-bar prominent. Juv. much darker above, with golden lines down back.

Voice: When flushed *kritt kritt* or *pit*; on the water a quiet *pirr*.

Occurrence: Breeds on small lakes and boggy pools in Scandinavian mountains. Very few pairs in extreme N. Britain. On migration individually and in small flocks on open sea, on water near to coast, rarely inland.

Behaviour: Very buoyant when swimming, with constantly nodding head. Pecks rapidly to right and left; tame.

Red-necked Phalarope, ♀ breeding plumage

Food: Small insects, spiders, crustaceans, worms, snails.

Grey Phalarope *Phalaropus fulicarius.* Rare passage migrant, mainly from Sep. to Nov. Stockier than Red-necked, with stouter bill, otherwise similar in winter plumage.

> House Sparrow	(S), (M)	IV–IX	BR,BL	

Whimbrel *Numenius phaeopus*
Family: Sandpipers Scolopacidae
F Courlis corlieu
G Regenbrachvogel

Distinctive character: Striking tittering call and the dark-striped crown.
Features: A small version of the Curlew, with bill somewhat shorter, thicker and less curved (more kinked at tip). Upperparts more contrastingly patterned, crown with two broad, dark brown stripes. Faster wingbeats than Curlew.
Voice: Flight call a whinnying *bibi-bibi . . .* , or rather like ♀ Cuckoo's *pu-hu-hu-hu . . . .* Song recalls Curlew's, but trill section rather harsher and less 'dying away'.
Occurrence: Breeds in northern Europe on moorland and wet heath in coniferous forest zone and up into the tundra; scarce breeder in northern Scotland. Likes to be near water but does not nest in cultivated areas like Curlew. On migration in small or large flocks at coast, mainly on mudflats, but also on rocky coasts. Rarer inland. Often together with Curlew.
Food: Insects, worms, small crustaceans, snails and other molluscs; in autumn, berries as well.

	– Black-headed Gull	M, (S)	IV–IX	SC

Curlew *Numenius arquata*
Family: Sandpipers Scolopacidae
F Courlis cendré
G Großer Brachvogel

Distinctive character: Largest European wader.

Features: Long, distinctly decurved bill, longer and more curved in ♀. Paler above than Whimbrel, lacking dark markings on head. Flight not particularly rapid.

Voice: Very melodious and atmospheric. Flight call a fluting *coor-lee* or somewhat hoarser *chrooi*. Alarm call repeated *kwu-wooi-wooi*. Loud fluting and bubbling song given by ♂ during rising and falling song-flight, ending in melancholy trill just before landing.

Occurrence: Wide, open areas, raised bog and fen, upland moors, overgrown lake margins, damp meadows. Also breeds on hay meadows following destruction of mires and wet meadows, but here breeding success limited by early and frequent mowing, application of fertilizers and by disturbance. Large flocks on mudflats and coastal grassland outside breeding season.

Food: Earthworms, insects and their larvae, small molluscs and crustaceans; berries and green parts of plants.

Breeding habits: April–June, 1 brood; well-camouflaged nest on ground, sited in low vegetation.

> Black-headed Gull	P, W, M	I–XII	BI, WI	

Bar-tailed Godwit *Limosa lapponica*
Family: Sandpipers Scolopacidae
F Barge rousse
G Pfuhlschnepfe

Distinctive character: Long, slightly upturned bill.

Features: Slightly smaller and shorter-legged than similar Black-tailed Godwit, with somewhat shorter and slightly upturned bill. ♀ has longer bill than ♂. Tail with narrow bars. Breeding ♂ mainly rust-red, heavily marked with black on the back; ♀ drabber. Winter plumage (drawing) with Curlew-like pattern. In flight legs extend only slightly beyond tail, white rump, no wing-bar.

Voice: Flight call a nasal, penetrating *kekeke*. Small flocks often silent. Song similar to Black-tailed Godwit's, beginning with *tuituitui* . . . , followed by a yodelling *dowee dowee dowee* .

Occurrence: Breeds in far north of Scandinavia and Soviet Union on damp tundra and mires at edge of conifer limit; on migration and in winter

Black-tailed
Godwit (winter)

Bar-tailed,
Godwit (winter)

in small to large flocks on coastal mudflats and sandy shores, very rarely on inland mud.

Food: Insects and larvae, worms, bivalves and snails, small crustaceans.

	< Feral Pigeon	M, W, (S)	I–XII	WI,WL

Black-tailed Godwit *Limosa limosa*
Family: Sandpipers Scolopacidae
F Barge à queue noire
G Uferschnepfe

Distinctive character: In flight white wing-bar and white base to tail contrast sharply with dark upperparts.
Features: A large, long-legged, long-billed wader, with slim, elegant appearance. Breeding ♂ (photo) has rust-brown neck and breast; ♀ has longer bill and slightly less intense colours. Juv. rufous-buff on neck and breast, with pale feather edging on back. In winter both sexes plain grey.
Voice: Nasal *geg* or *ved*, also repeated. Alarm call at breeding ground loud energetic *videvidevide*. In song-flight, often at great height, a loud, penetrating, somewhat wailing *kruttekrutte . . . .*
Occurrence: Bred originally on mires and in heath and steppe areas near to water. Now mainly found in extensively managed wet meadows. Breeds Iceland, and very locally from Britain and north-east and south east central Europe. Declined mainly because of more intensive use and destruction of meadows. Locally common on coast and on inland shallow water outside breeding season.
Food: Worms, snails, insects, small crustaceans, tadpoles, seeds.
Breeding habits: April–June, 1 brood; nest on ground, usually in tall grass.

– Feral Pigeon	M, W, (S)	I–XII	BR,BL, WL	

Woodcock *Scolopax rusticola*
Family: Sandpipers *Scolopacidae*
F Bécasse des bois G Waldschnepfe

Distinctive character: Evening courtship flight (roding) at tree-top height, accompanied by strange sounds.
Features: Squat, short-legged, large-headed wader with long straight bill. Highly camouflaged plumage, making bird very difficult to spot on ground. Seems neckless in flight, wings broad and rounded, bill held angled towards ground. When flushed, usually flies away silently (sometimes slight wing-noise) in weak zig-zag cruves, only to drop down again not far away. Crepuscular and nocturnal.
Voice: Not very vocal except when

roding; occasionally a high-pitched *tsveet* when disturbed. When roding ♂ alternates deep, wooden, *kvorr-kvorr-kvorr* with very high-pitched sharp *pitsick*.
Occurrence: Breeds, in extensive woodland, usually in open mixed deciduous woodland, rich-herb- and shrub-layer, and small damp areas or clearings. Widespread but usually rare; declined owing to forestry practices and disturbance in breeding season. On migration also in smaller patches of woodland, sometimes even in parks.
Food: Earthworms, insects and their larvae, spiders.
Breeding habits: March–July, 1–2 broods; nests on ground, often beneath tree.

| | – Feral Pigeon | R, M, W | I–XII | |

Snipe *Gallinago gallinago*
Family: Sandpipers Scolopacidae
F Bécassine des marais G Bekassine

Distinctive character: When flushed, flies up ('towering') just a few metres from the observer, in rapid zig-zag flight, calling frequently.
Features: Medium-sized wader with very long bill. Camouflage pattern above – brown back with black markings and yellowish stripes; two dark stripes on crown.
Voice: Repeated nasal *etch* when flushed. Song is a rhythmically repeated *chicka-chicka-chicka* . . . or *chepe-chepe-chepe*, given by ♂ and ♀, either from a song-post or in flight. ♂ makes high undulating flights over breeding ground, plunging downwards to produce a humming or bleating sound (so-called drumming) *wuwuwuwuwu* . . . , by vibrating the spread outer tail feathers.
Occurrence: Breeds in fens, damp meadows and other wetland areas with low vegetation. Widespread but not common. Marked decline due to habitat destruction. Outside breeding season common at lake margins, on muddy areas, small ponds and ditches.
Food: Worms, snails, small crustaceans, insect larvae.
Breeding habits: April–July, 1 brood; nest very well hidden on ground.

| < Blackbird | P, W, M | I–XII | |  |

199

Jack Snipe *Lymnocryptes minimus*
Family: Sandpipers Scolopacidae
F Bécassine sourde
G Zwergschnepfe

Distinctive character: Usually flies up from almost beneath observer's feet, landing again after short flight (does not 'tower').
Features: Much smaller than Snipe, with relatively short bill. Dark above with two broad yellowish stripes.
Voice: Usually silent when flushed, occasionally gives a low, hoarse *etch*. Song, heard mainly at dusk over breeding ground, is a strange sound, like a distant galloping horse.
Occurrence: Breeds on large wet mires with sedge and cottongrass in northern Scandinavia and Soviet Union, from the coniferous forest zone up into the willow region. On migration and in winter on overgrown lake margins, wet meadows, ditches, at damp areas in grazed fields, at coast and inland. Regular but scarce and local.
Behaviour: Not very sociable, most active in twilight, very difficult to see on ground because very secretive and sits tight when danger threatens.
Food: Worms, snails, insects, spiders.

Great Snipe *Gallinago media* is an uncommon breeding bird in Scandinavia and north-east Poland, and a very rare visitor to rest of Europe. It is slightly larger than Snipe but hard to distinguish in the field.

	< Blackbird	M, W	IX–5	O

Arctic Skua
Stercorarius parasiticus
Family: Skuas Stercorariidae
F Labbe parasite
G Schmarotzerraubmöwe

Distinctive character: Steals food from other seabirds, by pursuing and diving at them until they drop or disgorge their food.
Features: Two colour phases with intermediates: a light form with whitish underside and dark neck band (sometimes missing) and a uniformly dark form. Two pointed central tail feathers extend beyond tip of tail, but scarcely visible in juv.
Voice: Hoarse gull-like mewing *ee-yair* or *ay-yair*, often repeated.
Occurrence: Breeds in northern Europe in open areas with low vegetation, usually at the coast or on grassy islands, and in some regions inland on boggy moorland (Scotland) heath and on the tundra. Outside breeding season at sea, more often near coast than Long-tailed Skua. Regular migrant on North Sea coast, less common on other coasts.
Food: Mice, lemmings, small and juv. birds, eggs; mainly fish outside breeding season.

The largest skua, **Great Skua** (or Bonxie) *Stercorarius skua*, breeds on islands off north Scotland and is seen on migration along North Sea and Channel coasts. It is the size of a Herring Gull and can be distinguished by its dark plumage with conspicuous white flashes on the wings and by the lack of tail streamers.

– Black-headed Gull	S, M	IV–XI		

Long-tailed Skua
Stercorarius longicaudus
Family: Skuas
Stercorariidae
F Labbe longicaude
G Falkenraubmöwe

Distinctive character: Long tail streamers, very elegant flight.
Features: More delicately built than other skuas, with sharply delineated dark cap with white neck and upper breast. Tail streamers sometimes broken off. Juv. difficult to distinguish from young Arctic Skuas but slimmer and with narrower wings, central tail feathers just as short, but rounded. Tern-like silhouette, flies with rapid, elastic wingbeats.
Voice: A somewhat Buzzard-like pee-ay or sharp *kiu*; alarm call a series of short, hard *kriepp* calls.
Habitat: Northern Europe, breeding on upland heath above tree-line and on tundra. Outside breeding season a bird of the high seas; rare migrant on coasts, especially of North Sea.
Food: On breeding grounds mainly lemmings and other small mammals, young birds and small birds, insects; at sea mainly fish (often robbed from other seabirds).

Pomarine Skua *Stercorarius pomarinus* has two colour phases (dark one less common) like the somewhat smaller Arctic Skua. Distinguished by the blunt and twisted elongated central tail feathers, which are, however, sometimes broken. Uncommon migrant along coasts.

	– Black-headed Gull	(M)	V–XI	O

Kittiwake *Rissa tridactyla*
Family: Gulls Laridae
F Mouette tridactyle G Dreizehenmöwe

Distinctive character: Jet-black wing-tips without white spots.
Features: Yellow bill, short dark legs. (Juv. see drawing).
Voice: Flight call a whining *gak* or *gog*, as well as a harsh *kekeke*; at breeding site a loud, penetrating *kitti-weeek*.
Occurrence: Breeds in large colonies on tall, steep sea-cliffs; in some places also on houses and other buildings. Outside breeding season a bird of high seas, juv. occasionally seen inland after storms or in the winter.

Behaviour: Often picks food from water surface; occasionally dives from the air.
Food: Small fish, molluscs, small

Kittiwake, juv.

crustaceans, refuse.
Breeding habits: May–August, 1 brood; nest of earth and mud usually on projection or narrow ledge.

> Black-headed Gull	S, M	I–XII		

Little Gull *Larus minutus*
Family: Gulls Laridae
F Mouette pygmée G Zwergmöwe

Distinctive character: Smallest gull; tern-like flight.

Features: In breeding plumage (photo), resembles larger Black-headed Gull, but hood is black and extends further down neck, lacks white around eye, wing-tips rounded and without black. In flight distinguished by blackish underwings with broad white rear edge. Winter plumage (drawing) with dark head markings, upperside of wings grey. Juv. in flight has zig-zag on upperwings.

Voice: High *kik-ki-ki* or tern-like *kyek*; courting ♂ has *kik-kek-kik-kek*, often delivered in soaring flight.

Occurrence: Breeds on shallow lakes with rich vegetation, often together with Black-headed Gulls. A few pairs in the Netherlands and northern Germany, larger numbers in Poland and east Baltic area. Outside breeding season at sea, on coasts,

Little Gull
winter

and regularly on large inland lakes.

Food: Mainly flying insects, small fish, small crustaceans.

Breeding habits: May–July, 1 brood; colonial breeder in marshy sites.

	< Black-headed Gull	(S), M, W	I–XII	BR

Black-headed Gull *Larus ridibundus*
Family: Gulls Laridae
F Mouette rieuse
G Lachmöwe

Distinctive character: Commonest gull inland.

Features: Chocolate-brown face mask (not extending down back of neck) with crescent-shaped white mark around eye. Wing-tips black, bill and legs dark red. In winter (drawing) head white with dark ear-patch. Juv. much brown on head and upperparts; dark trailing edge to wings dark tip to tail. In flight narrow, pointed wings with white leading edge.

Voice: Very loud, *kvarr* in winter *ke-ke-ke* or *piee*.

Occurrence: Breeds in colonies at overgrown lake margins; commonly in reed- or sedge-beds and on small islands. Widespread and very common at coast and on inland waters (and fields) during winter.

Food: Very varied diet: especially worms, insects, small fish, crustaceans, carrion, refuse.

Black-headed Gull, winter

Breeding habits: April–July, 1 brood; nest often on a sedge tussock.

The **Mediterranean Gull** *Larus melanocephalus* slightly larger and heavier-looking than Black-headed. Primaries pure white, not black in ad.; hood darker and extends further down nape. Occasionally breeds in S. England.

Well known	R, M, W	I–XII		

Common Gull *Larus canus*
Family: Gulls Laridae
F Goéland cendré
G Sturmmöwe

Distinctive character: Like a small Herring Gull, but lacks red bill spot.
Features: Rounded white head, relatively narrow yellow bill and dark eyes; feet greenish-yellow. In winter head finely streaked brownish. Juv. (drawing) mottled brownish above, bill dark. In flight black wing-tips with white spots (ad.) dark brown terminal tail band (juv.).
Voice: Higher and more penetrating than Herring Gull; flight call *kia kia . . .* or *kyow kyow*; alarm call *e-e-e-eeee-e-eee-e.*
Occurrence: Breeds mainly near coast, in colonies in coastal meadows, bog and heath with low vegetation. Common in Scandinavia, Scotland, occasional breeder inland in central Europe. Mainly coastal out-

Common Gull, juv.

side breeding season, but also on inland waters and at lakes in parks.
Food: Worms, insects, fish, mice, plant material, refuse.
Breeding habits: April–June, 1 brood; nests on ground in low vegetation.

	> Black-headed Gull	R, W, M	I–XII	

206

Herring Gull *Larus argentatus*
Family: Gulls Laridae
F Goéland argenté G Silbermöwe

Distinctive character: Commonest coastal large gull; often follows ships.
Features: Plumage white except for blue-grey upperwings and black wing-tips. Bill powerful, yellow with red spot; eyes yellow; feet flesh-pink. In winter head has brownish streaks. Juv. mottled brown with broad black terminal tail band; attain full breeding plumage in fourth year.
Voice: Repeated *kyow* or *keeya*; alarm call at breeding ground *gagaga*. Juv. have a high-pitched *psiie*.
Occurrence: Breeds in coastal meadows, dunes, shingle banks and small islands, and in some areas on rock ledges and house roofs. Outside breeding season usually at coast, common at rubbish-tips, more rarely inland.
Food: Very varied. Crustaceans, bivalves, gastropods, starfish, fish, birds, eggs, small mammals, refuse and carrion.
Breeding habits: April–July, 1 brood; nest usually on ground, either bare or lined, depending on surroundings.

The similar **Iceland Gull** *Larus glaucoides* has pale wing tips at all stages. Breeds in Greenland. Uncommon on coasts of north-western Europe in winter.

Well known	P, W, M	I–XII		

Lesser Black-backed Gull *Larus fuscus*
Family: Gulls Laridae
G Goéland brun
G Heringsmöwe

Distinctive character: Size of Herring Gull with dark back.

Features: Similar to Herring Gull but slightly less bulky, and with wings extending further beyond tail. Back and upperwings dark slate-grey, legs yellow. In winter head streaky and legs yellowish-pink. Juv. difficult to separate from young Herring Gulls, but in second year or older birds the upperparts are darker.

Voice: Slightly deeper and less piercing than Herring Gull: *kyow kyow kywow* or *kyee kyee kyee . . .* ; alarm call similar to Herring Gull – *gagagga*, but quieter.

Occurrence: Breeds on low-lying coasts and islands, preferring taller vegetation than Herring Gull; also on inland mires. In Britain breeds mostly in western parts. Outside breeding season mainly at coasts, but regular at inland lakes as well. Usually hunts over open sea but not uncommonly visits rubbish tips.

Food: Fish, crustaceans, molluscs, mice, carrion, worms, insects, young birds, eggs, refuse.

Breeding habits: May–July, 1 brood; colonial, often with Herring Gulls.

| | – Herring Gull | S, W, M | I–XII | |

Great Black-backed Gull *Larus marinus*
Family: Gulls Laridae
F Goéland marin
G Mantelmöwe

Distinctive character: Our largest gull. Head and bill held well forward in flight, appearing rather like a bird of prey.

Features: Black back and wings, large elongated head, powerful yellow bill and flesh-coloured legs. Juv. very similar to young Herring Gull, but head usually paler. Flight slow with regular wingbeats and long periods of gliding.

Voice: A jubilant *krau krau krau . . .*, deeper and slower than Herring Gull; alarm call a sonorous *gagagaga*.

Occurrence: Breeds on rocky and stony coasts in north and western Europe, particularly on small rocky islands, in Britain mainly in west and north. Outside breeding season on low-lying coasts and often at rubbish tips.

Behaviour: More predatory than other gulls; often chases other birds to rob them of their food, overpowers seabirds and their young (commonly young Eiders), but also catches rabbits and rodents on land.

Food: Fish, crustaceans, worms, insects, birds (mainly young), mammals, carrion, refuse.

Breeding habits: April–July, 1 brood; nest usually on ground with little plant cover, often in open.

The **Glaucous Gull** *Larus hyperboreus* of the Arctic is almost as big as the Great Black-backed but is more like the Herring Gull in appearance. However, lacks dark wing tips on all ages. Rare but regular on coasts of north-western Europe in winter.

> Herring Gull	P, M, W	I–XII	

Caspian Tern *Sterna caspia*
Family: Terns Sternidae
F Sterne caspienne
G Raubseeschwalbe

Distinctive character: Largest tern, almost as large as Herring Gull, with very powerful red bill.
Features: Striking black cap, streaked pale in winter plumage. Juv. has light brown markings on cap and back mottled dark brown. In flight the dark primaries are usually obvious. Gull-like flight with slow wingbeats.
Voice: Heron-like hoarse and nasal *kraay-or* or *kraay/kraayar*. Hoarse *chaay-kraay* often heard at breeding grounds; alarm calls *rre*, and *gagaga* when attacking.
Occurrence: Nests in sometimes large colonies on flat sandy shores, small offshore islands and at salt lagoons. Breeds on Baltic coasts of southern Sweden and Finland, rare and irregular breeder in East Germany. Regular visitor to southern Baltic and (more rarely) to North Sea; very rare visitor to Britain, occasionally inland.
Food: Fish up to 23cm long, also young birds, eggs and insects.
Breeding habits: May–July, 1 brood; colonies usually sited where all-round visibility is good, on gravel or sand.

| | < Herring Gull | V | IV–X | O |

Roseate Tern *Sterna dougallii*
Family: Terns Sternidae
F Sterne de Dougall
G Rosenseeschwalbe

Distinctive character: A very pale, almost white tern with extremely long tail streamers.
Features: Ad. in summer plumage very pale pearl-grey above, with a black cap; underparts white, with delicate pink tinge to breast visible at close range. The relatively short wings show a blackish area at the tips. Tail streamers white and very long, projecting far beyond wings when the bird is perched and often waving about in the wind in flight. Legs bright red and long black bill deep red at base. In winter plumage, forehead pale and bill all black. Juv., black bill and legs, prominent dark scaly markings on back, much shorter tail streamers.

Voice: A characteristic, diagnostic, soft *chuwik* and a loud, hoarse rasping *raaaaach*.
Occurrence: Breeds very locally on islands and undisturbed beaches at a few sites on the coasts of Britain and Ireland, migrating to coasts of W. Africa in autumn. Rarest European tern, it has declined alarmingly in recent years, partly through hunting in the winter quarters also habitat disturbance and reduction in food supplies in the breeding areas.
Behaviour: Much as for Common Tern, but when foraging often quarters the sea at a higher level. In flight very buoyant, with shallow wingbeats like Sandwich Tern.
Food: Fish.
Breeding habits: June–July, 1 brood; colonial, nesting in shallow depression among low vegetation or between rocks.

– Common Tern	(S)	V–IX	BI, BR, BD, BL	

Sandwich Tern *Sterna sandvicensis*
Family: Terns Sternidae
F Sterne caugek
G Brandseeschwalbe

Distinctive character: Relatively large tern with shaggy crest on back of head.
Features: Long black bill with yellow tip. In winter plumage has white forehead. Juv. (drawing) with brown markings on back. Slim and narrow-winged in flight, with shallow wing strokes.
Voice: Vocal Shrill, grating *kjirrik* or *krrivi*. Alarm call short, sharp *krik* or *irk*. At breeding colonies often gives a *krekrekre* . . ., and *trirr* (young birds).
Occurrence: Entirely on coasts; breeds in colonies on sand and shingle banks, often on islands, peninsulas, or inaccessible spits, often next to colonies of other terns or gulls. Outside breeding season in coastal waters rich in fish.
Food: Small fish up to 17 cm long.

juv.

Sandwich Tern

Breeding habits: May–July, 1 brood; nests are simple scrapes in the sand or shingle, with little lining.

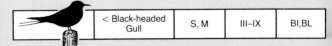

	< Black-headed Gull	S, M	III–IX	Bl,BL

Distinctive character: Smallest tern, with white forehead even in breeding plumage; frequently hovers.

Features: Easily identified by small size, yellow bill with black tip, and by white forehead. In winter plumage crown whitish, grading into black of back of head. Juv. have brownish crown, and upperparts with dark wavy markings. Narrow-winged and somewhat plump-bodied in flight. Wingbeats much quicker and more jerky than those of other terns; hovers for much longer before diving.

Voice: When agitated, a hoarse *vett vett vett* . . . ; high-pitched harsh *kirrit, kirri-ik* or hard *gik gik*.

Occurrence: Breeds on sand and shingle beaches, flat, rocky coasts, lagoons and on gentle banks of inland waters; usually in small colonies close to colonies of other terns. Uncommon breeder in Britain, where local on coasts only; scarce inland on migration.

Food: Small fish, small crustaceans, insects.

Breeding habits: May–July, 1 brood; up to 2 replacement clutches; nests usually amongst sparse vegetation, but often on bare ground. Eggs and young extremely well camouflaged.

< Common Tern	S, M	IV–X	BI, BL	

Common Tern
Sterna hirundo
Family: Terns Sternidae
F Sterne Pierre-Garin
G Flußseeschwalbe

Distinctive character: Only white tern which can be seen regularly inland.
Features: Very slim and elegant. Bill intense red, with black tip. Relatively long legs. When perched, tail streamers do not extend beyond wings. Winter ad. and juv. have dark bill and whitish forehead. In flight the dark outer primaries are noticeable, contrasting with pale, translucent inner primaries when seen from below.

Voice: Vocal. Flight call a short, repeated *kick*, *kirikirikiri* or *kree-yair* (warning call, accented on first syllable).
Occurrence: Breeds in colonies on sandy coasts, in dunes, on gravel banks of undisturbed rivers and on low bare banks of lakes and ponds. The inland central European population has declined markedly owing to river management, although in some places they breed successfully on artificial nesting rafts.
Food: Small fish, insect larvae, small crustaceans, tadpoles.
Breeding habits: May–August, 1 brood; nest a shallow hollow, usually on shingle or sand, amongst sparse vegetation.

	< Black-headed Gull	S, M	IV–X	

Arctic Tern *Sterna paradisaea*
Family: Terns Sternidae
F Sterne arctique
G Küstenseeschwalbe

Distinctive character: Uniformly red bill and short legs.
Features: Hard to distinguish from Common Tern. Tail streamers are longer and extend beyond wings when at rest; bill is uniform blood-red; in flight from below, all the primaries are translucent. See drawing for juv.
Voice: Not quite as harsh as Common Tern, and calls usually shorter: *kree-errr*; also a soft *gik*.
Occurrence: Breeds exclusively on coast, usually with other terns in large colonies on sand and shingle banks, mainly in northern Europe. Occasionally occurs inland on migration. Very long migrations; European breeders reach the Antarctic on their travels, thereby covering over 20,000 km each year.

Arctic Tern, juv.

Food: Fish and small crustaceans.
Breeding habits: May–July, 1 brood; nest is a shallow hollow in the sand, shingle or between sparse vegetation.

– Common Tern	S, M	IV–X	BI	

215

Black Tern *Chlidonias niger*
Family: Terns Sternidae
F Guifette noire
G Trauerseeschwalbe

Distinctive character: In flight looks almost like a large, dark swallow.
Features: Small tern, very dark in breeding plumage; head and front part of body sooty-black, wings light grey above and below. In winter plumage (drawing) white below, with dark patch at side of neck, and dark on top of head. Juv. similar to winter ad., but darker above.
Voice: Not very vocal. Flight call a short *krek* or *kik* or a nasal *kyek*; in courtship *kriayr* and high-pitched *kiehk*.
Occurrence: Breeds on shallow, marshy lakes and ponds with rich vegetation; rather local (does not breed in Britain). Regular migrant in most of Europe: wetlands and coast.
Food: Insects, their larvae, tadpoles, small fish.
Breeding habits: May–July, 1 brood;

Black Tern, juv.

winter

colonial; nests usually placed on clumps in water, or floating on old reeds and other plant material.

	< Common Tern	M	IV–X	BR

Puffin
Fratercula arctica
Family: Auks Alcidae
F Macareux moine
G Papageitaucher

Distinctive character: A small auk with a big head and huge, brightly coloured, triangular bill.
Features: Small and fat. Ad. are black above and white below, with whitish sides to the head and black throat band; the legs are bright red, and the bill is red, yellow and grey-blue, very deep but flattened sideways. In winter the face is duller, the bill somewhat smaller and less bright and the legs yellowish, but still unmistakable. Juv. are much less conspicuous, having a grey face and a much smaller, dark bill.
Voice: At the breeding colonies the birds make creaking, grunting and groaning sounds.
Occurrence: Breeds on rocky coasts and islands with grass or turf tops, spending the winter months mostly far out to sea. Breeding colonies exist in Iceland, Norway, north-west France, Ireland, and in north and western Britain.
Behaviour: Highly sociable. Groups often stand upright together outside their burrows or fly in lines low over the sea with very fast whirring wing-beats. When returning from fishing trips, they carry several fish together (up to 10) held crossways in the bill.
Food: Fish, especially sand-eels, also crustaceans, molluscs, marine worms.
Breeding habits: May–August, 1 brood; colonies nest in rabbit burrows or in similar hollows on cliff slopes, or under boulders.

< Mallard	R	Mainly III–VIII		

Guillemot *Uria aalge*
Family: Auks Alcidae
F Guillemot de Troïl G Trottellumme

Distinctive character: Common cliff-nesting seabird.
Features: Duck-sized seabird with narrow, pointed bill. Sits upright. Often with narrow white eye-ring and narrow line behind eye (bridled form). In winter (drawing) cheeks, throat and foreneck white, dark line behind eye.
Voice: Grating *aaarrr . . .*, *uarr . . .* or *arr-ah-oorr*; much individual variation. Juv. somewhat moaning *tuhii tuhii.*
Occurrence: Breeds in large, dense colonies on narrow ledges and small projections on steep seacliffs. Outside breeding season at sea, usually at least a few kilometres from coast.

Guillemot,
winter

Food: Mainly fish such as herring, sprat, and cod, also molluscs, worms and crustaceans.
Breeding habits: May–July, 1 brood; 1 egg, laid directly on to rocks.

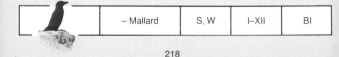

	– Mallard	S, W	I–XII	BI

Razorbill *Alca torda*
Family: Auks Alcidae
F Petit pingouin G Tordalk

Distinctive character: Large, laterally compressed bill.
Features: Similar to Guillemot but with larger head, short, thick neck and deep bill. Upperparts completely black. In winter totally white below, with black extending only to just below the eye. Juv. with smaller, uniformly black bill (lacking the white lines); easily confused with juv. Guillemots, but bill shorter and less pointed. On water appears dumpy, with the relatively long pointed tail held cocked while swimming. Flies with very fast wingbeats, long tail extending beyond outstretched feet.
Voice: Not very vocal; occasional grating calls such as *arrr*, *orrr* or *uorr-o*.
Occurrence: Breeds as pairs or small groups on steep cliffs on coasts or uninhabited islands, often in the midst of or on the edge of Guillemot colonies. Outside breeding season occurs at sea or in small numbers scattered along coast.
Food: Small sea fish, crustaceans, worms.
Breeding habits: May–July, 1 brood; nests in small cavities and crevices on steep sea cliffs.

< Mallard	S, (W)	I–XII	BI	

Black Guillemot *Cepphus grylle*
Family: Auks Alcidae
F Guillemot à miroir
G Gryllteiste

Distinctive character: Very characteristic breeding plumage.

Features: Small auk with mainly black plumage and striking white wing patches; feet bright red. In winter (drawing) white below, grey with pale feather edgings above. Juv. with dark feet. In flight the white wing-coverts are conspicuous.

Voice: High-pitched prolonged whistle – *sseeee . . .* or *peeeeih*; also repeated *sist sist . . .* or *deesa deesa*.

Occurrence: Breeds in small, loose colonies amongst rocks at the base of cliffs, on the lower slopes of bird steep cliffs and (commonly) on small rocky islands. Outside breeding season mostly in shallow coastal waters.

Behaviour: Flight more agile than Guillemot and often quite high. Feeds deep on sea-bed, unlike other auks.

Black
Guillemot

winter

Food: Crustaceans, small fish, bivalves, gastropods.

Breeding habits: May-August, 1 brood; eggs usually laid in small hollows on sparse nest lining.

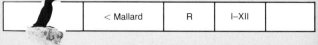

	< Mallard	R	I–XII	

220

Doves, Owls,
Kingfishers, Woodpeckers
and Allies

Pigeons and Doves – Columbiformes

Pigeons and doves have dumpy bodies and relatively small heads. In flight they are powerful and rapid, and often make clattering wing noises at take-off. During the breeding period they produce a milk-like substance from the inner lining of the crop on which the young are fed during their first few days of life. In the breeding season their songs are often audible from afar and are therefore very useful for distinguishing the species. The nest is usually simple, consisting of just a few twigs, and the clutch is normally two white eggs. There are five species in Europe. One of these, the Feral Pigeon, is descended from escaped tame pigeons which themselves derive from the wild original type, the Rock Dove *Columba livia*.

Cuckoos – Cuculiformes

Cuckoos are slim, long-tailed birds with two toes facing forward and two facing backwards. Fewer than half of all the cuckoo species are brood parasites. In central and northern Europe there is a single species with its well-known call; in flight it somewhat resembles a Sparrowhawk.

Owls – Strigiformes

Owls, like raptors, are birds of prey, catching live, mostly vertebrate prey. They have large forward-facing eyes and are mainly active at night or at dusk. Their feathers have special soft edges which give them an almost silent flight. They detect their prey mainly by their sensitive hearing. Owls have rather thick heads which can be turned through a wide angle. Many species have noticeable 'ear' tufts. They vary widely in size from the starling-sized Pygmy Owl up to the eagle-sized Eagle Owl.

For the nocturnal species a knowledge of their calls is essential for identification.

There are ten species in central and northern Europe, of which two are very rare. The **barn owls** (1 species here) are distinguished on anatomical grounds from the **true owls**, and are placed in a separate family.

Swifts – Apodiformes

Of all bird groups the swifts are the best adapted to the air. They are distinguished by their long, sickle-shaped wings and short tails. The bill is very short and broad and functions as an efficient insect trap. The feet are small, with all four toes directed forwards. The young are extremely nidicolous. There are two species in central and northern Europe.

Nightjars – Caprimulgiformes

There is one species in northern Europe. As the name suggests they are active in the dusk and at night. By day they sit tight on the ground or lengthways along a branch. Like owls they too have soft plumage, and are patterned rather like tree bark. Like swallows (to which they are not related) they have long, pointed wings and hunt insects in the air. Their broad skull with its deep oral cavity enables the mandibles to be opened very wide They build no nest, but lay their eggs directly on the ground.

Kingfishers and Allies – Coraciiformes

The groups in this order contain species which feed on small animals and which nest in holes. There are four families in Europe, each with a single representative.
Kingfishers are brightly coloured, small to medium-sized birds with large heads and long, powerful bills. Most live in tropical forest regions and excavate nest holes in steep banks. The European Kingfisher is found in wetlands and feeds mainly on fish.
Bee-eaters are slim and have pointed wings, like swifts and swallows; unlike them they are brightly coloured. The bill is long and pointed and slightly decurved. They are elegant insect feeders, catching their prey in the air, and they nest in holes which they dig for themselves.

They are found mainly in the warmer regions; our single species, the European Bee-eater, breeds regularly only in southern and eastern Europe.
Rollers look rather like jays; they have powerful bills, slightly hooked at the tip. Their colourful plumage is distinctive. They hunt large insects and small vertebrates from a prominent vantage perch. In Europe, the single species is found mainly in the south and east and is rather scarce.
Hoopoes are easily identified by their erectile crest and black-and-white-barred wings. There is only one species worldwide. It has a distinctive soft call, audible from afar.

Woodpeckers and Allies – Piciformes

A large order, containing barbets, honeyguides, toucans, jacamars and puffbirds, as well as woodpeckers, the sole European family.
Woodpeckers are small to medium-sized insectivorous woodland birds. They are adapted in a variety of ways to life in the trees: they have powerful feet with two toes facing forward and one set out to the side; the hind toe is scarcely used in climbing and is missing altogether in some species, such as the Three-toed Woodpecker. Their tail feathers (especially the central ones) are stiffened and used as a prop when climbing; the bill is very powerful and chisel-shaped and is used to peck open wood when feeding, to excavate nest holes and to produce territorial drumming. The tongue is very long, and can be extended a long way outside the bill to catch hidden insects. Incidentally, woodpeckers have an important ecological role in woodlands, creating nest sites for other hole-breeders.

One of the 10 species found in the region, the Wryneck, (which does not excavate its own nest hole) differs from the other woodpeckers in its camouflaged plumage, much softer tail feathers and relatively short, weak bill.

Stock Dove *Columba oenas*
Family: Pigeons and doves Columbidae
F Pigeon colombin G Hohltaube

Distinctive character: Breeds in tree holes.

Features: Often hard to distinguish from Feral Pigeon, but somewhat slimmer and with grey rump, and thin black wing-bars (often not prominent). In flight distinguished from the larger Woodpigeon by narrower wings with black margins and tips, and lack of white wing patches. Flight straight and rapid.

Voice: Alarm call a short *hru*. ♂ courtship song (heard as early as March) a hollow monotonous *gooo-roo-o . . .*, accented on first syllable.

Occurrence: Breeds in open deciduous and mixed woodland, pine woods and parks with old trees. Also in trees at field margins, orchards and even in some dune aeas. Often uses old Black Woodpecker holes, and needs nearby open country for feeding. Outside breeding season often found with other pigeons on fields.

Food: Seeds of grasses, herbs and trees, berries, acorns, beech nuts, green parts of plants, vegetables, clover.

Breeding habits: March–October, 2–3 broods; hole-nester (will use nest-boxes); uses plenty of stems, twigs and leaves as lining.

| | – Feral Pigeon | R, W | I–XII | |

Woodpigeon *Columba palumbus*
Family: Pigeons and doves Columbidae
F Pigeon ramier G Ringeltaube

Distinctive character: Bright white patches on wings and neck, visible in flight.
Features: Longer-tailed than Feral Pigeon, with purplish-pink breast. In flight rounded belly and soft whistling wing noise, as well as white patches, also noticeable. Loud wing clapping when flushed and in courtship flight.
Voice: Muffled, cooing and far-carrying *goo-goo-gu-gooroo*.
Occurrence: Breeds in open wooded landscapes with meadows and fields, or small boggy areas, often in trees at field margins. Increasingly to be seen in urban parks, feeding alongside Feral Pigeons and Collared Doves.
Behaviour: Often forms large flocks on fields outside breeding season. In spring performs frequent courtship flights over territory.
Food: Depending on the season, seeds of grasses and herbs, berries, acorns, beech nuts, grain, green leaves and buds, crops (rape, clover, cabbage); in urban areas also stale bread.
Breeding habits: April–November, 2–3 broods; flat nest made of dry brushwood, usually high up in tree, sometimes in a bush or on a building.

> Feral Pigeon	P, M, W	I–XII		

Collared Dove
Streptopelia decaocto
Family: Pigeons and doves Columbidae
F Tourterelle turque
G Türkentaube

Distinctive character: Commonest pigeon/dove in villages and towns after Feral Pigeon.
Features: Pale, slim; long-tailed dove with dark half collar at back of neck. Breast flushed pink.
Voice: In flight, especially before landing, a characteristic nasal *kwair kwair*. Territorial song a monotonous tri-syllabic *coo-cooo. coo*, usually accented on second syllable. Flight rapid and rather like bird of prey; wings produce whistling sound.

Occurrence: Has expanded its range from the south-east across Europe over recent decades. Now found as a resident in towns and villages, especially where there is an abundance of food, as in parks, zoos, silos, grain stores, farmyards, etc.
Behaviour: ♂ indulge in courtship flights early in the year: they fly steeply up, descending in a glide with wings curved downwards, uttering the nasal flight call. Fond of food put out for small garden birds.
Food: Seeds, buds and green parts of plants, grain, berries, fruit, bread.
Breeding habits: March–November 2–4 broods; nest is a flat, often flimsy platform of small twigs, usually in a tree or bush, sometimes on a building.

	< Feral Pigeon	R	I–XII	

226

Turtle Dove *Streptopelia turtur*
Family: Pigeons and doves Columbidae
F Tourterelle des bois
G Turteltaube

Distinctive character: Our smallest dove. Swift, nimble flight.
Features: Delicate dove with rust-brown, dark-spotted wings and prominent black and white markings at side of neck. ♀ slightly paler than ♂. Juv. browner and lacking neck marking. On take-off and landing the black tapered tail with narrow white border is noticeable. Flight rapid with slight rocking motion. Often claps wings at take-off.
Voice: Territorial song is a soft pur-

ring *turrr turrr . . .*; alarm call a short *ru*.
Occurrence: Breeds in wooded fields and banks, river valley woodland, woodland edges, orchards, and sometimes in well-wooded parks and gardens. Prefers warm, dry lowland sites. Commoner in south and eastern England.
Behaviour: Much shyer than Collared Dove. Often flies in pairs or small groups to feed in fields.
Food: Seeds and fruits of herbs and grasses, seeds of conifers, fewer cultivated plants than Collared Dove.
Breeding habits: May–September, usually 2 broods; flat nest made of dry brushwood in a tree or tall bush.

| < Feral Pigeon | S, M | IV–X | | 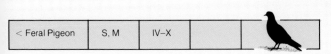 |

Feral Pigeon *Columba livia*
Family: Pigeons and doves Columbidae
F Pigeon biset G Straßentaube

Distinctive character: Very common in towns and cities.
Features: Very variable – from blue-grey (colour of original Rock Dove) to rust-brown and black to almost pure white; usually with white or pale grey rump.
Voice: Well-known cooing *guh-goorooguh* is part of courtship display, heard almost throughout the year.
Occurrence: Very common and associated with human habitation in villages and towns, but particularly in large cities. Feeding of pigeons has been banned in some places because of the damage caused to buildings by their droppings.

Behaviour: Very sociable and normally seen in flocks, like their wild ancestors. Become quite tame where fed regularly and will sometimes even come to the hand. Also take food from high balconies.
Food: Different seeds, including those of trees, grain, acorns, buds, seedlings, leaves, berries, bread, refuse.
Breeding habits: Mostly March–September, but also in winter, normally 3–4 broods; nest of stems and twigs, is a flat platform, normally in a sheltered position on a building.

Wild, pure **Rock Doves** now rare, are confined to north and west coasts of Britain and Ireland (commoner in Mediterranean region). They resemble Stock Doves but have paler grey wings with two short black bars on each and a white rump.

	Well known	R	I–XII	

Cuckoo *Cuculus canorus*
Family: Cuckoos Cuculidae
F Coucou gris G Kuckuck

Distinctive character: Sparrowhawk-like flight and distinctive call.
Features: Most often seen in flight. Unlike Sparrowhawk the wings are pointed. ♀ also occurs in rarer rufous colour form.
Voice: *cuc-coo* is territorial song of ♂. It is delivered from a high perch in a tree from the end of April to July and can be heard over a long distance. ♀ has a loud bubbling trill at breeding time.
Occurrence: Found in all near-natural habitats from the high mountains right down to coastal dunes. Prefers varied landscape with plenty of cover. Density highly dependent upon that of host species. Also in villages and towns in some areas.
Food: Mostly larvae of butterflies and moths, including hairy ones avoided by other birds. Also beetles, grasshoppers, dragonflies and other insects.
Breeding habits: May–July; lays eggs individually in nests of certain host species; hosts (depending on locality) include, among others, Redstart and Black Redstart, Robin, Pied Wagtail, Reed Warbler and Great Reed Warbler, *Sylvia* warblers, pipits, Dunnock and Red-backed Shrike. Each Cuckoo ♀ lays eggs of one type of coloration throughout its life and is therefore adapted to a particular host. The young Cuckoo normally hatches first and pushes the other eggs or nestlings out of the nest one after the other.

< Feral Pigeon	S	IV–IX		

Long-eared Owl *Asio otus*
Family: Owls Strigidae
F Hibou moyen-duc
G Waldohreule

Distinctive character: Long 'ear' tufts. These can however be laid flat, when they are no longer visible.
Features: Slim, long-winged owl with orange-yellow eyes; plumage with tree-bark pattern.
Voice: ♂ has far-carrying low *hoo*, heard as early as February. Alarm call a loud barking *wick*, often repeated. Contact call of young birds is a high-pitched and rather plaintive *tsee*.
Occurrence: Breeds in coniferous forests and plantations, light woodland, at woodland edges, in windbreaks, parks and in trees in fields. Hunts in the open over low vegetation. In winter often in communal roosts of up to 20 or more birds, sometimes found in parks, cemeteries and even in large gardens.
Behaviour: By day sits upright close to tree trunk, where its camouflaged plumage makes it difficult to spot. Does not emerge until dusk. Hunts mainly in quartering flight.
Food: Voles, mice and small birds.
Breeding habits: March–June, 1 brood; mainly nests in old Carrion Crow or Magpie nests, sometimes in old nests of birds of prey or squirrel dreys.

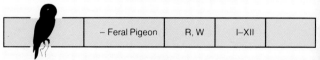

| | | – Feral Pigeon | R, W | I–XII | |

Short-eared Owl *Asio flammeus*
Family: Owls Strigidae
F Hibou des marais
G Sumpfohreule

Distinctive character: Lives in damp habitats and often hunts by day.

Features: Similar to Long-eared Owl but with short 'ear' tufts, often invisible. Plumage lighter and more contrasting. Eyes sulphur-yellow surrounded by broad black circles. In flight appears paler and more narrow-winged than Long-eared Owl. Wing tips dark; wings often held in V shape; tail wedge-shaped.

Voice: Territorial ♂ have soft *boo-boo-boo . . .* in spring; ♀ replies with *cheee-oop*. Ad. alarm call at nest is a barking *kwe*. Contact call of young fledglings is a snoring *kshiya*.

Occurrence: Breeds in open habitats with low yet thick vegetation on mires and overgrown lake margins, heath, dunes, and damp meadows or reedbeds. In winter often found at coastal marshes and agricultural land.

Behaviour: Slow searching flight over open country, occasionally hovering. In spring ♂ has high courtship flight over breeding ground, with slow deep wingbeats; often a series of wingclaps audible.

Food: Mainly small voles and mice, when these are scarce other rodents and small birds.

Breeding habits: March–July, 1–2 broods; nest made of a few dry stems in a shallow hollow.

– Feral Pigeon	P, W, M	I–XII		

Tawny Owl *Strix aluco*
Family: Owls Strigidae
F Chouette hulotte G Waldkauz

Distinctive character: Our commonest woodland owl, with well-known hooting call.

Features: Compact owl with large, round head and dark eyes. Two colour forms: a bark-coloured grey form and a commoner red-brown form. In flight also appears more compact than Long-eared Owl, and undersides of broad wings are barred.

Voice: ♂ territorial song, a shuddering, tremulous *huuu-hu-huhuhuh* heard in autumn and winter, but mainly in early spring. ♀ has frequent loud *ke-wick*.

Occurrence: Breeds in fairly open deciduous and mixed woodland adjoining open spaces or water; also in parks, cemeteries and gardens wth old deciduous trees. Up to about 1,500 m in the Alps.

Behaviour: Hunts from a perch or in flight; startles roosting birds and catches them in flight. Will even attack people near to nest when young are hatched.

Food: Very varied. Mainly mice, but also birds, voles, rats, moles and shrews, frogs, toads, fish and beetles.

Breeding habits: March–June, 1 brood; nests in holes in trees, more rarely in old nests of birds of prey or in buildings.

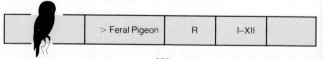

| | > Feral Pigeon | R | I–XII | |

Ural Owl *Strix uralensis*
Family: Owls Strigidae
F Chouette de l'Oural G Habichtskauz

Distinctive character: Very large owl.

Features: Similar to Tawny Owl but much larger and paler; well-developed facial disc with relatively small eyes. Long tail and barring on wings and tail gives somewhat Goshawk-like appearance in flight.

Voice: ♂ Spring territorial song is *voovoovoo* . . . , carries up to 2 km. ♀ call somewhat hoarser.

Occurrence: Breeds in varied forest with old, not too dense trees. In northern Europe mainly in coniferous or mixed forest, in central Europe also in pure Beech woodland. Rare breeding bird in eastern Poland and in Czechoslovakia. Not recorded in Britain.

Behaviour: Active at dusk and at night, but sometimes by day as well when young are being fed and in winter. Like Tawny Owl hunts mainly from woodland perch, but regularly hunts in the open, for example over mires or clearings.

Food: As varied as Tawny Owl. Mainly voles, but also shrews and birds (to size of Black Grouse), also frogs and insects.

Breeding habits: March–June, 1 brood; in central Europe mostly nests in old nests of birds of prey, in northern Europe in holes in trees or in nest boxes.

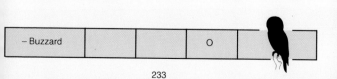

– Buzzard			O	

Tengmalm's Owl *Aegolius funereus*
Family: Owls Strigidae
F Chouette de Tengmalm
G Rauhfußkauz

Distinctive character: Characteristic nocturnal territorial song.
Features: Small owl with a large, round head and relatively distinct facial disc with dark brown border at the sides. Dark brown above, speckled white. Legs feathered down to talons. Juv. chocolate-brown with white spots on wings and tail. In flight wings and tail relatively long, and flight path direct, not undulating like Little Owl.
Voice: Alarm call a sharp *tseeuk*. ♂ territorial song is a fluting, slightly vibrating *u-u-u-u-u-ua-a*, rising slightly at end and often audible over several hundred metres.
Occurrence: Breeds in well-structured wooded habitat with old beech or pines, offering suitable holes and crevices. Also likes thick spruce groves for resting by day, and small mires, glades or felled areas for hunting. Very rare vagrant to Britain.
Behaviour: Highly nocturnal; mostly hunts from a perch.
Food: Mainly voles and mice, but also shrews, other small mammals and birds up to size of thrushes.
Breeding habits: March–June, 1 brood; nests mainly in old Black Woodpecker holes, but increasingly in special nest-boxes.

		< Feral Pigeon	V	X–III, V–VI	O

Pygmy Owl
Glaucidium passerinum
Family: Owls Strigidae
F Chouette chevêchette
G Sperlingskauz

Distinctive character: Smallest European owl.

Features: Small head with low forehead, lacking distinct facial disc. Flight either undulating like woodpecker, or straight and direct; shows short wings and rounded, often spread tail.

Voice: Alarm call *gyu*, often repeated; ♀ often makes a high-pitched *tsiii*. Territorial song in breeding season is an easily imitated *pyu pyu pyu . . .*, changing to *pyu uu pyu uu . . .* when excited. Outside breeding season both sexes give a rapidly rising series of whistles ('musical scale').

Occurrence: Breeds in tall coniferous or mixed forests, usually near to a clearing or small boggy area. Scandinavia, central and eastern Europe. Widespread but not common in Alpine foothills. Not recorded in Britain.

Behaviour: Mainly active at dusk, but often seen by day. Often sits at top of a spruce tree, jerking tail. Hunts small mammals and birds from a perch or in surprise attack; stores prey in holes in trees.

Food: Mainly small mammals such as voles; in winter also birds, especially tits, Goldcrests and finches.

Breeding habits: April–June, 1 brood; prefers to nest in old Great Spotted Woodpecker holes.

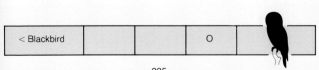

< Blackbird | | | O | |

Eagle Owl *Bubo bubo*
Family: Owls Strigidae
F Hibou grand-duc G Uhu

Distinctive character: Largest owl.
Features: Large head with orange-red eyes and well-developed 'ear' tufts. ♀ larger and heavier than ♂. In flight the wings are long, broad, rounded at the tip and pale below.
Voice: Song is a deep, far-carrying *boohoo*, usually heard in February and March, but also in October. ♀ also sings, but more rarely and at a slightly higher pitch.
Occurrence: Richly structured landscape with areas of woodland and open country, often near water. Breeds on cliffs, steep slopes and also in quarries. Mainly hunts in the open. Not found in Britain (though escaped captive birds sometimes seen).
Behaviour: Active in twilight and at night, sometimes earlier during breeding season. Hunts either from a perch or from the air.
Food: Mammals and birds to size of hares and Capercaillie; rats, mice, hedgehogs, rabbits, waterbirds.
Breeding habits: March–July, 1 brood; nests on ledges of steep rocky cliffs.

The **Snowy Owl** *Nyctea scandiaca* is a larger uncommon Arctic owl which has bred on Shetland. Older ♂ are almost pure white; the large ♀ and young ♂ have fine dark spots on a white background. Sometimes migrates long distances south.

> Buzzard

O

Scops Owl *Otus scops*
Family: Owls Strigidae
F Hibou petit-duc G Zwergohreule

Distinctive character: Monotonous territorial song, from April–June.
Features: Small, slim owl, with bark-like camouflaged plumage. Distinct 'ear' tufts, though these not always visible.
Voice: Territorial song is a monotonous *dyup*, repeated every 2–3 seconds, reminiscent of Midwife Toad but somewhat longer. Both sexes sing for hours on end after pairing, sometimes in a duet.
Occurrence: Breeds in varied semi-open landscape, in warmer parts of southern half of Europe, with good supply of large insects: parks, orchards, avenues or edges of open broad-leaved woodland. Widespread in Mediterranean region; very rare breeder in southern Switzerland, southern Austria, Hungary and Czechoslovakia; marked decline in central Europe. Rare vagrant to Britain.
Behaviour: By day remains well hidden, sitting vertically with erect ear tufts in a tree, bush or wall crevice. Hunts in twilight and at night, usually from a perch.
Food: Crickets, butterflies and moths, beetles, grasshoppers, spiders, woodlice, earthworms, small frogs, birds and mammals.
Breeding habits: May–July, 1 brood; nests in tree-holes, often in old woodpecker holes, also in holes in walls and in nest-boxes.

< Blackbird	V	IV–XI	O	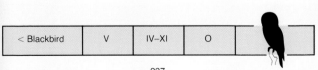

Little Owl *Athene noctua*
Family: Owls Strigidae
F Chouette chevêche G Steinkauz

Distinctive character: Often sits by day on fence posts or telegraph poles.
Features: Small, squat, short-tailed owl with flat crown and large yellow eyes; bounding, undulating flight, like woodpecker.
Voice: Alarm call a loud, penetrating *keeu, kwitt* or *kya.* ♂ territorial song is a drawn-out, nasal *gooo*, heard as early as March.
Occurrence: Breeds in open country with individual trees, copses or avenues. Likes meadows and pasture with pollarded willows, fruit trees and the margins of small, open woods. Also at edges of villages and farms. Absent from closed forest and above about 700 m. Widespread in lowland, but has declined owing to lack of breeding sites, and with use of pesticides; increasing in some areas with use of artificial nest-boxes.
Behaviour: Mainly active at dusk and night, but often seen by day. Hunts either from perch or in low flight; also hunts insects on ground.
Food: Mainly mice, also birds (mostly young) such as sparrows, buntings, larks and Starlings; frogs, lizards, earthworms, beetles, grasshoppers.
Breeding habits: April–July, 1 brood; nests in holes in trees or walls, also in special artificial nest-tubes.

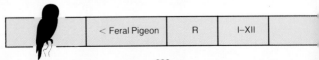

	< Feral Pigeon	R	I–XII	

Barn Owl *Tyto alba*
Family: Barn Owls Tytonidae
F Chouette effraie G Schleiereule

Distinctive character: Conspicuous pale heart-shaped facial disc.

Features: A pale owl with long legs, black eyes and no ear tufts. In flight shows long slim wings and very pale underparts.

Voice: Very vocal at breeding site from February/March onwards – making snoring and screeching sounds throughout the night; ♂'s territorial song is a hoarse, shrieking *kreehreehreeh* . . . .

Occurrence: Mainly in cultivated areas; breeds in church towers, barns, gables, which allow free flight access. Hunts in open areas. Population reduced by snowy winters and in years with low numbers of small mammals. Also threatened by loss of suitable breeding sites, intensification of farming and losses caused by road traffic and power lines. Widespread in lowland areas but very thinly spread.

Behaviour: Mostly nocturnal; hunts from perch or in flight; mainly uses hearing to locate prey.

Food: Mainly mice, shrews (especially in poor mouse years); other small mammals, few birds.

Breeding habits: April–October, 1–2 (3) broods; nests in undisturbed buildings and in special Barn Owl boxes.

– Feral Pigeon	R	I–XII	SC	

Swift *Apus apus*
Family: Swifts Apodidae
F Martinet noir G Mauersegler

Distinctive character: Long, sickle-shaped wings and shrill calls.
Features: Blackish plumage with pale chin and throat. Juv. have pale forehead and larger pale area on throat.
Voice: Very vocal. High-pitched shrill scream *sriieh* or short *sri*, *see* or similar.
Occurrence: Originally a cliff-nester but now mainly breeds in colonies in buildings such as church towers, chimneys and tower blocks. Very common, especially in towns.

Behaviour: Spends most of its life airborne, often for weeks at a time outside breeding season. Very sociable. In breeding season often seen flying fast in tightly knit flocks between houses, screaming as they go. In bad weather hunt low over water or wetlands.
Food: Small flying insects and spiders; especially flies, hymenopterans, aphids, beetles.
Breeding habits: May–August, 1 brood; nests in dark crevices, often in holes in walls or holes in eaves; shallow nest is built of stems, leaves, hair and other material collected in flight and glued together with viscous saliva.

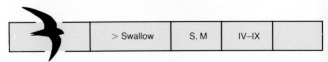

	> Swallow	S, M	IV–IX	

Alpine Swift *Apus melba*
Family: Swifts Apodidae
F Martinet alpin G Alpensegler

Distinctive character: White under-side with brown breast-band.
Features: Noticeably larger and paler than Swift. Lower wing-beat frequency, often glides with wings held low.
Voice: In flight an extended trill *trirr* . . . , rising and falling, easily distinguished from that of Swift; reminiscent of Canary in timbre and the individual syllables can be distinguished, unlike in Swift's call.
Occurrence: Breeds on high rock faces, on rocky coasts and, more rarely, on tall buildings. Mainly Mediterranean species. Rare breeder in Austria and Switzerland; in Germany just a few pairs on a church tower in Freiburg. Rare vagrant to Britain.
Behaviour: Very like Swift, but flight even faster: normal flight 60–100 km/h, courtship flights of up to 250 km/h reported.
Food: Like Swift exclusively small flying or wind-borne insects and spiders.
Breeding habits: May–August, 1 brood; nests in crevices and cracks on steep, high cliffs, also in gables and nest-boxes on tall buildings. Nest material collected in the air and stuck together with saliva.

> Swift	V	IV–IX	O	

Nightjar
Caprimulgus europaeus
Family: Nightjars
Caprimulgidae
F Engoulevent d'Europe
G Ziegenmelker

Distinctive character: Almost perfect camouflage and nocturnal purring song.
Features: Slim, long-winged and long-tailed, with relatively flat head and large black eyes. Upperparts with bark-like pattern. Small bill can be opened very wide to reveal large oral cavity surrounded by bristles. ♂ has white spots on wing tips and tail. Rather Cuckoo-like in flight.
Voice: Flight call *kuik*, or when disturbed a harsh *vack*. ♂ song is a continuous purring – *errr . . . orrrr-errr . . . .*, mainly heard in the evening twilight or at dawn.
Occurrence: Breeds mainly in light pine woods on sandy soil, also in thick forest with clearings or felled areas, and in dry heathland and dunes. Rather patchily distributed and uncommon.
Behaviour: Crepuscular and nocturnal. By day sits tight with eyes almost closed on the ground or lengthways on a branch. Hunts from low perch such as a branch or stone. ♂ claps wings together in display flight.
Food: Flying insects such as moths and beetles.
Breeding habits: May–August, 1–2 broods; clutch laid on ground, without nest.

| | – Blackbird | S | IV–X | SC |

Kingfisher *Alcedo atthis*
Family: Kingfishers Alcedinidae
F Martin-pêcheur G Eisvogel

Distinctive character: Very rapid flight, low and straight over the water; bright iridescent blue back.
Features: In size, behaviour and colouring unmistakable, but despite that easily overlooked when sitting quietly near the bank. ♀ has red base to lower mandible.
Voice: Loud, high-pitched penetrating *teeht*, *chee* or *chee-tee*, often rapidly repeated. Song consists of assorted calls and high trills.
Occurrence: Breeds on slow-flowing, clear streams and rivers with vertical steep banks more than ½ m tall, for tunnelling; more rarely in banks near still water. Outside breeding season also on fish ponds, small pools and even on the sea coast. Widespread, but affected by river 'improvement' schemes, pollution, and by cold winters.
Behaviour: Often sits on riverside perch above water waiting for small fish; solitary.
Food: Mostly small fish such as minnows, sticklebacks, small carp and trout.
Breeding habits: March–September, 2(3) broods; Kingfishers excavate a tunnel in the bank, usually gently sloping upwards and up to about 1 m long, at the end of which they make a round nest chamber.

< Blackbird	R	I–XII		

Bee-eater *Merops apiaster*
Family: Bee-eaters Meropidae
F Guêpier d'Europe G Bienenfresser

Distinctive character: Frequently glides and soars, showing pale translucent, triangular and pointed wings and projecting central tail feathers.
Features: Very colourful and attractive, difficult to confuse with any other species. Juv. lack long tail feathers.
Voice: Common and often heard from a distance; flight call *rruup* or *pruurr*, often repeated several times, sometimes as a duet; in disputes often gives a drawn-out *kreeh* alarm call *quitquitquit* . . . .
Occurrence: Open, warm and varied country with good supply of large insects; breeds on steep river banks, on dry, sandy slopes or sand quarries, more rarely on level ground. Common in southern Europe, also in Hungary, southern Czechoslovakia and a few pairs in Austria (Burgenland); irregular breeder further north. Rare vagrant to Britain.
Behaviour: Hunts insects from a perch such as a dry branch or wire, also in the air like swallows and martins.
Food: Mainly stinging insects such as bees, wasps, bumblebees and hornets; also butterflies, beetles and flies.
Breeding habits: May–July, 1 brood; both sexes excavate nest tunnel, about 1.5 m long with a nest-chamber at the end, in steep bank.

| | – Blackbird | (S), (M) | V–X | BR |

244

Roller *Coracias garrulus*
Family: Rollers Coraciidae
F Rollier d'Europe G Blauracke

Distinctive character: Intense blue and violet plumage, especially in flight.

Features: Almost crow-sized blue bird with red-brown back; also crow-like in flight.

Voice: Loud, harsh *rrak-rrak-rrak* . . . or (alarm call) drawn-out *krah*. Song, delivered in tumbling courtship flight, a crow-like *kraraa-kraraa-krera* . . . and *rerrerrerr* . . . .

Occurrence: Breeds in light woodland with old trees and many holes, especially in oak or pine stands; also in tree-lined avenues, isolated trees in fields, and in parks; in southern Europe also in steep river banks, in cliffs or even in old walls. In central Europe breeds only in East Germany, Czechoslovakia, Poland and in a few places in Austria. Rare vagrant to Britain.

Behaviour: Often perches in exposed position as on a pole, telephone wire or branch waiting for insects; drops to ground on to prey, returning to perch.

Food: Mainly beetles and other large insects, also lizards, young mice and worms.

Breeding habits: May–July, 1 brood; nests in holes in trees, often in old Black or Green Woodpecker holes; also uses nest-boxes. In the south of Europe often in holes in the ground, rocks or walls.

< Carrion Crow	V	IV–X	O	

Hoopoe *Upupa epops*
Family: Hoopoe Upupidae
F Huppe fasciée G Wiedehopf

Distinctive character: Fan-like erectile crest.
Features: Long, curved bill. Flight irregular, like a huge butterfly, showing contrasting black and white barred wings and tail.
Voice: Harsh, scratchy calls in territorial conflicts. Song of ♂ is a far-carrying low *poo poo poo.*
Occurrence: Breeds in warm, open country, especially in dry, extensively cultivated areas, in vineyards, light river-valley woodland and in parks, orchards and pasture. Nests in holes in old trees, in crevices in rocks and walls. Has declined over most of range. Scarce migrant in Britain, very rarely breeds.
Behaviour: Not very sociable. Feeds on ground, walking with continual changes of direction; raises crest when excited or on landing.
Food: Mainly large insects such as beetles, crickets, caterpillars, cockchafer grubs; spiders, worms, snails; also small lizards.
Breeding habits: May–July, 1 brood; nests in various holes, often those of woodpeckers, also in roof spaces, holes in walls and rocks and similar recesses.

| | – Blackbird | (M), (S) | III–X | BR |

Wryneck *Jynx torquilla*
Family: Woodpeckers Picidae
F Torcol fourmilier G Wendehals

Distinctive character: Territorial song, reminiscent of Hobby.
Features: Woodpecker relative with bark-coloured plumage which with its short bill looks like a passerine.
Voice: In territorial conflicts utters a hissing *kshree* or *vet-vet* . . . ; *tip-tip* when disturbed at breeding hole. Song a monotonous and slightly moaning crescendo *kyeeu-kyeeu-kyeeu* . . . given by both sexes, often as a duet.
Occurrence: Breeds in light broad-leaved woodland, copses in fields, parks, wooded avenues and orchards, on river banks and in wet areas with open tree cover or individual trees; avoids the interior of closed woodland; commonly found breeding near Green Woodpecker. Feeds on ground. Widespread but nowhere common. Outside breeding season also found in open areas. Much reduced in Britain (now breeds only in Scotland – a few pairs), where a scarce migrant.
Behaviour: Excavates ants' nests with bill and extracts the pupae with its long, sticky tongue. When threatened, makes snake-like movements with head and neck extended forward.
Food: Insects, especially pupae of small ant species.
Breeding habits: May–August, 1–2 broods; clutch laid in tree hole or nest box (no nest lining).

< Blackbird	(S), (M)	IV–X	BR	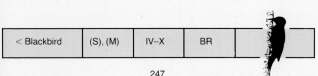

Grey-headed Woodpecker *Picus canus*
Family: Woodpeckers Picidae
F Pic cendré
G Grauspecht

Distinctive character: Loud, descending song, mostly heard in spring.
Features: Somewhat smaller than Green Woodpecker, greyer, especially on head and neck, and with narrower moustachial stripe. ♂ has red on forehead and front of crown; ♀ lacks red.
Voice: Contact call a *kyu*; in territorial conflicts a strained *kjik*. ♂ territorial song (rarely ♀) is a descending series of pleasant *ku-ku-ku* . . . notes which is easy to imitate. Drumming begins in winter (lasts 2 seconds, at 20 strikes/second).

Occurrence: Breeds in open broad-leaf and mixed woodland, often in Beech or river-valley woods; in thickets, parks, orchards and cemeteries. In mountain areas also found in coniferous woods to about 1,300 m. Widespread resident in central and eastern Europe and in central Scandinavia. Not recorded in Britain.
Behaviour: Lives well hidden and is solitary outside breeding season but is not particularly shy. Comes to feeding stations in winter.
Food: Mainly ants and their pupae; other insects, fruit, seeds, fatty scraps and suet at birdtables in winter.
Breeding habits: April–July, 1 brood; excavates its own hole in tree (usually broad-leaf); also takes over old woodpecker holes.

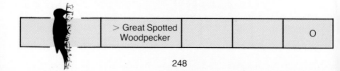

	> Great Spotted Woodpecker			O

Green Woodpecker *Picus viridis*
Family: Woodpeckers Picidae
F Pic vert G Grünspecht

Distinctive character: Loud resounding and laughing song.
Features: A large, green woodpecker with bright red crown. ♂ has red moustache with black edging, all black in ♀. Juv. are heavily barred below (except on neck), with a more orange colour on upper head. Conspicuous yellow rump in flight.
Voice: Flight call (and near hole) a hard *kjek* or *kjook*. Laughing territorial song, *klee-klee-klee . . .*, not descending like that of Grey-headed Wood-

pecker. ♀ has softer and quieter song. Drums only very rarely, in short bursts.
Occurrence: Breeds at edges of broad-leaf and mixed woodland, in copses in fields, orchards, parks and gardens with old trees; in Alps also in coniferous woods. Widespread and fairly common.
Behaviour: Digs holes up to 10 cm deep to grub out ants' nests, even beneath snow in winter. Does not visit feeding stations.
Food: Mainly ants, sometimes other insects, worms and snails, fruit.
Breeding habits: April–July, 1 brood; often nests in old holes; new holes excavated in rotten wood.

< Feral Pigeon	R	I–XII		

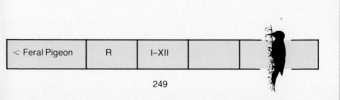

Black Woodpecker *Dryocopus martius*
Family: Woodpeckers Picidae
F Pic noir
G Schwarzspecht

Distinctive character: A black woodpecker almost as big as a crow, with very powerful, pale bill.

Features: ♂ has red cap, ♀ has only rear of crown red. Tongue relatively short, extending only about 5 cm beyond tip of bill. Flies fairly straight with irregular wingbeats, rather like a Jay, less undulating than other woodpecker species.

Voice: Typical flight call is a far-carrying *prree-prree-prree* . . . , often followed by a descending *klierr* on landing. Territorial song in spring *kweekweekwee* . . . . Drums with relatively slow strike rate (each burst lasts 2–3 seconds) – loud and audible over long distance.

Occurrence: Breeds in richly varied mixed and coniferous forest with old trees; nest hole usually in old beech or pine trees. Widespread resident over much of Europe. Not recorded in Britain.

Behaviour: Uses powerful bill blows to get at timber-dwelling insects; its feeding signs – elongate, deep holes – are often found on spruce trees attacked by heart-rot. Often 'dismantles' decaying tree stumps to get at the nests of horse ants.

Food: Mainly large ants and wood-boring beetles.

Breeding habits: March–June, 1 brood; excavates a large hole with vertically oval entrance (7–15 m from ground); also often takes over old holes.

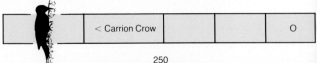

< Carrion Crow | | O

250

White-backed Woodpecker
Picoides leucotos
Family: Woodpeckers Picidae
F Pic à dos blanc
G Weißrückenspecht

Distinctive character: Lack of white shoulder patch (see Great Spotted Woodpecker).

Features: Larger and heavier than Great Spotted and with longer bill. Upper back black, lower back white; streaked flanks; undertail-coverts delicate pink. Crown red in ♂, black in ♀.

Voice: Less vocal than Great Spotted. Alarm call a soft *kjik* or harder *gek gek gek* . . . . Drum lasts longer than Great Spotted's and accelerates towards the end (30–40 strikes in about 1.6 seconds). Drumming bursts often interspersed with a muffled *kig-kig-kurr*.

Occurrence: Breeds in virgin-type mixed forests, with a high proportion of dead and dying tees. Uncommon resident in northern, eastern and south-east Europe. Rare breeder in eastern central Europe; found in some montane forest in Alpine area and in Bavarian Forest. Endangered because of low population density and its high sensitivity to disturbance and forestry operations.

Behaviour: Removes bark and digs deep holes in rotten wood when feeding; often works on fallen trunks.

Food: Mainly larvae of wood-boring beetles; ants, fruit, nuts, will take suet at feeding stations.

Breeding habits: April–June, 1 brood; excavates hole in dying wood.

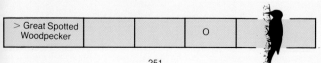

> Great Spotted Woodpecker			O		

Great Spotted Woodpecker
Picoides major
Family: Woodpeckers *Picidae*
F Pic épeiche G Buntspecht

Distinctive character: By far the commonest woodpecker.

Features: Contrasting black and white plumage, striking white shoulder patches; undertail bright red, flanks unstreaked. ♂ has red patch at back of head. Juv. have red crown. Undulating flight.

Voice: Hard metallic *chick* or *kix*, rapidly repeated when excited, and can be heard throughout the year. ♂ and ♀ make a series of hoarse scolding sounds when chasing each other in spring. Both sexes drum on dry branches, but also on wooden and metal posts, weather-vanes and on metal parts of roofs. Drum bursts short (about 0.5 seconds, dying away at end).

Occurrence: Breeds in all kinds of woods, especially those with oak and hornbeam, and in copses, parks, wooded gardens, often in villages and even towns and cities.

Behaviour: Widens natural clefts ('anvils') to hold fruits and cones while pecking at them for food.

Food: In summer mainly wood-boring insects and their larvae, other insects, young birds, eggs, fruits; in winter seeds of conifers, nuts, suet (sometimes visits feeding stations or bird tables).

Breeding habits: April–July, 1 brood excavates a new hole each year usually in a diseased tree, thus creating sites for other hole-nesting species.

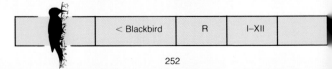

		< Blackbird	R	I–XII	

Syrian Woodpecker *Picoides syriacus*
Family: Woodpeckers Picidae
F Pic syriaque
G Blutspecht

Distinctive character: Differs from Great Spotted Woodpecker in lack of black band behind ear region connecting moustache with black rear of head; voice important.

Features: Very similar to Great Spotted Woodpecker; juv. of the two species very difficult to separate.

Voice: Calls softer than those of Great Spotted Woodpecker, similar to those of Middle Spotted: *gyik*, *gik* or *dshik*, also a series of *kirr* and *gyik* calls combined, such as *gyik-gyik-kirr*. Drum bursts slightly longer than Great Spotted (usually 20 strikes/second), but more seldom heard; usually about 5–6 drum bursts a minute; ♀ drums less often, the individual bursts being shorter.

Occurrence: Breeds in river valleys, near-natural dry oak and mixed forests. In central Europe mainly in vineyards, orchards and parks, but not in forest. Has spread into Hungary, Czechoslovakia, south Poland and Austria in recent decades. Recently hybrids between Syrian and Great Spotted have been found in Bavaria. Not recorded in Britain.

Food: As for Great Spotted, wood-boring insects and their larvae, but also fruits, berries and nuts throughout the year.

Breeding habits: April–June, 1 brood; like Great Spotted excavates holes in diseased trees.

– Great Spotted Woodpecker			O		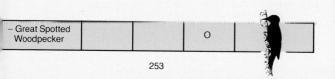

Middle Spotted Woodpecker
Picoides medius
Family: Woodpeckers Picidae
F Pic mar G Mittelspecht

Distinctive character: In all plumages, striking red cap with no black border.

Features: Similar to Great Spotted but somewhat smaller and with weaker bill. Flanks have dark streaks; belly yellowish, grading into pink on undertail-coverts.

Voice: Calls less frequently than Great Spotted: soft *gik*; and a scolding *gegegeg* . . . heard throughout the year. Drums seldom. Territorial song is a nasal, plaintive, slow *gair-gair* . . . .

Occurrence: Only in lowland areas. Breeds in near-natural open broad-leaf woodland with old Oaks and Hornbeams, particularly in river-valley woodland, orchards, and also in larger parks with old Oaks. Restricted to warmer regions of central, eastern and south-east Europe. Patchy distribution. Not recorded in Britain.

Behaviour: When foraging, relies less on intensive pecking than Great Spotted, often gleaning caterpillars and other insects from foliage and branches and even attempting to catch flying insects. Uses 'anvils' but does not excavate its own.

Food: Mainly insects, from bark or twigs; fruits, cherry stones; at feeding stations will take suet and seeds.

Breeding habits: April–June, 1 brood; nest hole in rotten wood, often in a horizontal branch.

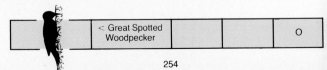

| | < Great Spotted Woodpecker | | | O |

Lesser Spotted Woodpecker
Picoides minor
Family: Woodpeckers Picidae
F Pic épeichette G Kleinspecht

Distinctive character: Smallest European woodpecker, about the size of a sparrow. Voice important.

Features: Weak bill, back barred black and white; no red on underside. ♂ has red cap with black border, ♀ has no red colour at all in the plumage.

Voice: Territorial song is a shrill *kee-kee-kee* . . . , somewhat reminiscent of Kestrel; heard most often in spring. ♂ and ♀ drum in long yet weak, uniform bursts (length 1–1.5 seconds), on thin branches.

Occurrence: Breeds in open, broad-leaf and mixed woodland, favouring swampy and river-valley woodland and riverside trees; also in parks with old willows or poplars and in orchards. Widespread but not common.

Behaviour: Often clambers vertically in typical woodpecker fashion on thin branches and twigs, especially in crown layer of trees. Often wanders about with other small birds in winter and may then visit feeding stations.

Food: Mainly insects and their larvae, taken from leaves and twigs. In winter mainly beetles wintering beneath the bark; sunflower seeds at bird tables.

Breeding habits: April–July, 1 brood; nest hole in diseased or dead wood, often on the underside of relatively weak branches.

| – House Sparrow | R | I–XII | | 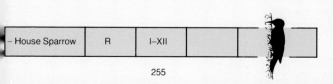 |

Three-toed Woodpecker
Picoides tridactylus
Family: Woodpeckers Picidae
F Pic tridactyle
G Dreizehenspecht

Distinctive character: ♂ and ♀ totally lacking red in plumage.
Features: A black and white woodpecker almost the same size as Great Spotted; wings black, back white but often with dark markings. ♂ has yellow patch on crown.
Voice: Less vocal than Great Spotted. When excited, a soft *kjig* or *gik*, increasing to a rapid twitter when more agitated. Contact calls of fledglings recall Fieldfares. ♂ and ♀ drum from late winter, most frequently in April and May; drum bursts which accelerate slightly towards the end,

are quite long (about 1.3 seconds, 20 strikes).
Occurrence: Breeds in Scandinavia in near-natural spruce woods (taiga) where there are many dead or dying trees. Also in the Alps, Carpathians and Balkan mountains. In central Europe only in the Alps, and higher ranges elsewhere (Bavarian Forest Böhmerwald, Tatras) above about 700 m. Not recorded in Britain.
Behaviour: Not very shy. Seeks food mainly beneath bark; pecks rows of small holes in tree bark (bark ringing) and later consumes the exuding sap.
Food: Mainly larvae and pupae of tree beetles; tree sap (especially in spring).
Breeding habits: May–July, 1 brood; excavates new hole each year in dead or dying conifer.

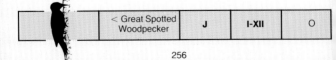

	< Great Spotted Woodpecker	**J**	**I-XII**	O

Songbirds

Passerines – Passeriformes

This order contains over half of all the world's species. In Europe they are represented by 24 ecologically very diverse families in the Songbird suborder (Oscines).

Songbirds are mostly small, but some are almost Buzzard-sized. They have a special vocal apparatus (the syrinx) with more than three pairs of singing muscles. Another characteristic feature is the toe arrangement – three toes pointing forward and one pointing back.

All young songbirds are nidicolous and altricial, that is they are born naked, blind, helpless, and unable to walk. The nestlings have brightly coloured gape flanges and oral cavities, and when the adult bird approaches the nest they beg for food by opening their bill wide (gaping) and stretching their necks upwards, revealing the conspicuous mouth pattern. The families are as follows:

Larks are small, relatively compact, mostly ground-nesting birds. Most species are streaked brown, with the sexes usually similar. Four species can be found in northern Europe.

Swallows are small, slim songbirds with elongated bodies, pointed wings and more or less deeply forked tails. Bill and legs are short. Swallows feed exclusively on insects, caught in flight. Four species exist in northern and central Europe.

Pipits and wagtails live mainly on the ground and are insectivorous. Pipits have lark-like camouflaged plumage, but they are much more slender and elegant, and have characteristic, often conspicuous song-flights. Wagtails have very long tails, long, thin legs and bright contrasting plumage. Eight species are found regularly in northern Europe.

Waxwings are unmistakable with their pink-brown plumage and obvious crest. Only one species in Europe.

Dippers, of all songbirds, are the best adapted to water. They can swim and dive, and search for food mainly under water. Often sit bobbing on a stone in the water. One European species.

Wrens are birds of the New World, with the exception of a single species, which occurs also in Europe. Its small size, rotund appearance with constantly cocked tail and loud voice make the Wren easy to identify.

Accentors are drab sparrow-like birds. They are best located by their voice. Two species exist in Europe, one restricted to high mountains.

Thrushes, chats and flycatchers have rather long legs and slender insectivore bills. They have particularly fine songs. They mostly search for their prey – insects – on the ground. Juveniles usually have a spotted plumage. 20 species occur regularly in central and northern Europe.

Warblers also have loud, musical songs. Most species are small and have inconspicuous plumage. Bill relatively long and narrow. 24 species can be seen in central and northern Europe.

Kinglets are the smallest songbirds, and the smallest of all European birds. They have yellow and orange crowns, and live mostly in dense coniferous woodland, where they are often hard to spot. Two species in Europe.

Reedlings are long-tailed birds of bushes or reedbeds. One species, the Bearded Tit, is an irregular breeder in large reedbeds.

Long-tailed tits, despite their very long tails, attract attention usually by their calls; not often seen singly; restlessly perform acrobatics on thin twigs and catch small insects with their tiny bills. The sole European species builds a very elaborate, attractive nest.

Tits are sturdily built small birds with short, pointed bills and relatively short tails. They climb skilfully among the foliage and are only rarely seen on the ground. All tits are hole nesters, and feed on insects and seeds. Six species exist in northern Europe.

Nuthatches are robust songbirds with a powerful bill and short tail. They climb on tree bark, often hanging upside down. They reduce holes to the right size by sticking mud around the entrance. The sole northern European species is common throughout the region.

Wallcreepers are found only in the high mountains of Europe and Asia. The Wallcreeper is a specialist rock climber and is not difficult to identify.

Treecreepers have plumage patterned like tree bark, and a long, curved bill. They climb up trees in a spiral, supporting themselves, like woodpeckers, with the tail. The two European species are very similar.

Penduline Tits are rather like the true tits in appearance, with a short, pointed bill. In behaviour, too, they resemble tits as they move acrobatically and skilfully on thin twigs and in reeds. The sole European species constructs an elaborate nest.

Orioles live mainly in Africa and south-east Asia. They are thrush-sized birds and the males of most species have attractive plumages. The only species in Europe is a shy bird of woodland.

Shrikes often impale their prey on thorns or wedge them in branch forks. They live mainly in bushy country, where they sit on a high exposed perch keeping a lookout for their insect and small vertebrate prey. Four species in central and northern Europe.

Crows are the largest songbirds. Most are dark-coloured and many are quite colourful. They are very adaptable and intelligent. Their songs are very poorly developed. Nine species breed in central and northern Europe.

Starlings are very lively and sociable birds. Most have short tails and powerful pointed bills. The single northern European species is a common hole-nester throughout the region. Easily identified by its behaviour, calls and song (incorporating many imitations).

Sparrows are rather like finches, but their tails are either only slightly forked or not forked at all. They are closely related to the weaver-birds of Africa. They either nest in holes, or, like weaver-birds, build nests in the open with over-arching roofs. Three central and northern European species.

Finches are small, seed-eating birds with pointed, more or less conical bills. In many species the males are brightly coloured, the females usually much drabber. Bill and tail shape are important characters as are their calls and songs. Fourteen species exist in northern Europe.

Buntings are rather elongated, finch-like songbirds with short, powerful bills. Most live in open country with bushes and trees. Males are usually much more colourful than the females. Eight species exist in northern Europe.

Crested Lark *Galerida cristata*
Family: Larks Alaudidae
F Cochevis huppé G Haubenlerche

Distinctive character: Conspicuous crest.
Features: More dumpy and short-tailed than Skylark, with somewhat more powerful legs, and longer slightly decurved bill. Less contrasting upperparts. Flight light and easy with nervously flapping wingbeats, showing broad wings and buff outer tail feathers.
Voice: Flight call a musical *djui*; when excited *dee-jee-ju* or *dee-dee-deer-dlee*. Song consists of short and long whistled or twittering phrases,

and often contains imitations of other bird calls, and even human whistles.
Occurrence: Dry open wasteland, steppe, semi-desert, embankments, factories, sportsfields, also in cities; even breeds on flat roofs with a gravel covering. Distribution patchy. In small flocks outside breeding season. Very rare vagrant to Britain.
Behaviour: Very approachable. Song often delivered from low or medium-high perch, but also in circling flight.
Food: Seeds of grasses and wild herbs; green parts of plants; small insects and spiders.
Breeding habits: April–June, 2 broods; simple ground nest made of loosely intertwined stems.

| | > House Sparrow | V | | O |

Woodlark *Lullula arborea*
Family: Larks Alaudidae
F Alouette lulu G Heidelerche

Distinctive character: Atmospheric, musical song.
Features: Smaller and noticeably shorter-tailed than Skylark. At close range pale supercilia, meeting at nape, and black and white marking at bend in wing. When nervous, repeatedly raises small, rounded, otherwise inconspicuous crest.
Voice: Soft, melodious call *did-loee* or, when disturbed, *titroeet*. ♂'s song made up of many different, mostly soft and melancholy phrases, falling towards the end – such as *dleed-leedleedleedleedlee* or *deedideedi-deedideedi*, repeated in a specific sequence. Repertoire of more than 100 different phrases.
Occurrence: Mainly in woodland clearings in light, dry pine forests or on wooded heathland. Often nests near Tree Pipit. Declined over much of range; distribution rather patchy. In Britain confined to south.
Behaviour: The only European lark that commonly perches in trees. As a song perch often uses tips of young pines, which bend under its weight.
Food: Insects, spiders, buds, green parts of plants.
Breeding habits: March–August, 2–3 broods; carefully-built nests with deep cup, well hidden.

– House Sparrow	R	I–XII	BR	

Skylark *Alauda arvensis*
Family: Larks Alaudidae
F Alouette des champs G Feldlerche

Distinctive character: Sustained trilling song.
Features: Plumage camouflaged; small crest can be raised when excited. Trailing edges of wings and outer tail feathers conspicuously white.
Voice: Flight call a pleasant hard *chirrup* or *chreeoo*; song nearly always performed in flight, often high up, and audible from afar. A mixture of warbles, or trills and whistles, following on from each other without a break; often includes imitations of other birds such as Redshank and Green Sandpiper.

Occurrence: Breeds in all kinds of open country, especially agricultural fields and pasture, and low-growing and wet meadows. Common throughout nearly all of Europe.
Behaviour: Flies directly upwards into steeply ascending song-flight, singing continuously, and then remains for several minutes 'hanging' in sky while singing; occasionally circles low, with wings quivering. Normal flight is slightly undulating and fluttering. Hardly ever perches on trees.
Food: Insects, spiders, seeds, green parts of plants.
Breeding habits: April–August, 2–3 broods; well-hidden nest made of grass in a hollow scraped in the ground.

	> House Sparrow	P, W, M	I–XII	

Shore Lark *Eremophila alpestris*
Family: Larks Alaudidae
F Alouette hausse-col
G Ohrenlerche

Distinctive character: Our only lark with yellow on head, chin and throat.
Features: Sandy grey above, whitish below. The yellow and black head markings are much less distinct in winter, especially in the ♀. Breeding ♂ has small black 'horns' which are hardly visible in winter. ♀ and some ♂ lack these 'horns'. In flight slimmer than other larks, and with rather more pointed wings.
Voice: Flight call a pure, tinkling *seet-dit-dit*, *tsee-tui-tsee* or *tsee-tsee*; alarm call *pseet* or a Snow Bunting-like *peeu*. Song usually a rapid, high-pitched twitter, delivered in short phrases; sometimes also a sustained twittering like Skylark.
Occurrence: Breeds in open mountain habitats on dry, stony plateaux, above the willow zone in northern Europe, also breeds in Balkan mountains. Winters in small flocks on North Sea and Baltic coasts, often mixed with Skylarks; coastal meadows, waste land and fields with short vegetation. Very scarce visitor to Britain (east coast); has bred in Scotland.
Behaviour: Moves jerkily on ground and crouches, and is therefore easily missed.
Food: Insects, spiders, seeds and green parts of plants.

> House Sparrow	W, P	X–IV	BR	

Sand Martin *Riparia riparia*
Family: Martins and swallows Hirundinidae
F Hirondelle de rivage
G Uferschwalbe

Distinctive character: Smallest European swallow.
Features: Noticeably smaller than House Sparrow. Tail weakly forked. Brown above, below white with brown breast band (drawing).
Voice: Vocal. Scratchy *chripp* or *chrr* and a rapidly repeated *brbrbr*; alarm call a sharp *tsier*. Song low twittering, usually heard close to nest.
Occurrence: Steep, sandy banks and sand quarries with steep walls, usually close to water, including at the coast. Endangered by disturbance during breeding period and by reuse of old sand workings.
Behaviour: Very sociable, often breeding in large colonies. Regularly feeds far out over water. After breeding season they frequently gather to roost in large flocks in reedbeds.
Food: Small flying insects.
Breeding habits: May–August, 2

Sand Martin, in flight

broods; both sexes excavate a 60–100 cm long horizontal tunnel with an oval entrance hole, in a steep bank; holes usually arranged next to each other in lines.

	< House Sparrow	S, M	III–X	

Distinctive character: Spread tail reveals row of pale spots.

Features: Resembles Sand Martin but is larger and more powerfully built; tail is hardly notched at all. Plumage brownish above; no breast band; dark underwing-coverts contrast with paler flight feathers. Flight rapid, agile and swift-like.

Voice: Vocal. Sparrow-like *chrri*, *trt trt* or *pit pit*. Song a prolonged chattering, interspersed with calls and trills.

Occurrence: Breeds on sunny, sparsely vegetated cliffs in the Alps and Mediterranean area; a few pairs in Bavaria. Outside breeding season and in bad weather often hunts over water.

Behaviour: Very skilful and agile in flight, following rock structure close

Crag Martin, in flight

to cliff face. Less sociable than other swallows.

Food: Small flying insects.

Breeding habits: April–July, 1–2 broods; nests below overhangs in spots protected from rain and wind, in clefts and holes in cliffs. Nest made of mud and open at top.

< House Sparrow	V		O	

Swallow *Hirundo rustica*
Family: Martins and Swallows Hirundinidae
F Hirondelle de cheminée
G Rauchschwalbe

Distinctive character: Commonest swallow in rural areas.
Features: Very slim with unusually long tail streamers (drawing). Upperparts and breast band metallic blue, forehead and chin red. Juv. less brightly coloured and with shorter tail streamers. Flight elegant and rapid, rather more direct than House Martin's.
Voice: Common flight call *vit-vit*; alarm call a penetrating and ringing *tsidit*, often repeated. Song a pleasant, rather prolonged twittering chatter, usually with a rattling end section.
Occurrence: Common throughout open countryside and in villages,

especially on farms; usually feeds over green fields. In mountains found up to level of mountain pastures.
Behaviour: In bad weather often flies low over fields and water. Very

Swallow, in flight

sociable, especially outside breeding season.
Food: Small flying insects.
Breeding habits: May–September, 2–3 broods; nests mostly inside buildings (stables and barns), on a beam next to a vertical wall; nest basin-shaped, made of mud and twigs.

	< House Sparrow	S, M	III–XI	

266

House Martin *Delichon urbica*
Family: Martins and swallows Hirundinidae
F Hirondelle de fenêtre
G Mehlschwalbe

Distinctive character: White rump and pure white underside.
Features: More compact than Swallow, tail much less forked and lacking long streamers. Metallic blue-black above; juv. dark brown, lacking sheen. More fluttering flight than Swallow, with higher wing-beat frequency. Often glides.
Voice: Flight call *prrt*, *trrtrr* or *chrrp*; alarm call shrill high-pitched *seer*, often repeated. Song very unobtrusive, dry twittering, less varied than Swallow's.
Occurrence: Common in towns and villages; in cities very much rarer;

also breeds in quarries and in mountains up to 2,000 m.
Behaviour: Usually hunts higher up than Swallow; always very sociable.

House Martin, in flight

Food: Small flying insects.
Breeding habits: May–September, 2–3 broods; nests colonially on the outsides of buildings, usually immediately under the eaves; also on bridges and cliffs; hemispherical mud nest, closed except for a small entrance hole.

< House Sparrow	S, M	IV–XI		

Meadow Pipit *Anthus pratensis*
Family: Pipits and wagtails Motacillidae
F Pipit farlouse G Wiesenpieper

Distinctive character: Perches on trees more rarely than Tree Pipit. Chirping warning calls near nest.
Features: Distinguished from very similar Tree Pipit mainly by voice and habitat. More olive above, breast with less yellow and more delicately streaked. Usually less upright posture than Tree Pipit; spends more time on ground. Flight undulating and rather unsteady.
Voice: When flushed, repeated high-pitched shrill *ist*; contact call a soft *psip*. Song made up of high, thin notes turning into a hard trill towards the end, usually introduced by an accelerating series of *tsip* sounds.
Occurrence: Breeds on moorland, wet meadows, heath, dunes and waste ground; in mountains on meadows up to tree-line. In winter often on fields and coasts.
Behaviour: Inconspicuous and easily overlooked when on ground. Song-flight less frequent than Tree Pipit's, often starting from ground perch. Also sings from ground, when song tends to be more monotonous.
Food: Mainly insects and other small animals, collected on the ground; small seeds.
Breeding habits: April–July, 2 broods; loosely constructed ground nest, usually well hidden under a tuft of grass.

| 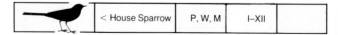 | < House Sparrow | P, W, M | I–XII | |

Tree Pipit *Anthus trivialis*
Family: Pipits and wagtails Motacillidae
F Pipit des arbres G Baumpieper

Distinctive character: Characteristic song.
Features: Slimmer than House Sparrow, with yellowish breast and throat, streaked with dark brown. Legs reddish.
Voice: When flushed a somewhat hoarse *psee*, often repeated at intervals; near nest a rhythmically repeated *tsitt*. Song louder, fuller and more musical than Meadow Pipit's, consisting of various longer phrases, some reminiscent of Canary, increasingly drawn out towards the end.
Occurrence: Breeds on margins of broadleaf and coniferous forest, in herb-rich clearings, mires and patches of heathland with scattered trees or bushes. Occurs up to tree-line in mountains.
Behaviour: Sings mainly from high tree top or in short song-flight, in

Song-flight

Tree Pipit

which the bird takes off from perch just before the climax of the song and then 'parachutes' down (drawing) to the same or a different perch.
Food: Mainly insects, spiders.
Breeding habits: May–July, 1–2 broods; nest well hidden in ground vegetation.

– House Sparrow	S, M	IV–X		

Rock Pipit *Anthus petrosus*
Family: Pipits and wagtails Motacillidae
F Pipit maritime G Strandpieper

Distinctive character: Dark legs; inhabits rocky shores.
Features: Larger than Tree and Meadow Pipits, with greyer, darker plumage, less streaked above. Underside dirty buff with heavy obscure streaking. Narrow eye ring, occasionally extending into indistinct short supercilium (may be more prominent in summer).
Voice: Slightly deeper, louder, hoarser than Meadow Pipit – *eesst eesst* or *sit sit*; repeated *tsit* near to nest. Song, often in flight, is made up of several long and high phrases, louder and more musical than Meadow Pipit's such as *tri tri tri . . .* , *tsveetsveetsvee . . .* or *fooifooifooi . . . .*

Occurrence: Breeds on rocky shores around British Isles and in north-west France and Scandinavia. Outside breeding season also on other types of coast and very occasionally at inland waters.
Food: Mostly insects, spiders and molluscs.
Breeding habits: April–June, 1–2 broods; nests in rock crevices under low vegetation.

The **Water Pipit** *Anthus spinoletta* breeds beside fast-flowing streams in the mountains of central and southern Europe, wintering in lowland areas usually near water (north to southern Britain). It has a prominent white supercilium, and in summer plumage crown and nape are pale blue-grey and underparts pinkish-white (usually unstreaked).

	> House Sparrow	R, W, M	I–XII	

Tawny Pipit *Anthus campestris*
Family: Pipits and wagtails *Motacillidae*
F Pipit rousseline G Brachpieper

Distinctive character: Looks rather wagtail-like.

Features: Larger and slimmer than Tree Pipit, and with longer legs and tail. Plumage sandy and almost unstreaked, with clear eye-stripe. Juv. streaked above and on breast.

Voice: Call sparrow- or lark-like: flight call *chrill* or *psia*, often *tseehp* on take-off. Song a monotonous, repeated *tseerluee*, *chleeu* or *treeih*.

Occurrence: Breeds in steppe country, in dry open habitats with stony or sandy soils, in clearings in pine forests, in vineyards, heathland and in dunes. Threatened in some areas by afforestation of heathland and recultivation of gravel and sand workings. Very scarce passage migrant in Britain.

Behaviour: Often moves plover-like over bare soil with its body held horizontal. Frequently sings in circling, undulating song-flight, gliding down at the end with vibrating wings.

Food: Small soil insects, spiders and slugs.

Breeding habits: May–August, 1–2 broods; nest made of dry grass and roots, lined with fine grass and long hairs.

> House Sparrow	(M)	IV–X	O	

271

Yellow Wagtail *Motacilla flava*
Family: Pipits and wagtails Motacillidae
F Bergeronnette flavéole
G Englische Schafstelze

Distinctive character: Uniform bright yellow underside (and yellowish upperparts in Yellow Wagtail).

Features: Somewhat smaller and shorter-tailed than Pied Wagtail. Yellow Wagtail *M. f. flavissima*, the British race, has yellow-green upperparts and yellow supercilium; female much duller, above and below. Blue-headed Wagtail *M. f. flava*, the central European race, has slate-grey head and short white supercilium; ♀ somewhat paler with head more brownish-grey. About six other races in north, south and east Europe.

Voice: Flight call heard frequently, a sharp *pseep*; alarm call *sreesree*. Simple song of short elements such as *sree sree . . . tsip tsip tsipsi . . . .*

Occurrence: Less dependent upon water than other wagtails; breeds on boggy ground, marshes, damp heathland, meadows and pasture in lowland sites; also on fields and cultivated land; avoids woodland and mountains. In Britain, apart from Yellow Wagtail (breeder), several races occur as scarce passage migrants.

Behaviour: Often found close to grazing animals. Sings from the ground, from song perch or in ascending and descending song-flight with shallow wingbeats.

Food: Mostly insects, their larvae and spiders.

Breeding habits: May–July, 1–2 broods; loose nest of stems, grasses and roots in a hollow beneath thick ground vegetation.

	> House Sparrow	S, M	III–X	

Grey Wagtail *Motacilla cinerea*
Family: Pipits and wagtails Motacillidae
F Bergeronnette des ruisseaux
G Gebirgsstelze

Distinctive character: Repeatedly wags very long tail up and down.
Features: Yellow underside like Yellow/Blue-headed Wagtail, but has much longer tail, uniformly grey back and darker wings. ♂ has black chin and throat; winter ♂, ♀, and juv. have white chin and throat. In flight yellow undertail and greenish-yellow rump; white wing-bar sometimes visible.
Voice: Sharp metallic *tsitsiss*, alarm call near nest a shrill *sisseeht* or *seeht tsicktsick*. Song: high-pitched shrill twittering phrases made up of call-like notes, such as *tseep tseep tseep*, *tsee tsee tsee*, *tsit tsit tsit*.
Occurrence: Breeds along fast-flowing mountain streams and shallow rivers (to 1,900 m). In lowlands mostly at reservoirs, bridges and gravel pits. Outside breeding season also on lakes and ponds in parks, watercress beds, coast.
Behaviour: Flutters from stone to stone to catch insects; flies rapidly and often low over water surface. Often sings in flight.
Food: Insects, spiders, small aquatic worms and crustaceans.
Breeding habits: March–July, 1–2 broods; nest made of twigs, grass and moss, lined with hair, and sited in a crevice in rocks, between roots or under bridges; usually close to bank.

> House Sparrow	R, M	I–XII		

Pied Wagtail *Motacilla alba*
Family: Pipits and wagtails Motacillidae
F Bergeronnette d'Yarrell
G Trauerbachstelze

Distinctive character: Long black tail with white outer feathers; tail constantly bobbed up and down.
Features: Legs long, thin and black. Pied Wagtail *M. a. yarrellii*, the British race, black crown and upperparts, black throat and breast and white forehead, cheeks and belly; ♀ back dark grey. White Wagtail *M. a. alba*, the continental race, pale grey back. ♀ of both races are less contrasting; often less black on head. In winter all have white chin, throat, dark breast-band. Juv. brown-grey above, without black, buff on head and throat.
Voice: Penetrating *tsick*, *chizzik*, *tslipp* or *tsilipp*, often repeated near nest a series of *klik* calls. Song is a rapid twitter made up of elements similar to call notes. Reacts to birds of prey with loud twittering.
Occurrence: Common everywhere in open country, especially near water; breeds in towns and villages, farms, gravel pits; outside breeding season often seen on lakes and rivers, meadows, fields and wet areas.
Behaviour: Runs rapidly with short steps, nodding head rhythmically backwards and forwards. Feeds mainly on sparsely vegetated or bare ground, roads, flat roofs etc; catches insects in short feeding flights.
Food: Insects, larvae, spiders, small worms and snails; in winter seeds.
Breeding habits: April–August, 2–3 broods; rough nest of twigs, stems, leaves and moss, sited in recess or cavity, on roof gable, bank, under stones, in piles of logs, etc.

	> House Sparrow	P, W, M	I–XII	

Waxwing
Bombycilla garrulus
Family: Waxwings Bombycillidae
F Jaseur boréal
G Seidenschwanz

Distinctive character: Crest, silky plumage and high-pitched calls.
Features: Very colourful, but looks uniform brown from a distance. In ♀ the waxy red wing markings are smaller, as are the yellow wing markings in juv. birds. Flight swift and direct, starling-like but looks slimmer.
Voice: Call on take-off and in flight a high, trilling *sreer*, sounds softer at close range. Calling flocks often audible over distance. Song a sus-

tained humming and chattering, incorporating typical flight calls and other squeaky and noisier elements.
Occurrence: Breeds in open spruce taiga with rich undergrowth and in birch woods in northern Scandinavia and Soviet Union. In autumn and winter usually seen further south and west (as far as Britain) in small numbers; in some years larger numbers occur during 'irruptions'.
Behaviour: Very sociable, usually feeds on berry-bearing bushes, shrubs and trees, often in parks and gardens; tame.
Food: Mainly insects in breeding season; otherwise almost entirely berries, especially rowan, viburnum, hawthorn, and fruit.

| – Starling | W, M | X–VI | O |  |

Dipper *Cinclus cinclus*
Family: Dippers Cinclidae
F Cincle plongeur G Wasseramsel

Distinctive character: Only songbird that can swim and dive.
Features: Rotund, Wren-like appearance, with short tail and strong legs and feet. Juv. slate-grey above, with dirty white throat and breast (caused by dark feather edges).
Voice: Sharp, scratchy, flight call – *srit* or *tsit*, and a harsh *tserrp*. Song: a rhythmic chattering series of whistles, trills, harsh twittering and scratchy elements, often incorporating imitations of other birds. Both sexes sing,

even in winter. Song often drowned by sound of rushing water.
Occurrence: Breeds on fast-flowing clear streams and rivers up to 2,000 m; widespread in upland areas, otherwise rare. In winter also seen occasionally at slow rivers and lake sides away from breeding site.
Behaviour: Often sits on stone in the water, bobbing; flies rapidly, direct and low over water.
Food: Mainly aquatic insects and their larvae; also worms, small crustaceans and fish fry.
Breeding habits: March–July, 2 broods; large, roofed moss nest, in thick overhanging bank vegetation, under a bridge, or in special nest-box.

| | – Starling | R, (W) | I–XII | |

Wren
Troglodytes troglodytes
Family: Wrens Troglodytidae
F Troglodyte mignon
G Zaunkönig

Distinctive character: Tail usually held cocked when excited.
Features: Tiny and squat, with short tail.
Voice: Alarm call a loud, hard *teck teck teck* . . . , often also *tetetet te tete* . . . , or a churring *tserrr* . . . . Contact call of fledged young sounds like *tseep* and is hard to locate. Song loud and ringing with trills, ending in fluting sounds or with a high, sharp note.
Occurrence: Often close to water;

breeds in woods with thick undergrowth, and in scrub; also in parks and overgrown gardens; in Alps to about 2,000 m. Widespread and common, but populations hit hard by cold winters.
Behaviour: Very lively; creeps about close to ground like a mouse, frequently disappearing into reeds or brushwood, or amongst the roots at a bank or into a wood pile. Flight direct with rapid wing-beats. Sings nearly all the year, usually from a low perch.
Food: Insects, their larvae, small spiders and worms.
Breeding habits: April–August, 2 broods; spherical nest made of moss with entrance hole at the side, usually low in the undergrowth, in ivy or amongst roots of fallen trees.

< House Sparrow	R, W	I–XII		

Dunnock *Prunella modularis*
Family: Accentors Prunellidae
F Accenteur mouchet
G Heckenbraunelle

Distinctive character: Inconspicuous, slightly resembles ♀ House Sparrow, but has thinner bill.

Features: Head and breast slate-grey, flanks with dark streaks; at close range, brown ear-coverts and red-brown iris visible. Juv. have brown-grey head with dark streaks, and stronger streaking on underparts.

Voice: High, piping alarm call is a drawn-out *tseeh*. Contact call often a high-pitched, clear *deedeedee*; and outside breeding season, especially in autumn, a high, far-carrying *tseedit* or *tseetseetsee*. Song a pleasant continuous hurried twitter, gently rising and falling, and of variable loudness and phrase length. Each ♂ has several different phrase types.

Occurrence: Common breeder in coniferous and mixed woodland, in parks, cemeteries and overgrown gardens with thick shrubbery; in moorland scrub and in mountains up to dwarf pine region.

Behaviour: Hops on ground in hunched posture, skulking, and seldom leaving cover. Often sings at tops of hedges and young conifers.

Food: Insects, spiders; in winter small seeds (poppy).

Breeding habits: April–July, 2–3 broods; compact moss nest with twig base, often in young spruce or bush.

	– House Sparrow	R, W	I–XII	

Alpine Accentor *Prunella collaris*
Family: Accentors Prunellidae
F Accenteur alpin
G Alpenbraunelle

Distinctive character: Flight and behaviour lark-like, not a bird of cover like Dunnock.
Features: Larger, squatter and more colourful than Dunnock. From a distance looks a uniform grey-brown, but at close range the rust-red patterning on flanks, pale throat markings and yellowish base to bill are all visible; dark wing patch bordered with white. In flight shows white tips to tail feathers.
Voice: Vocal. Soft *trru trru* or *treer treer* . . . ; alarm call a loud *tuutitit*. Song a sustained chatter with deep trills, somewhat slower than Dun-

nock's, rather reminiscent of Skylark.
Occurrence: Breeds amongst rocks in sunny spots, on stony Alpine grassland and on rock slopes. Common in vicinity of mountain huts. In summer mostly above about 1,300 m, in winter lower down, but visiting villages only in hard weather. Widespread in the Alps and Tatras and other major mountains of central and southern Europe. Rare vagrant to Britain.
Behaviour: Seeks food in the open; sings mainly from perch, but also in flight.
Food: Insects, spiders, worms, snails; in winter mainly seeds.
Breeding habits: May–August, 1–2 broods; usually nests in a hollow in ground, a cleft in the rock, or beneath low shrubs.

> House Sparrow	V	III–VI, VIII–I	O	

Robin *Erithacus rubecula*
Family: Thrushes and allies Muscicapidae
F Rouge-gorge familier G Rotkehlchen

Distinctive character: Large dark eyes and orange-red breast.

Features: Rounded shape, relatively long legs; juv. lacks red, and is strongly mottled with brown.

Voice: When disturbed, a sharp *tsick*, often rapidly repeated ('ticking'); a high-pitched, penetrating *tsee* when an aerial predator appears. Tuneful and rather melancholy song, heard almost throughout the year, is a clear descending series of notes; the rather long phrases usually start with high-pitched, pure fluted notes and die away towards the end.

Occurrence: Breeds in all kinds of woodland, especially in broadleaf and mixed woods with rich undergrowth, also in parks and gardens with trees or bushes. Widespread, right up to tree-line. Also common in coastal areas in winter.

Behaviour: Often feeds on the ground. Bobs, and flicks wings and tail. Rather tame and often quite inquisitive. Sings from March from cover of trees and bushes, often until late in the evening. Visits bird tables in winter.

Food: Insects, snails, worms, berries, fruits.

Breeding habits: March–July, 2–3 broods; cup-shaped nest made of old leaves, grass and moss, on ground in thick undergrowth, in a hollow near ground, or between tree roots.

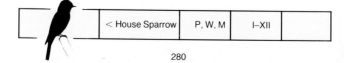

| | < House Sparrow | P, W, M | I–XII | |

Bluethroat *Luscinia svecica*
Family: Thrushes and allies Muscicapidae
F Gorge-bleue à miroir
G Blaukehlchen

Distinctive character: Flirts tail frequently and jerks it up and down.
Features: Similar to Robin in shape and size, but has slightly longer legs. Base of tail rust-red at sides. Central European race *L. s. cyanecula* has white spot on blue throat, northern European race *L. s. svecica* has red spot ♀ (drawing) and winter ♂ have dark-bordered white throat. Juv. similar to young Robins, but as adults have red base of tail.
Voice: Alarm call a hard *tack* or whistling *hooit*. Song is a hurried delivery of long phrases, made up of pure and ringing, sharp and strained notes, together with imitations of many other species; often begins with an accelerating run of cricket-like chirps.
Occurrence: Breeds in willow thickets with reeds, in ditches, ponds, lakes and rivers, and in swampy river-valley woodland. Scarce migrant

Bluethroat, ♀

in Britain (has bred).
Behaviour: Sings from medium-high perch or in flight.
Food: Insects, worms, berries.
Breeding habits: April–June, 1 brood; nest well hidden, usually near ground.

< House Sparrow	(M)	III–V, VIII–X	BR	

Nightingale
Luscinia megarhynchos
Family: Thrushes and allies Muscicapidae
F Rossignol philomèle
G Nachtigall

Distinctive character: Loud, atmospheric warbling and fluting song.
Features: Uniform brown above, except for red-brown tail. Underside slightly paler and without markings. Juv. resembles young Robins, but larger and with red-brown tail.
Voice: A Willow Warbler-like *hueet*; alarm call a deep, grating *karrr*. Song very varied and attractive, with warbling and crystal-clear fluting phrases, interspersed with deep, hard *chook chook chook*, cricket-like chirping and long, swelling crescendo of 'sad' notes e.g. *peeoo peeoo peeoo* ('sobbing').
Occurrence: Breeds in broadleaf or

mixed woodland with thick undergrowth, in river-valley woodland, parks, cemeteries and overgrown gardens; patchy distribution.
Behaviour: Not very sociable; keeps

Nightingale, singing

in cover. Feeds on ground, moving very elegantly and often cocking tail. Sings from thick bushes, often at night as well.
Food: Insects, worms, berries.
Breeding habits: May–June, 1 brood; loose nest in thick ground vegetation.

		> House Sparrow	S, M	IV–IX	

Thrush Nightingale *Luscinia luscinia*
Family: Thrushes and allies Muscicapidae
F Rossignol progné
G Sprosser

Distinctive character: Song less varied, slower and less warbling than Nightingale's, and lacking crescendo section.
Features: Difficult to distinguish from Nightingale on basis of plumage. At close range by darker, more olive-brown upperparts, lightly mottled breast and less rusty tail.
Voice: When disturbed has Nightingale-like calls – a deep, sonorous *karr* or a clear *tseeh*. Song loud and far-carrying like Nightingale's, interspersed with tuneless rattles and Reed/Sedge Warbler-like calls; known to imitate Song Thrush and Woodcock.
Occurrence: Often breeds in wetter habitats than Nightingale: thick bushy areas close to water; swampy woodland with alder, birch and willow scrub. Replaces Nightingale in southern Scandinavia and eastern Europe; both species overlap in some areas, such as northern Germany. Rare vagrant to Britain.
Behaviour: Similar to Nightingale, but when excited makes twisting movements of tail.
Food: Insects, spiders, worms, snails, berries.
Breeding habits: May–June, 1 brood; loose nest made of old leaves, grass and brushwood, usually in a hollow beneath thick scrub.

> House Sparrow	(M)	V–X	O	

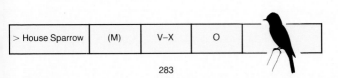

283

Spotted Flycatcher
Muscicapa striata
Family: Thrushes and allies Muscicapidae
F Gobe-mouches gris
G Grauschnäpper

Distinctive character: Sits upright on a perch and catches passing insects in the air.
Features: Slim and inconspicuous, with large, dark eyes. Grey-brown above, whitish below. Head and breast with light streaking. Juv. spotted above.
Voice: When disturbed a short *tk*, a sharp *pst* or *tsek*, often *tsee-tk-tk*. Song unremarkable and seldom heard, a halting sequence of short individual elements and double notes such as *tsi-tsi-tsi-sri-tru-zr*.

Occurrence: Breeds in light broadleaf and mixed woodland, in wooded fields, parks, and gardens, often in inhabited areas. Widespread breeding bird but has declined markedly in some areas recently.
Behaviour: Fairly solitary. Hunts mainly in crown regions of trees; often returns to the same perch after hunting foray. Often flicks wings and tail on landing and when excited. Sometimes flutters in mid-air when hunting.
Food: Flying insects; also berries in autumn.
Breeding habits: May–August, 1–2 broods; nests in open cavities and on ledges; loose nest made of moss, feathers and hair, sited in a hole in a tree or wall, under eaves, on a trellis or half-open nest-box.

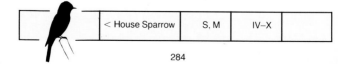

| | < House Sparrow | S, M | IV–X | |

Red-breasted Flycatcher *Ficedula parva*
Family: Thrushes and allies Muscicapidae
F Gobe-mouches nain
G Zwergschnäpper

Distinctive character: Smallest European flycatcher.
Features: Grey-brown above with pale eye-ring. Cream-coloured below, conspicuous white at base of outer tail feathers. Full-adult ♂ has orange-red throat with grey side of head; first-year ♂ tinged either orange on throat or, like ♀, without red. Juv. have pale feather edges above.
Voice: Alarm call a melodious *dooi*, and often a high-pitched *tsit*, or Wren-like *tsrr*. Song is a descending, pure-toned whistling phrase, a little like Willow Warbler – *tink tink tink . . . dlu tink dlu tink dlu dlu dlu . . . .*
Occurrence: Breeds in damp old broadleaf woodland, especially Beech; also in parks in some areas, and in coniferous and mixed woodland. Eastern species found as far west as northern Germany and southern Bavaria (mainly in hills to about 1,300 m). Scarce passage migrant in Britain.
Behaviour: Flicks tail frequently, with wings drooping. Mainly stays high in tree-tops, catching insects in typical flycatcher manner. Difficult to spot without knowing call.
Food: Mostly flying insects.
Breeding habits: May–July, 1 brood; moss nest sited in hole in tree, usually high up.

< House Sparrow	(M)	IV–XI	O	

Pied Flycatcher
Ficedula hypoleuca
Family: Thrushes and allies Muscicapidae
F Gobe-mouches noir
G Trauerschnäpper

Distinctive character: Repeatedly flicks wings and tail.
Features: ♂ deep black (drawing) to grey-brown above, with clear white wing patch and white forehead. ♀ grey-brown above, wing-patch (smaller) and underside dirty white. Winter ♂ like ♀ but sometimes with white on forehead.
Voice: Alarm call a sharp *pit*, often repeated. also a hard *tk*. Song an ascending and descending *voo-tee-voo-tee-voo-tee*, reminiscent of Redstart.
Occurrence: Breeds in broadleaf, coniferous and mixed woodland, and in parks and gardens with good sup-ply of nest-holes; patchy distribution In Britain breeds in north and west but more widespread on migration.
Behaviour: Hunts flying insects from a perch, seldom returning to same position. Also takes insects

Pied Flycatcher, ♂

from ground. Usually sings only ir May.
Food: Flying insects; also berries ir the autumn.
Breeding habits: May–July, 1 brood large nest made of grass, leaves anc moss. in tree-hole or nest-box.

		< House Sparrow	S, M	IV–X	

Collared Flycatcher
Ficedula albicollis
Family: Thrushes and allies Muscicapidae
F Gobe-mouches à collier
G Halsbandschnäpper

Distinctive character: ♂'s conspicuous white neck band.

Features: As well as contrasting black and white plumage, ♂ has white rump and larger white wing-patch than Pied Flycatcher. ♀ difficult to distinguish in field from ♀ Pied Flycatcher, although wing-patch larger and rump paler, and has indication of neck band. Winter ♂ similar to ♀.

Voice: High-pitched, full and drawn-out *seep*, reminiscent of Nightingale's warning call; also hard, very short *tek*, often repeated. Song simpler, slower and higher-pitched than Pied's with characteristic *seep* calls between phrases: *sit-sit-sit-siu-see-siu-tree-see-tree-see-seep*.

Occurrence: Breeds in broadleaf woodland and parks with old trees, in cemeteries, orchards. Mainly an eastern species; very rare vagrant in Britain.

Behaviour: Very similar to Pied; usually hunts in tree-tops.

Food: Almost exclusively flying insects.

Breeding habits: May–July, 1 brood; like Pied nests in tree-holes and in nest-boxes. Both Collared and Pied Flycatchers are polygamous, that is a single ♂ may pair with more than one ♀.

< House Sparrow	V	V–IX	O	

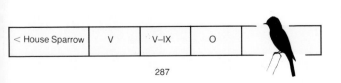

Black Redstart
Phoenicurus ochruros
Family: Thrushes and allies Muscicapidae
F Rouge-queue noir
G Hausrotschwanz

Distinctive character: Upright on high lookout; bobs and constantly quivers tail.
Features: Slim and long-legged, with rust-red rump and tail. ♂ easily identified from a distance by dark plumage with a pale wing patch. ♀ (drawing) dark grey-brown. Juv. blackish-brown, with only slight patterning.
Voice: Hard short *neet-tek-tek* when disturbed; rapid, voiceless *tektektek* near nest. Song: short rapid phrase in two sections: an ascending *jirr-titititeetee* then a condensed, scratchy *tschr-chts-treetutiti*.
Occurrence: Breeds on buildings and in original habitat of mountain rocks and scree to over 3,000 m. Widespread and usually common. A few sites in S. Britain. Commoner on migration and in winter.
Behaviour: Flies down to ground to

Black Redstart, ♀

catch insects; sings from high look-out e.g. T.V. aerial, often before dawn.
Food: Insects, spiders, berries.
Breeding habits: April–July, 2 broods; nests in holes in walls, under roofs and in half-open nest-boxes.

| | < House Sparrow | S, W, M | I–XII | BR |

Redstart
Phoenicurus phoenicurus
Family: Thrushes and allies Muscicapidae
F Rouge-queue à front blanc
G Gartenrotschwanz

Distinctive character: Quivers tail intermittently.
Features: Breeding ♂ often hard to spot despite colourful plumage; in autumn less colourful (washed-out) on head and below, with pale feather edgings. ♀ (drawing) has markedly paler underside than ♀ Black Redstart. Juv. heavily spotted below.
Voice: When disturbed a short *hooeet* or *hooeet-tuk-tuk*. Song pleasant and wistful, *hooet tray tray tray*, combined with harsh, slurred and purer notes, and often mimicry.
Occurrence: Breeds in light broad-leaf, coniferous and mixed woodland,

in parks, gardens and orchards with old trees; on Continent also in villages and at the edges of towns. Declined markedly in many areas in recent years. On migration often in coastal areas.

Redstart, ♀

Behaviour: Often perches on low twigs and flies to ground to collect insects. Sings from before dawn from treetop to other high perch.
Food: Insects, spiders, berries.
Breeding habits: May–July, 1–2 broods; nests in hole in tree or rock, wall ledges and in nest-boxes.

< House Sparrow	S, M	III–X		

Whinchat *Saxicola rubetra*
Family: Thrushes and allies Muscicapidae
F Traquet des prés G Braunkehlchen

Distinctive character: Often perches on exposed bush, post or wire.
Features: Squat and short-tailed; easily overlooked despite bright colours. ♂ has white stripe above eye, ♀'s is buffer (drawing).
Voice: Vocal. Hard, very short *tek tek* or *tsek tsek*, often alternating with soft *dju* calls. Song: a mixture of short, hurried phrases made up of scratchy, clinking and fluting notes; many phrases contain imitations of other birds or shortened forms of other bird's songs.
Occurrence: Breeds in open damp areas, extensively cultivated hay meadows, fallow and waste-land; essential requirement is availability of medium-sized bushes and other perches. Decreased due to destruction of damp habitats. In Britain, distribution patchy.
Behaviour: Flies low from perch to

Whinchat, ♀

perch; often flicks tail and wings. Sings from low perch or in brief song-flight.
Food: Insects, spiders.
Breeding habits: May–July, 1–2 broods; nest well hidden, usually under grass tussock.

		< House Sparrow	S, M	IV–X

Stonechat *Saxicola torquata*
Family: Thrushes and allies Muscicapidae
F Traquet pâtre
G Schwarzkehlchen

Distinctive character: ♂'s contrasting plumage.
Features: Slightly more rotund than Whinchat. ♀: head and upperparts brownish, lacking ♀ Whinchat's white base to outer tail feathers; supercilium only faint. Juv. has finely streaked breast.
Voice: When disturbed a hard, scratchy *trak*, usually repeated, or *weet kr*. Song: a short, hurried phrase with scratchy, rattling and whistled notes, often incorporating imitations of other birds.
Occurrence: Usually in drier places than Whinchat; breeds in open, stony country with gorse on embankments, but also on moorland and extensively cultivated meadows; to 1,400 m in mountains.
Behaviour: Feeds on ground more often than Whinchat; perches in more upright posture; watches out for passing insects from top of bush; constantly flicks wings and tail; flies low and jerkily. Often sings from top of bush, sometimes in short, dancing song-flight.
Food: Insects, small worms.
Breeding habits: April–August, 2–3 broods; usually nests in thick undergrowth.

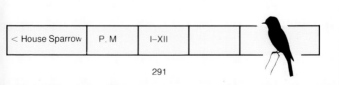

| < House Sparrow | P. M | I–XII | | |

291

Wheatear Oenanthe oenanthe
Family: Thrushes and allies *Muscicapidae*
F Traquet motteux
G Steinschmätzer

Distinctive character: Striking white rump and tail markings obvious in flight: broad black inverted T (drawing).

Features: Long black legs, relatively short tail and upright posture distinctive. ♂ has dove-grey back, black cheeks and wings, and white stripe above eye. ♀ and autumn ♂, brownish, without contrasting head markings. Juv. finely mottled.

Voice: Hard, hollow *tk*, usually repeated, often interspersed with *weet* or *yif* sounds. Song, not often heard, is a short, rapid, chattering phrase made up of hard, harsh notes and soft whistles.

Occurrence: Open stony or rocky country; waste land, upland pastures, dunes, moorland and heath; up to more than 2,000m in mountains. Common on coast when on migration.

Behaviour: Ground-living bird, often

Wheater,
in flight

perching on rocks or mounds. Bobs up and down, flicks tail.

Food: Insects, spiders, worms.

Breeding habits: April–July, 1–2 broods; nests amongst rocks, scree, holes in walls, old rabbit burrows.

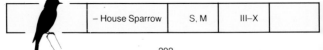

| | – House Sparrow | S, M | III–X | |

Rock Thrush *Monticola saxatilis*
Family: Thrushes and allies Muscicapidae
F Merle de roche G Steinrötel

Distinctive character: White patch on back of ♂, very variable in extent.
Features: has rust-red tail and underparts and grey-blue head. ♀ (drawing) and winter ♂ brownish, heavily spotted above, with buffish scaly pattern below.
Voice: Alarm call a hard, often repeated *tack* or soft *jeeh*, sometimes a Magpie–like chatter. Song is a fluting, somewhat strained twitter, often with clear imitations of other birds.
Occurrence: Breeds on sunny rocky slopes, with sparse plant cover, also in quarries and ruins; rare breeder in Austrian and Swiss Alps, and, in some years, in Bavarian Alps. Mainly in southern and eastern Europe. In Britain a very rare vagrant.
Behaviour: Fairly shy; often sits upright on open lookout perch (rock, building, tree). Remarkable song-flight in which the bird sweeps down

Rock Thrush, ♀

with tail spread out wide.
Food: Insects, spiders, worms, berries.
Breeding habits: May–July, 1 brood; loose nest amongst rocks.

| > House Sparrow | V | V–XI | O | 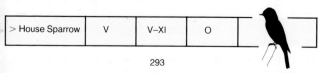 |

Mistle Thrush *Turdus viscivorus*
Family: Thrushes and allies Muscicapidae
F Grive draine G Misteldrossel

Distinctive character: Largest European thrush.

Features: Noticeably larger than Song Thrush, with longer wings and tail. Grey-brown above with large spots below; outer tail feathers tipped whitish. Juv. have upperparts with dark spots and pale streaks and uniform whitish throat. Resembles a pigeon in flight, with rounded belly and striking pale underwing-coverts; undulating flight.

Voice: Loud, dry rasping *tzrrr*, especially on take-off. Song reminiscent of Blackbird's, but more melancholy and less variable: short, fluting phrases, delivered at almost even pitch.

Occurrence: Tall broadleaf and coniferous woodland; wooded fields; also in parks in some areas; in mountains to tree-line. Widespread but usually rather less common than Song Thrush.

Behaviour: When feeding on ground, usually holds body upright with wings slightly drooping. Often sings from treetop.

Food: Worms, snails, insects, in autumn berries as well (including Mistletoe), fruit.

Breeding habits: March–June, 1–2 broods; nest made of grass, roots and twigs, strengthened with soil and lined with grass; usually 2–10m up and in a branch fork.

		> Blackbird	R, W	I–XII	

Song Thrush *Turdus philomelos*
Family: Thrushes and allies Muscicapidae
F Grive musicienne
G Singdrossel

Distinctive character: When flushed flies off with a high-pitched thin *tsip*.
Features: Small thrush with brown upperparts and large dark eyes; underside covered with small dark spots. Juv. streaked pale above. In flight buff underwing-coverts conspicuous.
Voice: Alarm call like Blackbird's, but less penetrating: *tchiktchiktchiktchik* . . . . Song loud and varied, made up of musical, fluting or chirping phrases, each repeated 2 or 3 times (often more): *yoodeet-yoodeet-*
yoodeet. Often imitates other birds, especially waders.
Occurrence: Widespread and common in all kinds of tall woodland, especially in open, mixed woodland with thick undergrowth, in copses, parks and gardens with old trees.
Behaviour: Often feeds on fields close to woodland, running for a short distance and then stopping abruptly. Smashes open snails against selected stone (anvils). Sings for long periods from tree-top perch in spring.
Food: Snails, worms, insects, in autumn also berries and fruit.
Breeding habits: March–August, 2 or more broods; sturdy, well-shaped nest with deep cup, lined with wood chips and mud; often sited close to trunk of young spruce tree.

< Blackbird	P, W, M	I–XII		

Blackbird *Turdus merula*
Family: Thrushes and allies Muscicapidae
F Merle noir G Amsel

Distinctive character: Very common garden bird.

Features: Bill and eye-ring of ♂ orange-yellow, plumage shiny black; ♀ dark grey-brown to blackish-brown with paler, weakly mottled breast. Juv. with reddish-brown plumage, strongly mottled below.

Voice: Vocal. *Tix tix* or *chook chook chook*; when excited a metallic *tsink tsink* and a shrill chatter. Song loud and melodious fluting ('organ-grinding'); the relatively slowly delivered and variable phrases are not repeated as in Song Thrush, and usually end in a somewhat higher-pitched short twitter.

Occurrence: Common everywhere in woods, copses, parks and gardens.

Behaviour: Mostly hops along ground when feeding, stops sud-

Blackbird, ♀

denly, cocks tail and flicks wings.

Food: Earthworms, snails, insects, berries, fruit.

Breeding habits: March–August, 3–5 broods; sturdy nest usually low in tree, bush or hedge, sometimes on window sill or balcony.

	Well known	R, W, M	I–XII	

Ring Ouzel *Turdus torquatus*
Family: Thrushes and allies Muscicapidae
F Merle à plastron G Ringdrossel

Distinctive character: Conspicuous white breastband of ♂.
Features: Similar in size and shape to Blackbird, but wings and tail slightly longer and show pale wing panel; underparts with suggestion of scaly pattern, especially in winter. ♀ has duller, less obvious breastband, browner plumage and more 'scaly' look. Juv. lack breastband and are heavily barred brown below with mottled throat.
Voice: Alarm call a hollow, hard *tok tok tok*; flight call a vibrating *tsriet*. Song consists of short, fluting phrases, repeated in manner of Song Thrush. Tone and ring similar to Blackbird or Mistle Thrush, but less attractive and less mellow: *deeru deeru, tree tree* or *chulee chulee*.
Occurrence: Hills, moors and mountains of Scandinavia, north and west British Isles. Fairly common in Alps and other high mountain ranges, in open spruce forest and in dwarf pine zone at around 1,000–2,000m; on migration also in valleys and lowland.
Behaviour: Flies rapidly and skilfully; fairly shy; often perches on tops of trees or on walls.
Food: Earthworms, snails, insects, berries.
Breeding habits: April–July, 1–2 broods; large nest made of grass, moss and heather, usually low down in a spruce or dwarf pine, sometimes on the ground.

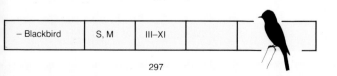

– Blackbird	S, M	III–XI		

Fieldfare *Turdus pilaris*
Family: Thrushes and allies Muscicapidae
F Grive litorne G Wacholderdrossel

Distinctive character: Striking plumage.

Features: Long-winged and long-tailed. In flight black tail contrasts with light grey rump and pale underwing-coverts.

Voice: Flight call a loud, harsh chatter: *shak shak shak* or, near nest, *trarrak*. Birds of prey and crows mobbed with a rattling *trrtrrtrrt*. Song fairly quiet warbling and strained twittering, often sings in flight.

Occurrence: Breeds in copses, at woodland margins, in river-valley woodland, light Birch forests, and in parks, and gardens with trees. Mainly north and east Europe. Widespread autumn and winter visitor to British Isles, where very rare breeder in north.

Behaviour: Feeds on ground, usually in upright posture; very sociable. In breeding colonies Fieldfares

Fieldfare, in flight

join together to attack nest predators. Flight undulating and heavy-looking.

Food: Worms, snails, insects, berries, fruit.

Breeding habits: April–July, 1–2 broods; colonial. Large nest in branch fork of tree or close to trunk.

| | > Blackbird | (S), W, M | I–XII mostly X–IV | BR |

298

Redwing *Turdus iliacus*
Family: Thrushes and allies Muscicapidae
F Grive mauvis G Rotdrossel

Distinctive character: Flight call: a high-pitched, drawn-out, slightly hoarse *tseeh*.
Features: At close range distinguished from slightly larger and paler Song Thrush by whitish stripe over eye, red-brown flanks, and breast with long streaks (not spots). In flight (drawing) red-brown underwing-coverts striking.
Voice: When disturbed a low muffled *chewk*, close to nest a rattling *trrt*; in addition to typical flight call also has a soft *kuk*. Song is a rapid, mostly melancholy, descending series of notes such as *tree tree tree tree* or *chirre cherre churre chorre*, followed by a rapid squeaky twitter; the first

(fluting) part of song very variable.
Occurrence: Breeds in light birch and coniferous forest in the north, up to the edge of tundra; a small population

In flight

Redwing

breeds in Scotland. In winter flocks to fields and open woods, parks, and gardens with berry-bearing bushes; common and widespread.
Food: Worms, snails, insects, mainly berries on migration (especially grapes).

< Blackbird	(S), W, M	I–XII mostly X–IV	BR	

Grasshopper Warbler *Locustella naevia*
Family: Warblers Sylviidae
F Locustelle tachetée
G Feldschwirl

Distinctive character: Sustained churring song, reminiscent of Great Green Bush Cricket.
Features: Narrow, rounded tail. Olive to yellowish-brown above, with dark streaking. Underside pale, faintly streaked. Juv. has reddish tinge above. Usually identified by song.
Voice: Alarm call *tschek tschek*, near nest a sharp *pitt pitt*. Song, audible from afar, is an even, mechanical whirring (reeling) on one pitch, starting quietly and often continuing for minutes; difficult to locate. Also sings by night.
Occurrence: Breeds in thick scrub in marshy areas, in damp meadows with tall grass, swampy and river-valley woodland. Also on heathland, in dry woodland clearings, and even in spruce plantations with tall grass. Very patchily distributed in Britain, not common.
Behaviour: Shy, keeps under cover and seldom flies out; may sing on exposed stem.
Food: Insects, spiders.
Breeding habits: May–July, 1–2 broods; deep cup-shaped nest made of old leaves, grass and stalks, usually near ground in thick vegetation.
The tiny **Fan-tailed Warbler** *Cisticola juncidis* is found in southern and south-western Europe and is a very rare and irregular breeder in the Netherlands, Belgium and southern Switzerland. Song: sharp, high-pitched *dsip dsip* . . . often in song flight.

	< House Sparrow	S	IV–X	

Savi's Warbler
Locustella luscinioides
Family: Warblers Sylviidae
F Locustelle luscinioide
G Rohrschwirl

Distinctive character: Reeling song.
Features: Tail broad, rounded and markedly graduated. Nightingale-like plumage, unstreaked; inconspicuous short stripe over eye.
Voice: Alarm call a short *tsik*, near nest *pit* or a harsh rattle. Song deeper than Grasshopper Warbler's and in shorter phrases, often beginning with accelerating ticking notes: *tik tiktiktik ... err*; sounds rather like Green Toad or Mole Cricket.
Occurrence: Breeds in extensive reeds and rushes, at overgrown lake margins. Patchy distribution. In Britain very rare breeder, confined to south-east.
Behaviour: Less skulking than Grasshopper Warbler; often sings high up on reed stems; frequently flicks wings and tail.
Food: Insects, spiders.
Breeding habits: May–July, 1–2 broods; large nest made of reed stems and leaves, close to water in reedbed.

Similar **River Warbler** *Locustella fluviatilis* has delicately streaked throat and breast. Lives well hidden in swampy woodland with rich undergrowth, water meadows and other swampy habitats. Song a 'chuffing' *dzedzedze* .... Eastern species spreading west – now reaches northern Germany in the north and southern Bavaria in the south.

< House Sparrow	(S)	IV–IX	BR, BL	

Marsh Warbler
Acrocephalus palustris
Family: Warblers Sylviidae
F Rousserolle verderolle
G Sumpfrohrsänger

Distinctive character: Loud, pleasant and very varied song: a series of brilliant imitations of other birds' songs, interspersed with a medley of dry, nasal, squeaking and rattling notes.

Features: Difficult to separate from Reed Warbler except by song. More olive-brown above and slightly plumper with larger wings.

Voice: Alarm call *tschak*, *twik* or *vit*. Song free-ranging, unstructured, rapid medley of imitations; species mimicked include Blue and Great Tits, Blackbird, Chaffinch, Swallow, Goldfinch, Pied and Yellow Wagtails, Skylark, Starling, House and Tree Sparrows, Quail and many others; in addition learns songs of African species on migration and incorporates these, too. Often sings at night.

Occurrence: Breeds in lush scrub near water, in tall-herb communities and nettle beds, in cereal and rape fields and in overgrown gardens. Rare and local breeder in Britain.

Food: Insects, spiders.

Breeding habits: May–July, 1 brood; nest looser and shallower than Reed Warbler's, made of stems and plant fibres and usually sited in tall herbs (meadowsweet, nettles), woven between stems.

	< House Sparrow	(S)	V–IX	BR, BD

Reed Warbler
Acrocephalus scirpaceus
Family: Warblers Sylviidae
F Rousserolle effarvatte
G Teichrohrsänger

Distinctive character: Found even in quite small stands of reed.
Features: Very similar to Marsh Warbler, separated in field with certainty only by voice. Bill somewhat thinner, forehead flatter, legs darker, upperparts redder brown. Juv. of both species similar in plumage coloration.
Voice: Alarm call hard *kra* or *vit*. Song similar to Sedge Warbler's, but slower, more relaxed and less varied: harsh, scratchy, nasal notes repeated two or three times, such as *tere-tere-tere-cheerk-cheerk-tsair-tsair-twee-twee-twee*.

Occurrence: Breeds in reeds and in thick bank-side bushes. On migration sometimes found in bushes away from water. Widespread and normally the commonest *Acrocephalus* warbler in reedy areas.
Food: Insects, spiders.
Breeding habits: May–August, 1–2 broods; sturdy, deep, cup-shaped nest slung between vertical reed stems, usually 1–1.5 m up.

The slightly larger **Cetti's Warbler** *Cettia cetti* (long, broadly rounded tail, dark red-brown above) lives in overgrown damp habitats. It is usually identified by loud, abrupt song. Mainly in south-west and southern Europe. Very local, uncommon breeder in southern Britain, also in Netherlands and Belgium to south-west Europe.

| < House Sparrow | S | IV–IIX | | |

Great Reed Warbler
Acrocephalus arundinaceus
Family: Warblers Sylviidae
F Rousserolle turdoïde
G Drosselrohrsänger

Distinctive character: Largest of our *Acrocephalus* warblers.

Features: Long, powerful bill, flat head profile, conspicuous stripe over eye.

Voice: Alarm call hard *karr*, near to nest *tsek tsek*. Song very loud and raucous, clearly separated phrases in regular tempo; deep rattling sections alternate with high-pitched musical ones. *karre-karre-karre-keet-keet-keet dree-dree-dree trr trr trr tseep-tseep-tseep*.

Occurrence: Breeds in reedbeds, especially in the edge zone, close to water, at lakes, ponds and rivers.

Declined in many areas owing to habitat destruction. Absent as breeding bird from British Isles and most of Scandinavia, but occurs irregularly as a vagrant, especially in late spring.

Behaviour: Somewhat slow and heavy in flight, with tail slightly spread. Often sings while clambering up reed stems. Not as retiring as Reed Warbler and therefore easier to see.

Food: Insects (including aquatic), spiders, tiny frogs.

Breeding habits: May–July, 1 brood, solid, deep, suspended nest made of reed leaves, usually about 1m from ground, slung between reed stems. Nest material dipped in water first to make it easier to work around reed stems; when it dries the nest is held very firmly and can withstand strong winds.

	> House Sparrow	V	V–X	O

Sedge Warbler
Acrocephalus schoenobaenus
Family: Warblers Sylviidae
F Phragmite des joncs
G Schilfrohrsänger

Distinctive character: Often makes short song-flight, landing nearby and continuing song.
Features: Streaked above but rump uniform in colour; dark crown and clear whitish stripe over eye distinctive.
Voice: When disturbed a hard *tsek*, *tsrr*, or rattling *karrr*. Song usually begins with a short *trr*; much longer phrases and faster tempo than Reed Warbler; interspersed with long, pleasant trills and many imitations.
Occurrence: Reedbeds, marshy and reedy willow thickets on banks or ditches. Mainly northern and eastern half of Europe; fairly common in Britain.
Behaviour: Fairly retiring, but often chooses exposed perch when singing.
Food: Insects and spiders.
Breeding habits: May–August, 1–2 broods; large nest usually near ground in reeds or willow scrub.

The very similar **Moustached Warbler** *Acrocephalus melanopogon* has more contrasting head markings, and has Nightingale-like *doo* notes in its song. Scattered in Mediterranean region and south-east Europe; very rare vagrant in Britain.

The **Aquatic Warbler** *Acrocephalus paludicola* has slightly yellower coloration than Sedge Warbler, a darker crown with a pale central stripe and bolder, pale and black streaks above. Lives mainly in extensive sedge beds in north-east and southern parts of central Europe; rare but regular migrant in Britain, mostly August–September.

< House Sparrow	S	IV–X		

Icterine Warbler *Hippolais icterina*
Family: Warblers Sylviidae
F Hypolaïs ictérine
G Gelbspötter

Distinctive character: Loud, hoarse song, with much mimicry.
Features: Plumage mainly yellowish; stance Reed Warbler-like; long orange bill.
Voice: Common call is a musical *deederoid* or *teytedwee*; alarm call hard *tetete* or sparrow-like *errr*. Song unstructured, rather hoarse and strained, but including musical whistling and long-drawn-out notes, together with many imitations, including Blackbird, Fieldfare, Starling, Swallow, Blue Tit, Chaffinch, Golden Oriole, Great Spotted Woodpecker; many phrases repeated one or more times. Usually sings hidden in tree-tops.
Occurrence: Breeds in light broad-leaf and mixed woodland, river-valley woods, parks with undergrowth, copses and gardens. Decreased in some areas in recent years. Mainly central and eastern Europe. Scarce but regular migrant in Britain.
Food: Insects and spiders.
Breeding habits: May–July, 1 brood; neat cup-shaped nest of stems, leaves, bark and cobwebs, 1–3 m in branch fork of bushes and young trees.

The slightly smaller and shorter-tailed **Melodious Warbler** *Hippolais polyglotta* has noticeably shorter wings. Usually distinguished from Icterine in the field only by song. Song less strident, faster and more chattering, often including imitations of sparrows. Breeds mainly in southern and western Europe, but spreading eastwards; scarce but regular migrant in Britain.

![bird silhouette]	< House Sparrow	(M)	mainly VIII–X	O

Blackcap *Sylvia atricapilla*
Family: Warblers Sylviidae
F Fauvette à tête noir
G Mönchsgrasmücke

Distinctive character: Loud, fluting song with clear phrasing.
Features: Grey-brown, greyer in autumn. ♂ has black cap, ♀'s is red-brown. Juv. has dusky red-brown cap.
Voice: Alarm call a hard *tak* or *tzek*, in rapid rattling series when highly excited. Often a soft *deedeedee* before flying off. Song starts with a soft, chattering section, developing suddenly into loud, clear fluting notes; imitations of other birds may be included in either section. In some areas the second section is reduced, sounding like *deeladeeladeela*.
Occurrence: Commonest *Sylvia* warbler. Breeds in open broadleaf and coniferous woodland, river-valley woodland, spruce plantations, parks and gardens.
Behaviour: Spends its time skulking in trees and bushes, ♂ usually sings from concealed perch.
Food: Insects and their larvae, spiders; berries in autumn.
Breeding habits: May–July, 1–2 broods; delicate nest made of twigs, stems and roots, with cobwebs woven around rim, usually hidden low in a thick bush.

The somewhat larger **Orphean Warbler** *Sylvia hortensis* has a mainly Mediterranean distribution, reaching as far north as southern Switzerland (rare). From Blackcap by dark hood merging into back, by white on outer tail feathers and by pale eyes. Song is thrush-like.

< House Sparrow	S, M, (W)	I–XI		

Barred Warbler
Sylvia nisoria
Family: Warblers Sylviidae
F Fauvette épervière
G Sperbergrasmücke

Distinctive character: Bright yellow eyes and Sparrowhawk pattern below.
Features: Large warbler with powerful bill, double white wing-bar and white in outer tail feathers. ♀ less barred beneath. Juv. has dirty white underparts, barring indistinct or lacking.
Voice: Alarm call a rattling *trtrtr* or *errr*, also a hard *tak tak*. Song similar to Garden Warbler's, but in shorter phrases often interspersed with typical rattling *errr* calls.

Occurrence: Woodland edges with thorn bushes, thorny field hedges, juniper heath, overgrown parks with hawthorn and blackthorn; often breeds near Red-backed Shrike. Mainly an eastern species; regular but scarce migrant in Britain, mainly in autumn.
Behaviour: Usually hides in thick scrub; movements seem clumsy; often flicks tail. Also sings in short song-flight, when rises a short distance with strong flapping wings only to disappear almost immediately into nearest cover.
Food: Insects, spiders, berries, fruits.
Breeding habits: May–July, 1 brood; large, loose, deep nest of grass stalks and roots, usually 0.5–2m up in thick bush or hedge.

	– House Sparrow	(M)	mainly VIII–X	O

Garden Warbler *Sylvia borin*
Family: Warblers Sylviidae
F Fauvette des jardins
G Gartengrasmücke

Distinctive character: Skulking and therefore difficult to find, except by song.

Features: Plump, no obvious markings. Head rounded, bill relatively short. Grey-brown above, somewhat paler below, and with hint of an eyestripe. Juv. more reddish-brown above.

Voice: Alarm call sustained regular *chek-chek-chek* and a harsh *tsharr* as well as a soft *Phylloscopus*-like *ooit*. Song musical and in long phrases with prolonged 'babbling', somewhat reminiscent of Blackbird owing to powerful 'organ-grinding' phrases; deeper in pitch than Blackcap. Sometimes mimics other species – Chaffinch's call. When agitated or nervous sings quiet and shortened strained phrases.

Occurrence: Common breeder in thick, tall scrub, lakeside thickets, bushy woodland margins, woods and parks with rich undergrowth; rarer than Blackcap in gardens. In mountains to about 2,000m, often in alder bushes.

Food: Insects, spiders, many berries in autumn.

Breeding habits: May–July, 1–2 broods; loose, untidy nest of grass stems and roots, often low in nettle bed or blackberry bushes.

< House Sparrow	S, M	IV–X		

Whitethroat *Sylvia communis*
Family: Warblers Sylviidae
F Fauvette grisette
G Dorngrasmücke

Distinctive character: Hurried scratchy twittering song.
Features: Relatively long tail with white outer feathers. Contrasting colouring, narrow white eye-ring. ♀ drabber, with brownish crown and cheeks.
Voice: Alarm call *hwett-hwett-wit-wit*, also hard *charr* and repeated *tshek*. Song made up of short, scratchy but pleasant elements often with imitations of other birds.
Occurrence: Breeds in thorny scrub, in hedgerows, often along embankments, in abandoned quarries and heavily overgrown gardens. Wide-spread but uncommon in some areas.
Behaviour: Very lively; often sings with raised crown and throat feathers from bush top, from where it takes off for short song-flight (drawing), return-

Whitethroat, song-flight

ing to cover again.
Food: Insects and spiders; in autumn also berries.
Breeding habits: May–August, 1–2 broods; deep, rough nest made of dry stems and roots, usually about 0.5m or less from ground.

	< House Sparrow	S, M	IV–X	

Lesser Whitethroat
Sylvia curruca
Family: Warblers Sylviidae
F Fauvette babillarde
G Klappergrasmücke/
Zaungrasmücke

Distinctive character: The rattling song.

Features: Slightly smaller than White-throat. From close range shows mask-like dark cheeks, contrasting with white throat, relatively short tail and lack of chestnut on wings (compare with Whitethroat).

Voice: Often calls *chek* and, when alarmed, an irregularly repeated *tak*, or short *vet* when aerial predator appears. Song in two parts: a quiet hurried warble, followed by a loud rattle on one note; the first part is audible only from close to and begins very high.

Occurrence: Breeds in semi-open country with thick bushes, at wood-land margins, in young spruce and pine clearings, in parks and gardens, and in the mountains right up to dwarf pine region. Widespread but rather patchy in distribution.

Behaviour: Skulking; flight jerky and flitting. Often sings in short bursts between feeding forays, or from a perch, and occasionally in brief horizontal song-flight.

Food: Insects and spiders, in autumn also berries.

Breeding habits: May–August, 1–2 broods; delicate, shallow nest made of fine twigs, dry grass and roots, 0.5–1m up in thick scrub or in young conifers.

< House Sparrow	S, M	IV–X		

Dartford Warbler
Sylvia undata
Family: Warblers Sylviidae
F Fauvette pitchou
G Provencegrasmücke

Distinctive character: Very small-bodied, short-winged, dark warbler with conspicuously long tail often held cocked.

Features: ♂ Dark brown above; dark grey head; deep brownish-maroon below with a whitish belly and a few white spots on throat; in winter, slightly duller and with more obvious white throat spots. ♀ much duller, with browner head, and paler below. Juv. lacks all reddish tones and appears generally brownish, with paler belly and darker flanks. Long tail, often held up at an angle, is always obvious.

Voice: When excited or nervous, a low, drawn-out, harsh *churr, chirrr,* or often *cherrr-tk.* Song is a short, scratchy but pleasing warble with a few whistled notes.

Occurrence: Dry bushy scrub areas in S.W. Europe. In Britain confined to extreme S. England, where it breeds on heathland with gorse, thick heather, and often with scattered low pines. In hard winters suffers heavy losses.

Behaviour: Very shy and skulking, but in sunny, still weather perches on tops of gorse. Flight weak, fluttering, tail moving jerkily, low down and for short distances. In spring performs short song-flights like Whitethroat.

Food: Insects and small spiders.

Breeding habits: April–July, 2–3 broods; compact cup-shaped nest of heather stalks, grasses, wool and moss, lined with fine grass, rootlets and hair, decorated with spiders' webs, built low in gorse, scrub or heather.

	< House Sparrow	R	I–XII	BR, BL

Wood Warbler *Phylloscopus sibilatrix*
Family: Warblers Sylviidae
F Pouillot siffleur
G Waldlaubsänger

Distinctive character: Found in Beech woods with sparse undergrowth; characteristic song.

Features: Somewhat larger than Chiffchaff and with longer wings; throat and breast yellow, contrasting with white belly; yellow stripe over eye. In summer after moult noticeably paler.

Voice: When excited a soft *duuh* or gentle *vitvitvit*. Song a descending shivering trill, beginning with *sip* calls: *sip-sip-sip-sipsirrrrr . . .* , often with a melancholy whistling *diuh diuh diuh diuh*.

Occurrence: Breeds in open broad-leaf and mixed woodland with sparse undergrowth, especially beech woods, rarely in pure coniferous forest; in mountains to 1,500 m. In Britain breeds more commonly in west.

Behaviour: Lives in canopy of tall mature deciduous trees. Usually sings from exposed branch or in horizontal song-flight, moving slowly from branch to branch, with wings fluttering. Often not hard to observe, but usually seen from below.

Food: Insects and their developmental stages, spiders.

Breeding habits: May–July, 1 brood, sometimes 2; almost spherical, 'oven-shaped' nest made of grass, leaves and sometimes ferns, in low vegetation; often camouflaged with old leaves.

< House Sparrow	S, (M)	IV–IX		

Distinctive character: Distinctive *chiff-chaff* song.

Features: Very like Willow Warbler, but looks less slim. Wings shorter, head more rounded; generally has dark legs and is olive-brown (less yellow) above; underside whitish. Juv. browner above.

Voice: Alarm call monosyllabic *hweet*, louder and slightly harder than Willow Warbler's. Song is monotonous and irregular repetition of two notes *chiff chaff chiff chiff chaff . . .*, often with a muffled *trr-trr* between the phrases. Often sings in autumn as well. (Some Willow Warblers introduce Chiffchaff notes into their own song).

Occurrence: Breeds in broadleaf and mixed woodland, with plenty of undergrowth, in river-valley woodland and tall, thick scrub, and in parks and gardens. In mountains to above tree-line. Common throughout most of Europe, including Britain (where small numbers winter).

Behaviour: Always on the move, flicking wings. Often sings high in the trees, dipping tail down with each note.

Food: Small insects, spiders.

Breeding habits: April–July, 1–2 broods; oven-shaped nest, like Willow Warbler's, but somewhat less compact, and with many dry leaves, usually hidden in vegetation at ground level.

	< House Sparrow	S, M, (W)	mainly III–X	

Willow Warbler *Phylloscopus trochilus*
Family: Warblers Sylviidae
F Pouillot fitis G Fitis

Distinctive character: Soft, melancholy song.

Features: Looks slim and delicate; best separated from very similar Chiffchaff by song; plumage somewhat yellower, with clearer and yellow lower stripe over eye. Legs normally (but not always) light brown. Juv. uniform yellowish below.

Voice: Alarm call soft *hoo-eet*, usually clearly disyllabic. Song fluting and melancholy, a pure, descending phrase *titi-dje-djoo-dooe-dooi-djoo*, a little like Chaffinch's in progression of pitch changes, but much more delicate and soft.

Occurrence: Breeds in open broadleaf and mixed woods, in clearings, wooded wetlands, willow scrub, wooded lake margins, parks and gardens with birch trees. Common throughout northern and central Europe.

Behaviour: Hops and flutters about in thick foliage, but not as restless as Chiffchaff. Often sings from exposed branch or top of young tree, especially in May and June.

Food: Small insects, spiders.

Breeding habits: May–July, 1–2 broods; oven-shaped nest made of grass and moss, well lined with feathers, amongst tall grass or hidden on ground under low branches.

< House Sparrow	S, M	III–XI		

Goldcrest *Regulus regulus*
Family: Goldcrests Regulidae
F Roitelet huppé
G Wintergoldhähnchen

Distinctive character: Very small, with Firecrest, Europe's smallest bird.
Features: Olive-green above, ♂ with bright yellow crown with a few orange-red feathers in the centre (often hidden); in ♀ crown uniform light yellow (photo). No stripe through or above eye. Juv. lacks the yellow and black crown markings.
Voice: Vocal. Very high-pitched, thin, but penetrating *sree-sree-sree-sree*. Song short, very high-pitched, thin phrases, rising and falling and with clear, slightly lower final flourish:

sisee sisee sisee sesee seritete – not a crescendo like Firecrest.
Occurrence: Breeds in thick coniferous forest or groups of conifers in mixed woodland, parks and gardens. Also found in thick scrub and in deciduous trees on migration. Widespread and common, especially in northern and central parts of Europe.
Behaviour: When foraging often hangs acrobatically on underside of twigs (more so than Firecrest). Sociable, often associating with Coal tits and Crested Tits in mixed flocks outside breeding season.
Food: Tiny insects and their development stages, spiders.
Breeding habits: April–August, 2 broods; thick-walled cup-shaped nest in branches of coniferous tree.

	< House Sparrow	P, W, M	I–XII	

Firecrest
Regulus ignicapillus
Family: Goldcrests Regulidae
F Roitelet triple-bandeau
G Sommergoldhänchen

Distinctive character: Black stripe through and white stripe above eye. Brighter general coloration than Goldcrest. Very small.

Features: Bright yellow-green above, paler below than Goldcrest. ♂ has orange-red crown, ♀ yellow. Juv. lacks crown markings, but has dark eyestripe.

Voice: Very high-pitched, sharp *si-si-si*. Song a short crescendo of similar-pitched notes, very high and thin, with accented end section: *seeseeseeseeseeseeseesirrr*.

Occurrence: Breeds in coniferous forest, but not as dependent upon conifers as Goldcrest; also in cemeteries, parks, gardens and scrub; on migration also in broadleaf woods and low bushes. Widespread and common in central and southern Europe. Rare and very local breeder in Britain (in southern half).

Behaviour: Lives hidden in thick, mainly coniferous woods, but not shy. Often hunts on upper sides of branches, and hovers at tips of twigs. Not as sociable as Goldcrest, only rarely joining mixed flocks of tits.

Food: Tiny insects and their developmental stages, spiders.

Breeding habits: May–August, 1–2 broods; thick-walled deep nest made of moss and cobwebs, on underside of conifer branch, usually well hidden.

< House Sparrow	(S), (W), (M)	I–XII	BR	

Bearded Tit *Panurus biarmicus*
Family: Reedlings Panuridae
F Mésange à moustaches
G Bartmeise

Distinctive character: Conspicuous long, cinnamon tail.
Features: Plumage mainly cinnamon-brown; ♂ has grey head with broad black moustache, and yellow bill and eyes. ♀ lacks colourful head and neck markings and has a brownish bill. Juv. similar to ♀, but with dark centre of back and sides of tail, the male with black lores.
Voice: Flight call a nasal, twanging *dsching*, often repeated. Alarm call short *pik* or *pik pik*. Song: short phrases made up of call-like elements: *dshing-dshik-pit-chret*.
Occurrence: Breeds in large reedbeds. Rare and irregular breeder in central Europe, with large population fluctuations owing to often high losses in hard winters. Scattered European distribution. Common in Netherlands, north-east Germany and Neusiedlersee (Austria); in Britain mainly in south-east.
Behaviour: Sociable. Skilful climber; flight slow and fluttering, often with tail slightly fanned, usually low over reeds, and rapidly diving into cover again.
Food: Insects, in winter mainly reed seeds.
Breeding habits: April–August, 2–3 broods; large, deep cup-shaped nest, near ground in thick reedbed.

	< House Sparrow	R	I–XII	BL

Long-tailed Tit
Aegithalos caudatus
Family: Long-tailed tits Aegithalidae
F Mésange à longue queue
G Schwanzmeise

Distinctive character: Very long, graduated tail, making up more than half total body length.

Features: British race and central European race (photo) have broad, blackish stripe over eye; northern and eastern race has pure white head (drawing). Juv. has shorter tail and very dark cheeks.

Voice: *sree. see-see-see* or *sitrr*; when excited, often *tserr* or *tschrrt*; flight call soft, constant *pt*. Song (seldom heard) a soft medley of chirps, twitters and trills.

Occurrence: Breeds in woods with rich undergrowth, especially near water; in copses and wooded mires, parks and gardens. Fairly common.

Behaviour: Very sociable; outside breeding season in small flocks which keep close together by constant contact calls. Weak, bounding flight.

Food: Small insects, spiders.

Long-tailed Tit,
British and central
European race

Breeding habits: April–June, 1–2 broods; very attractive, oval-shaped nest made of moss, lichen, plant fibres, cobwebs, feathers and hair, in tree or high in a bush, usually well hidden.

< House Sparrow	R	I–XII		

Marsh Tit *Parus palustris*
Family: Tits Paridae
F Mésange nonnette G Sumpfmeise

Distinctive character: Shiny black cap.

Features: Roughly size of Blue Tit. White cheeks and small black bib. Juv. has matt-black cap and is almost impossible to separate from young Willow Tit.

Voice: *tsichay, pitchew* or *pische dedededede*, the *de* notes much less drawn-out than Willow Tit's. Song made up of rattling phrase such as *tjitjitjitji . . . , checheche . . . ,* or a rhythmic *tsiwu tsiwu tsiwu . . . ;* a single ♂ may alternate several different phrase types.

Occurrence: Breeds in broadleaf and mixed woodland, copses, parks and gardens; usually in drier habitat than Willow Tit. Widespread and quite common.

Behaviour: Sometimes visits bird tables; likes hemp seeds and often takes these away, several at a time, to store individually in bark crevices, between dry leaves or similar hiding place.

Food: Insects, their larvae, spiders, seeds of thistles, grasses and many other plants.

Breeding habits: April–June, 1 brood; nest made of moss, hair and feathers, in hole in tree, between roots, and, rarely, in nest box.

	< House Sparrow	R	I–XII	

Willow Tit *Parus montanus*
Family: Tits Paridae
F Mésange boréale
G Weidenmeise

Distinctive character: Extended nasal *dair* call.
Features: Very similar to Marsh Tit and the same size, but cap is matt black, not glossy; cap also extends further down nape, giving thick-headed appearance. Bib slightly more extensive, flanks slightly darker. Has pale wing patch, which usually disappears in spring.
Voice: Typical call is a drawn-out, nasal *dair-dair-dair*, often also *tsee-tsee-dair-dair-dair*. Song: pure-toned, slightly descending series, *tsyu-tsyu-tsyu-tsyu* .... Song of

Alpine race is all on one note: *tsee-tsee-tsee* .... Occasional warbler-like phrases.
Occurrence: Breeds in woods on marshy ground, especially alder, willow and birch, but also in dry clearings with young trees; rarer in parks and gardens than Marsh Tit. Alpine race found in coniferous and mixed forest up to dwarf pine region. Locally common in Alps and in lowland areas. In Britain widespread, but rather local.
Food: Insects, their larvae, spiders, small seeds.
Breeding habits: April–June, usually 1 brood; scanty nest made of wood-chips, moss and animal hair; excavates hole in rotten wood of broadleaf tree; occasionally uses woodpecker holes or nest-boxes.

< House Sparrow	R	I–XII		

Coal Tit *Parus ater*
Family: Tits Paridae
F Mésange noir G Tannenmeise

Distinctive character: Smallest European tit; slightly smaller than Blue Tit.

Features: Relatively large head, striking white cheeks and large white nape patch. Juv. have yellowish undersides and cheeks.

Voice: Contact call high-pitched, thin *see* or *tseetseetsee*; when excited a high, nasal *tui* or *sitchu*; alarm call to aerial predator a very rapid, high-pitched *sisisi*. Song: delicate phrases made up of repeated elements such as *tsiweetsiweetsiwee* or *situi-situi-situi*. Sings throughout year (both sexes).

Occurrence: Breeds in spruce and fir forests, less commonly in pine from lowland up to tree-line in mountains; in parks and gardens with conifers. Also found in broadleaf woods outside breeding season. Common throughout.

Behaviour: An acrobatic feeder in the tops of conifers, nimble and constantly on the move. Often joins other tits and Goldcrests in mixed flocks outside breeding season. Often visits bird tables.

Food: Insects, their larvae, spiders, conifer seeds, nuts.

Breeding habits: April–July, 1–2 broods; matted nest made of moss and cobwebs, lined with plant fibres and hair. Nests in tree holes, stumps, holes in the soil or walls, and in nest boxes (as long as not too high up).

	< House Sparrow	R, (W)	I–XII	

Crested Tit *Parus cristatus*
Family: Tits Paridae
F Mésange huppée G Haubenmeise

Distinctive character: Black-and-white-speckled crest.
Features: Brown above, whitish below with cream-coloured flanks. Juv. have shorter and duller crest.
Voice: When excited often gives a purring, rolling *burrrurrr*, or *zee-zee-burrr-r*. Song: medley of calls, sometimes with a variable chattering phrase.
Occurrence: Breeds in pine, spruce and fir forests up to tree-line, also in small pockets of conifers within broadleaf woodland; very sedentary. Widespread, but rarer than Coal Tit. In Britain only in Caledonian forest of Scotland.

Behaviour: Like Coal Tit often moves about acrobatically high up in conifers, but sticks closer to cover so is not so easy to observe; also spends much time near ground. Not very sociable, usually seen only in pairs, even outside breeding season, but occasional small flocks. Visits feeders only in coniferous woods.
Food: Insects, their larvae, spiders, conifer seeds, nuts.
Breeding habits: April–June, 1–2 broods; nest made of moss and lichens, lined with wool and hair, sited in narrow tree-hole, stump, or sometimes in an old squirrel drey, or even an occupied nest of bird of prey. Usually excavates its own holes, using nest-boxes only if there is a lack of suitable natural holes.

< House Sparrow	R	I–XII	BL	

Blue Tit *Parus caeruleus*
Family: Tits Paridae
F Mésange bleue G Blaumeise

Distinctive character: Only native bird with blue and yellow plumage.
Features: Small, compact tit with small bill. ♀ slightly duller. Juv. much paler, with greenish-brown upperparts and yellow cheeks.
Voice: Alarm call a rising, nasal *tserretetet*, also *tsee-tsee-tsee*, *tooi* or a slightly harsh *chett*. Song: very clear, pure notes, followed by series of deeper trills, such as *tsee-tsee-tututu . . .* or *zeezeesirrr*.
Occurrence: Breeds in broadleaf and mixed woodland, especially with oak, in copses, parks and gardens. In winter often feeds in reeds. Common throughout.
Behaviour: Very lively, moves acrobatically and skilfully among thin twigs, even hanging upside down. Quite tame. Often in mixed tit flocks outside breeding season. Sings from February; often makes short, gliding butterfly-like courtship flights.
Food: Insects, their larvae, spiders, small seeds; suet, nuts.
Breeding habits: April–July, 1–2 broods; matted nest made of soft plant material, wool, hair and feathers, usually sited in tree hole, nestbox or hole in a wall, occasionally even in letter-box or similar site.

	< House Sparrow	R, W	I–XII	

Great Tit *Parus major*
Family: Tits Paridae
F Mésange charbonnière
G Kohlmeise

Distinctive character: Largest and commonest European tit.
Features: Striking black and white head, yellow underparts with a broad (♂) or narrow (♀) black stripe down centre. Juv. has yellowish cheeks, otherwise head is blackish-brown; altogether less contrasting.
Voice: Wide repertoire. Chaffinch-like *pink* or *tsipink* call; alarm call a rattling *cherr-r-r-r* or *terrr terrr*, also *tseetuit* and a drawn-out *seee*. Often imitates calls of Blue, Marsh and Coal Tits. Song: simple phrase consisting of repeated calls: *tsi-tsi-tay-tsi-tsi-tay* or *tsee-tay tsee-tay*.
Occurrence: Breeds in all types of woodland, in parks, gardens, even in urban areas.
Behaviour: Fairly tame; in some places hand tame. Feeds on ground more readily than other tits. Often in mixed flocks with other small birds outside breeding season. Often visits bird-tables.
Food: Insects, their larvae, spiders, seeds, nuts, suet.
Breeding habits: April–July, 1–2 broods; nest made of moss, roots, stems and wool, lined with hair and plant fibres; sited in hole in tree or wall, nest-box, sometimes in other man-made objects, even iron pipes.

< House Sparrow	R, W	I–XII		

Nuthatch *Sitta europaea*
Family: Nuthatches Sittidae
F Sittelle torchepot G Kleiber

Distinctive character: Dumpy and short-tailed; powerful woodpecker-like bill.
Features: Blue-grey crown and upperparts, creamy yellow below; ♂ with chestnut-brown flanks contrasting with rest of underparts, in ♀ paler brown and less contrasting.
Voice: Commonest call *tvit tvit tvit*, *tuitutui* or (when alarmed) a sharp *titi-tsirr*. Song a whistling, trilling *wiwiwi-wiwi . . .*, *twee twee twee twee . . .* or *trirrr . . .*, audible from afar. The individual phrases are fairly easy to imitate by whistling.
Occurrence: Breeds mainly in broadleaf and mixed woodland, in copses, parks and gardens; up to about 1,700 m in the Alps. Widespread and fairly common in southern Britain.
Behaviour: Climbs about tirelessly on tree trunks and branches, including the underside and often downwards with head facing ground. Often visits bird tables close to woods or parks. Not very sociable, usually seen only in pairs, even outside breeding season; joins roving tit flocks.
Food: Insects, their larvae, large seeds, nuts, suet.
Breeding habits: April–June, 1 brood; nest constructed of large quantities of fine strips of bark (especially pine bark) and dry leaves. Nests in woodpecker holes and nest-boxes; entrance holes that are too big are narrowed to right diameter by application of damp mud.

	– House Sparrow	R	I–XII	

Wallcreeper
Tichodroma muraria
Family: Wallcreepers
Tichodromadidae
F Tichodrome échelette
G Mauerläufer

Distinctive character: Long, rounded wings with red patches and white spots.
Features: Long, thin, curved bill, short tail. Breeding ♂ has blackish throat and upper breast, pale in ♀ and winter ♂. Flight butterfly-like; easily overlooked, despite striking plumage.
Voice: Calls throughout year, but often drowned by sound of wind or rushing water. Thin, piping *tooi*, or *tchruit*. Song, given by both sexes, is a series of clear, rising and in parts slightly scratchy whistles.
Occurrence: Breeds on steep cliffs with clefts and crevices, in deep ravines and gorges, especially those with waterfalls. Often at lower altitudes in winter, when also seen on buildings such as towers, castles or ruins. Widespread but not common in the Alps; rarely seen in lowland areas. Very rare vagrant to Britain.
Behaviour: Solitary. Climbs vertical rock faces with jerky movements, constantly flicking wings.
Food: Insects and their developmental stages.
Breeding habits: May–July, 1 brood; usually nests in deep cleft in rocks, often protected from predators above a mountain stream; occasionally nests on buildings.

> House Sparrow	V	IX–VI	O	

Short-toed Treecreeper
Certhia brachydactyla
Family: Treecreepers Certhiidae
F Grimpereau des jardins
G Gartenbaumläufer

Distinctive character: Song, a short, rising phrase.

Features: Size of Blue Tit, slim; long, delicate, decurved bill, long stiff tail, plumage bark-like grey-brown above, whitish below with brownish flanks.

Voice: Loud high *teet* or *teet teet teet*, also a high-pitched *sree* more drawn-out than Treecreeper's. Song a short rising phrase of high-pitched thin whistles, *toteeteetiroiti*.

Occurrence: Breeds in open broad-leaf and mixed woodland, especially with Oaks, Elms and Ash in parks and gardens with old trees and in open fruit-growing areas. Rare above about 800 m in the Alps, not found above 1,300 m. Widespread and fairly common throughout Europe, but absent from British Isles and Scandinavia.

Behaviour: When foraging, climbs up tree trunks in short hops; when it reaches the top of one tree it flies down to the bottom of another tree. Not very sociable, but in winter communal roosts of 10 or more birds may be found (as protection against cold).

Food: Small insects and their larvae, spiders; in winter also small seeds and suet.

Breeding habits: April–July, 1–2 broods; nest made of twigs, stems and moss, behind raised bark, in crevice in tree or wall, or in special treecreeper nest-box.

| | | < House Sparrow | V | IV–V, IX–X | O |

Treecreeper
Certhia familiaris
Family: Treecreepers Certhiidae
F Grimpereau des bois
G Waldbaumläufer

Distinctive character: Song, a descending series of notes, in two parts.

Features: Best distinguished from Short-toed by voice. Bill usually slightly shorter and less curved, white supercilium more prominent, crown more heavily streaked pale, paler above with rust-brown rump, and white below (British race with pale buffish flanks).

Voice: High-pitched, slightly vibrating *sree*, often repeated; alarm call *sree-tsi-tsitsi*; flight call *tititi*. Song quieter than Short-toed's, with longer phrases – a descending sequence of two trills, the first starting very high and falling slowly, the second starting almost as high, but descending more quickly.

Occurrence: Breeds in large areas of coniferous woodland, but also in mixed woodland; less commonly in parks and gardens with stands of conifers; in Alps up to tree-line. In Britain widespread and fairly common.

Behaviour: Feeding habits as Short-toed. Often found with tit flocks outside breeding season; both this and previous species visit feeding stations.

Food: Insects, their larvae, spiders, small seeds, suet.

Breeding habits: April–July, 1–2 broods; nest made of twigs, moss and stems, built behind raised bark, in crevice, or in special nest-box (with slit-like entrance hole).

< House Sparrow	R	I–XII			

Penduline Tit *Remiz pendulinus*
Family: Penduline tits Remizidae
F Rémiz penduline G Beutelmeise

Distinctive character: Pouch-like nest with tunnel entrance, suspended from twigs.

Features: About size of Blue Tit; the only small bird with chestnut back; conspicuous black face mask. ♀ slightly duller; juv. lacks black mask.

Voice: High-pitched drawn-out *tseeh* or *seeu*, similar to Reed Bunting, but thinner and purer. Song: soft, varied phrases, often containing the *seeu* call and shorter series of *tlu* sounds.

Occurrence: Breeds in river-valley woods, on overgrown banks with willows and poplars, at ponds, rivers and lakes. Mainly eastern Europe and Mediterranean, but increasing and spreading westwards in parts of central Europe. Rather commoner outside breeding season, but not often seen in winter. Very rare vagrant in Britain, but more frequent in recent years.

Behaviour: Mainly forages high in deciduous trees in summer, hanging acrobatically and skilfully from twigs like a tit. Often in small flocks in willow scrub and reeds in spring and autumn.

Food: Small insects, spiders; also seeds in winter.

Breeding habits: April–June, 1 brood; soft, pouch nest with entrance tunnel, suspended from end of twig, commonly above water.

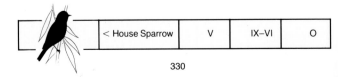

	< House Sparrow	V	IX–VI	O

Golden Oriole *Oriolus oriolus*
Family: Orioles Oriolidae
F Loriot d'Europe G Pirol

Distinctive character: Striking yellow and black plumage and whistling song of ♂ (easy to imitate).
Features: Often hard to spot, without knowing voice. ♂ unmistakable black and yellow; ♀ and juv. greenish above, light grey and streaked below, wings and tail blackish-brown. Older females resemble male.
Voice: Alarm call a harsh, nasal *kraa* or *kraawel*. Song: pleasant fluting *deedlio* or similar phrase, easy to imitate by whistling, the first part softer and less far-carrying.
Occurrence: Breeds in old broad-leaf woodland, in river valley woods, parks and avenues with old trees; in some places also in pine woods. Declining in many areas. Rare breeding bird in southern England, with a few also recorded on passage.
Behaviour: Shy. In breeding season stays concealed in crowns of trees. Flies rapidly in long, shallow undulations, with an arrow-like final swoop into cover, wings held close to body. Not very sociable.
Food: Larger insects, larvae (caterpillars), berries, fruit.
Breeding habits: May–July, 1 brood; delicate suspended cup nest made of grass stalks, wool, and sometimes paper, in branch fork, or woven between two horizontal branches, usually high up in deciduous tree.

< Blackbird	(S), (M)	IV–X	BR, BL	

Red-backed Shrike
Lanius collurio
Family: Shrikes Laniidae
F Pie-grièche écorcheur
G Neuntöter, Rotrückenwürger

Distinctive character: Sits on exposed perch in upright posture.
Features: ♂ has conspicuous plumage, the thick black eye-stripe often visible from distance. ♀ (drawing) is red-brown above, with a pale underside with crescent-shaped markings. Juv. has heavy scaly markings.
Voice: Alarm call *chek*, *geck* or a hard *trrt-trrt*, also a nasal *kevevi*. Song, not often heard, is a varied warble with strained calls, interspersed with frequent imitations of other birds.
Occurrence: Breeds on fens and heaths, at woodland margins with

thorn bushes, and in semi-open country with thorny hedgerows and scattered bushes. In Britain occurs in small numbers on passage.
Behaviour: Flight direct, sometimes

Red-backed Shrike, ♀

hovers. When excited waves tail from side to side. Impales prey on thorns or barbed wire when food is plentiful.
Food: Large insects, lizards, young birds, young mice.
Breeding habits: May–July, 1 brood; nests in thorn bushes at height of 1–3 m.

	< Blackbird	(S), M	V–X	BR, BD

Woodchat Shrike *Lanius senator*
Family: Shrikes Laniidae
F Pie-grièche à tête rousse
G Rotkopfwürger

Distinctive character: Crown and nape rust-red, conspicuous white shoulder patches.
Features: Somewhat broader head and shorter tail than Red-backed. Blackish above, pure white below. ♀ slightly paler, with browner upperparts and less clearly marked black mask. Juv. like young Red-backed, but paler and browner above, with paler shoulders and rump.
Voice: House Sparrow-like *cherrt*, or hollow chattering *che-che*, often repeated when excited. Song a sustained chatter with harsh, hard calls, and many imitations of other birds.
Occurrence: Breeds in open country with bushes and copses, in open orchards and heathland, and in wooded avenues. Mainly south and south-central Europe. Rare breeder in Switzerland, Austria, Czechoslovakia and Poland, and the warmer parts of southern Germany. Has declined in many areas following the destruction of habitat. Vagrant in Britain.
Food: Large insects, especially beetles and bumblebees.
Breeding habits: May–July, 1 brood; compact nest made of twigs, stems and roots, often about 2–6 m high in apple or pear tree.

| < Blackbird | V | IV–X | O | 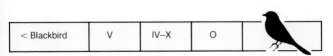 |

Lesser Grey Shrike
Lanius minor
Family: Shrikes Laniidae
F Pie-grièche à poitrine rose
G Schwarzstirnwürger

Distinctive character: Black mask, extending over forehead.
Features: A little smaller than Great Grey, with shorter bill and tail, but with proportionately longer wings. Tinged pink below. ♀ has narrower mask. Juv. has grey forehead and fine scaly markings above. White wing-bars obvious in flight.
Voice: In intraspecific conflicts a short *kshree kerrep* or sparrow-like chirp. Chattering song incorporates excellent mimicry of songs of other species such as Blackbird, warblers and tits.

Occurrence: Breeds in warm, open country with isolated trees and bushes, in wooded avenues, vineyards and orchards. Rare breeder in Hungary, Czechoslovakia and Poland, but almost extinct in Germany, owing to habitat destruction, pesticides, and a series of cool, wet summers. Also nearly extinct in Austria. Mainly south and eastern Europe. Rare vagrant to Britain.
Behaviour: Often perches upright on telephone wires; usually flies in straight line.
Food: Mainly large insects such as beetles and grasshoppers.
Breeding habits: May–July, 1 brood; carefully constructed cup-shaped nest made of twigs, grasses and roots; often nests high up in fruit tree or poplar.

| | < Blackbird | V | V–XI | O |

Distinctive character: Broad black eye-stripe, separated from grey crown by narrow white area.

Features: Noticeably larger than Red-backed Shrike. Wings relatively short, tail rather long and somewhat graduated. Looks a pale, black and white bird from distance. Some ♀ have fine crescent markings on breast. Juv. has darker wavy barring below.

Voice: Sharp *vaaek* or *shrrie* in two or three syllables. Sometimes a Magpie-like chatter. Song consists of short metallic or vibrating phrases, and continuous chattering, with imitations of other species.

Occurrence: Breeds on fenland and heath with groups of trees, in open country with hedgerows and in orchards. Has declined owing to habitat destruction. Does not breed in Britain.

Behaviour: Often waits horizontally on a high perch, on the look-out for prey. Flight slow and undulating; often hovers. Wedges superfluous food in branch fork, or impales it on thorns or barbed wire.

Food: Large insects, birds, mice, shrews, lizards.

Breeding habits: April–June, 1 brood; nest made of twigs, moss and stems, in taller bushes or high up in isolated tree.

< Blackbird	W	X–IV	O	

Jay *Garrulus glandarius*
Family: Crows Corvidae
F Geai des chênes G Eichelhäher

Distinctive character: Striking blue-and-black-barred wing-coverts.

Features: Crown with streaked erectile feathers. Black moustachial stripe. White wing patches and rump, conspicuous in flight (drawing).

Voice: When excited a loud and harsh screaming *kaaa* often repeated, also *shrehri* a soft *kahi* and a Buzzard-like *hee-ay*. Song very varied, low chatter, with ventriloquial notes and imitations.

Occurrence: Breeds mainly in mixed and broadleaf woodlands, in wooded parks and gardens, more rarely in coniferous woods. Up to about 1,700 m in the Alps. Common nearly everywhere.

Behaviour: Flight slow, with irregular wingbeats; often hops on ground when foraging; in winter often in small, loose flocks. Also visits bird tables.

Food: Varied. Mainly seeds, acorns,

Jay,
in flight

nuts, Beech mast, insects, worms, young birds, eggs.

Breeding habits: April–July, 1 brood; relatively small, shallow nest, usually well hidden in a tree or bush.

		< Carrion Crow	R, W	I–XII	

Nutcracker
Nucifraga caryocatactes
Family: Crows Corvidae
F Casse-noix moucheté
G Tannenhäher

Distinctive character: Hoarse, slightly nasal call; *krairr-krair*.

Features: In flight (drawing) the broad, rounded wings, the short tail with white terminal band, and white undertail-coverts are distinctive.

Voice: Characteristic call is often repeated many times, together with a Jackdaw-like *yek yek*. Song an insignificant low chatter interspersed with imitations of other birds.

Occurrence: Breeds in coniferous and mixed broadleaf woodland in southern Scandinavia, and in mountains of central and eastern Europe, in the Alps to 2,000 m; in winter often seen in Alpine valleys. In central Europe there are occasional invasions by the slender-billed Siberian race *N. c. macrorhynchos*, when they sometimes reach Britain.

Behaviour: Often perches right at the top of trees. Flies slowly and rather

Nutcracker, in flight

irregularly. In autumn lays up hoards of tree seeds, e.g. those of Arolla Pine.

Food: Seeds of conifers (mainly Arolla Pine), hazelnuts and walnuts, berries, fruit.

Breeding habits: March–May, 1 brood; nest made of twigs, grasses and lichens, held together with some mud, high in a conifer.

< Carrion Crow	V	mainly VIII–I	O	

Magpie *Pica pica*
Family: Crows Corvidae
F Pie bavarde G Elster

Distinctive character: Glossy black and white plumage and long, graduated tail.

Features: In flight the white primary patches are prominent (drawing). Juv. has much shorter tail and duller, less glossy plumage.

Voice: Vocal. A chattering *shak-shakshak* or *charrakakkak*, also *keke-kek* or *yekyekyek*. Song: a gurgling chatter with rattling and piping sounds.

Occurrence: Breeds in open country with hedges, copses and wooded avenues; in villages, parks and gardens with trees, even in urban areas; avoids dense woodland. In mountains to about 1,500 m. Widespread and common in many areas.

Behaviour: Walks and runs and hops on the ground with a wobbly gait. Alert and shy. Sociable usually

Magpie,
in flight

seen in pairs of small flocks.

Food: Worms, snails, insects, fruits, seeds, refuse, eggs, young birds, mice, frogs.

Breeding habits: April–June, 1 brood. large twig nest with loose, overarching roof and side entrance, usually high up in a tree or bush. Old Magpie nests are often used by Kestrels or Long-eared Owls.

		< Carrion Crow	R	I–XII	

Jackdaw *Corvus monedula*
Family: Crows Corvidae
F Choucas des tours G Dohle

Distinctive character: High-pitched call.

Features: Plumage mainly black, with grey rear head and nape; eye pale. Juv. has brownish-black plumage.

Voice: Vocal. Short, loud *kya* or *kyak*, often repeated; also a rattling *kyerr*, and when disturbed a high-pitched *yip*. Song, seldom heard, is a quiet chatter with crackling and mewing calls; ♀ also sings.

Occurrence: Breeds in broadleaf woodland with tree holes (such as Black Woodpecker holes), in cliffs and quarries, in isolated trees in fields, and in parks with old trees; on churches, castles and ruined buildings. Locally common, but rather patchy.

Behaviour: Pairs for life. Very sociable. Mostly feeds in small flocks in open country. Jackdaws often fly with flocks of Rooks, when they are distinguished by their smaller size,

Jackdaw, in flight

higher-pitched calls and faster wing-beats.

Food: Insects, worms, snails, fruits, seeds, grain, young birds, mice.

Breeding habits: April–June, 1 brood; colonial breeder in holes in trees, rock crevices, holes in walls and nest-boxes. Often makes large twig nest.

< Carrion Crow	R, W	I–XII		

339

Chough
Pyrrhocorax pyrrhocorax
Family: Crows Corvidae
F Crave à bec rouge
G Alpenkrähe

Distinctive character: In flight, broad wings with primaries spread like fingers and high, explosive calls.
Features: Entirely glossy blue-black plumage with bright red legs and red decurved bill. Juv. duller, without gloss; yellowish bill which gradually turns orange. In flight the outer wings are long and the primaries well spread, producing untidy appearance.
Voice: Explosive *keeah*, similar to Jackdaws' but higher and thicker. *kruk-uk*.
Occurrence: Breeds along rocky coasts inland quarries crags in W. Britain and Ireland; and in mountains in S. Europe.
Behaviour: Sociable. Performs acrobatic manoeuvres in the air.
Food: Insects, grubs, worms, slugs, also grain.

Alpine Chough,
in flight

Breeding habits: April–June, 1 brood; nest of twigs, roots and stems is built in rock crevices, caves, on cliff ledges and in old mineshafts.
The **Alpine Chough** *Pyrrhocorax graculus* is very similar but has a shorter, less curved bill which is yellow. Breeds above the tree line in high mountains in S. Europe.

	< Carrion Crow	R	I–XII	BR, BL

Raven *Corvus corax*
Family: Crows Corvidae
F Grand corbeau G Kolkrabe

Distinctive character: Largest crow, with very deep call.
Features: Very powerful black bill. Plumage black with bluish sheen. In flight wedge-shaped tail distinctive.
Voice: Very varied. A deep, sonorous *grok*, *krah* or *kroar*, as well as a hollow *klong*, a wooden *k-k* and, when alarmed, *kra-kra*. Song a varied chatter with call-like rattles and clicks, and with much mimicry.
Occurrence: Breeds in a variety of habitats, such as open continuous wooded country, mountains, coasts, tundra and steppe. In Britain confined to north and west.
Behaviour: Flies with heavy wing-beats, producing a wing-whistle; often soars.
Food: Carrion, insects, worms, snails, small mammals, birds.
Breeding habits: February–May, 1

Raven, in flight

brood; large nest made of branches and twigs, sited in a recess on steep cliff face or high in a tree (in lowland sites).

> Carrion Crow	R	I–XII	

Carrion Crow *Corvus corone corone*
Family: Crows Corvidae
F Corneille noir
G Rabenkrähe

Distinctive character: Adaptable bird associated with settlements and cultivated land.
Features: Carrion Crow and Hooded Crow (*C. c. cornix* – drawing) are regarded as races of the same species. Hooded Crow has light grey back and underparts. Hybrids occur in areas of overlap.
Voice: Vocal *kraa*, *werr*, *kirrk* or *konk*; alarm call a short *krr*. Song is a ventriloquial chatter with piping and grating calls and much mimicry.
Occurrence: Common breeder in open country, in moorland, on the coast, in parks and gardens, even in urban areas. In mountains to 2,000 m.

Hooded Crow replaces Carrion Crow in northern, eastern and south-east Europe, and in north-west Scotland and Ireland.
Behaviour: Usually seen in pairs or

Hooded Crow, in flight

small flocks, never in huge flocks like Rook.
Food: Worms, snails, insects, mice, eggs, young birds, carrion, fruits, vegetable matter, refuse.
Breeding habits: March–June, 1 brood; large sturdy nest made of twigs and earth, usually high up in a tree.

		Well known	R, W	I–XII	

Rook *Corvus frugilegus*
Family: Crows Corvidae
F Corbeau freux G Saatkrähe

Distinctive character: Bare, whitish patch at base of adult's bill.
Features: Black, with metallic violet-blue sheen; steep, angled forehead. Belly and thigh feathers tend to be looser than Carrion Crow's ('trousered' appearance).
Voice: More nasal and hoarser than Carrion Crow: *kroh, krah* or *korr*; also higher *kja* and a mechanical-sounding *krrr*. Song chattering and rattling, interspersed with metallic and cawing calls.
Occurrence: Open country with copses; edges of broadleaf and coniferous woodland, parks, even in urban areas. Somewhat patchy distribution.

Behaviour: Very sociable. In winter gathers together in large (sometimes huge) flocks to feed in fields and large parks.
Food: Insect larvae such as grubs

Rook, juvenile

and wireworms; snails, mice, seeds, vegetable matter, refuse.
Breeding habits: March–June, 1 brood; colonial breeder in tree-tops; large nest made of twigs, stems and earth.

– Carrion Crow	R, W	I–XII		

343

Starling *Sturnus vulgaris*
Family: Starlings Sturnidae
F Étourneau sansonnet G Star

Distinctive character: Wobbly gait.
Features: Short-tailed and thick-set, with long, pointed yellow bill. In autumn bill is brown and plumage heavily spotted with white caused by white feather fringes; fringes gradually wear away towards spring, revealing the green-violet breeding plumage. Juv. uniform grey-brown with pale throat and dark bill. In flight shows pointed triangular wings.
Voice: Hoarse *tcheerr* or *err*; shrill *shreen*; alarm call a hard *vett vett*. Song: a varied, sustained chatter, made up of whistling, crackling, clicking and rattling calls; many imitations of other birds and other sounds.
Occurrence: Common throughout, especially where there are trees with natural holes or nest-boxes. Found in broadleaf and mixed woodland, open cultivated areas, parks and gardens. Absent from Spain, Portugal and much of Mediterranean coast. British population swollen by many winter immigrants.
Behaviour: Hunts on ground, with a rather wobbly walk, constantly probing soil with bill; does not hop. Very sociable, and often in large flocks outside breeding season.
Food: Insects, snails, worms, fruit (especially grapes), berries.
Breeding habits: April–July, 1–2 broods; untidy nest made of straw, stems and leaves, sited in hole in tree or rocks, or in nest-box.

| 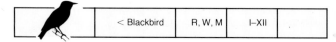 | < Blackbird | R, W, M | I–XII | |

Snow Finch *Montifringilla nivalis*
Family: Sparrows Passeridae
F Niverolle des Alpes
G Schneefink

Distinctive character: Black and white markings on wings and tail (especially obvious in flight).
Features: Large and finch-like. Breeding ♂ (drawing) has grey head, black bill and black throat patch; ♀ more brownish-grey on head and with fainter throat markings, the white in wing slightly less extensive. In winter (photo), ♂ and ♀ have yellow bill and lack black throat patch.
Voice: Short, nasal *pchie, tsutsiek* or *vehk.* Alarm call a soft-trilling *pshrrrt,* rather like Crested Tit. Song a simple, somewhat stuttering twitter of repeated notes: *titt-titt-che.*

Occurrence: Breeds in Alpine rock zone in Pyrenees, Alps, Appennines, and Balkan mountains, usually above about 1,900m. In winter also seen at cable-car stations and mountain

Snow Finch, breeding plumage

huts, but only rarely in valleys.
Behaviour: Very sociable, usually breeding in small groups. Often forms larger flocks outside breeding season.
Food: Insects, seeds.
Breeding habits: May–July, 1–2 broods; nests in clefts and small holes, and on buildings in some areas.

> House Sparrow			O	

House Sparrow *Passer domesticus*
Family: Sparrows Passeridae
F Moineau domestique
G Haussperling

Distinctive character: Very common town bird.
Features: ♂ has contrasting plumage; ♀ (drawing) and juv. drab grey-brown.
Voice: Alarm call a penetrating *tete-tet ched-ched*; flight call *che-ip* or *chilp*. Song a well-known rhythmic chirping: *chilp chelp . . . .*
Occurrence: Everywhere where there are houses; very common in villages, towns and farmyards; also at mountain huts.
Behaviour: Very sociable; often in noisy loose flocks, continuously chasing each other with chirping and scolding calls. Hops easily on ground.

Likes to bathe in dust. ♂'s often perform courtship display together, with wings drooped and tail raised.
Food: Insects, their larvae, seeds, fruits, berries, buds, grain, refuse.

House Sparrow,

scraps.
Breeding habits: April–August, 1–4 broods; untidy, roofed nest made of stems, stalks, paper, rags; usually under a roof, or in a hole in a wall or tree.

	Well known	R	I–XII	

346

Tree Sparrow *Passer montanus*
Family: Sparrows Passeridae
F Moineau friquet G Feldsperling

Distinctive character: Much less conspicuous in behaviour than House Sparrow.
Features: Somewhat smaller and slimmer than House Sparrow. Easily distinguished by chestnut-brown crown and nape, black spot on cheek, and smaller black throat patch. Juv. has grey-brown head and dark grey throat.
Voice: Flight call or when excited a hard *tek tek tek*, often combined with *tsuwit*, also *chet chet*. Song similar to House Sparrow's – a rhythmic stammering chirping, but shorter and noisier.

Occurrence: Less dependent on human habitations than House Sparrow. Breeds in open country with hedges, copses and orchards, in parks and at edges of towns and villages.
Behaviour: As sociable as House Sparrow, but less noisy. Often found at outskirts of villages in winter. Visits bird tables, but shyer than House Sparrow. Both sparrows are less quarrelsome at feeding stations than, for example, finches.
Food: Insects, seeds, fruits, buds, oats, grain, scraps.
Breeding habits: April–August, 2–3 broods; roofed nest made of stems and stalks, lined with feathers; sited in hole in tree or rock, nest-box, or sometimes in old Sand Martin tunnel.

| < House Sparrow | R, W | I–XII | | |

Chaffinch *Fringilla coelebs*
Family: Finches Fringillidae
F Pinson des arbres G Buchfink

Distinctive character: Commonest finch.

Features: Breeding ♂ has bright blue-grey crown, brownish-grey in winter. ♀ (drawing) olive-brown above, grey-brown below. Bright white wing markings and outer tail feathers prominent in flight.

Voice: Alarm call a loud, short *pink*, similar to Great Tit. When excited a soft *fooeet* or repeated *rrhee* (rain call), and, when flushed, a short *yip*. Song: a loud warbling descending phrase, accented at the end: *tsitsitsitsyetsya-chitter-reetyu-kik*.
The final *kik* note, an imitation of Great Spotted Woodpecker, is omitted in some regions.

Occurrence: Common in all areas with trees.

Behaviour: Feeds mostly on the ground, walking with jerky head

Chaffinch, ♀

movements. Outside breeding season often in large flocks.

Food: Seeds, fruits, insects, spiders, grain.

Breeding habits: April–July, 1–2 broods; attractive, solid cup-shaped nest, relatively high up in tree or bush.

	– House Sparrow	R, W, M	I–XII	

Brambling *Fringilla montifringilla*
Family: Finches Fringillidae
F Pinson du nord G Bergfink

Distinctive character: White rump, usually obvious when flying up.

Features: Breeding ♂ (not illustrated) has black back, head and bill, with orange breast and shoulders. In ♂ outside breeding season (photo) the black areas are mottled brownish, full breeding plumage appearing in early spring as the feather edges wear away. ♀ (drawing) has grey cheeks, blackish streaks on crown and brown markings on back.

Voice: A distinctive wheezy *chee-e* or *kvayeek*, flight call a short *yek*, repeated on take-off. Song not very loud, a combination of Greenfinch-like calls such as *dzeee* and rattling.

Occurrence: Common breeding bird in Birch woods and coniferous forests in the north of Europe. In winter

Brambling, ♀

in often large flocks in Beech woods, parks, gardens and in open fields. Also visits bird tables. A very few pairs breed in north Britain.

Food: Insects and their larvae; in winter Beech mast, large seeds, grain, nuts.

– House Sparrow	(S), W, M	mainly IX–IV	BR	

Serin *Serinus serinus*
Family: Finches Fringillidae
F Serin cini G Girlitz

Distinctive character: Smallest European finch, with very short conical bill.

Features: Much yellow in plumage (♂); ♀ more grey-green, streaked below, like male has yellow rump which is often conspicuous in flight. Juv. brownish, with heavy dark streaks and no yellow rump.

Voice: Flight call high-pitched trilling *tri-ri*, *kirr* or *kirrlit*; alarm call a drum-out *chayee*. Song: a sustained high-pitched jingling twitter, all on one pitch.

Occurrence: Breeds in cemeteries, parks, gardens, orchards and vineyards, in light broadleaf and mixed woods up to about 1,200 m. Absent from north and north-west Europe, but a few pairs breed in southwest Britain.

Behaviour: Flight rapid and shallowly undulating. Often feeds on ground. Usually seen in pairs or small groups. Sings from tree-top, telephone wire, or in bat-like song-flight in which it flies in wide circles at tree-top height and continues to sing loudly on landing.

Food: Fine seeds, green parts of plants, insects.

Breeding habits: April–July, 2 broods; elaborate nest made of roots, stems and moss, and lined with feathers, hair and plant fibres, usually built at medium height in a conifer, hedge or bush.

| | < House Sparrow | (S), (M) | II–XI | BR |

Citril Finch *Serinus citrinella*
Family: Finches Fringillidae
F Venturon montagnard
G Zitronengirlitz

Distinctive character: Small and inconspicuous; best identified by voice.

Features: Face, rump and underside plain yellow; nape and sides of neck grey; two yellow-green wing bars; no yellow on tail. ♀ darker and less yellow, and lightly streaked above and below. Juv. browner, streaked above and below.

Voice: Flight call high-pitched, slightly nasal *dit dit*, often rapidly repeated; when disturbed *tsiay*. Song, similar in tone to Goldfinch and about the same length as Serin, is a lively twitter, often ending in a drawn-out wheeze.

Occurrence: Resident in Alps, Pyrenees and other ranges in central and south-west Europe, also in Corsica and Sardinia. Relatively common in open coniferous forest in Alps from about 1,400 m to tree-line. A few pairs in Black Forest.

Behaviour: Sociable. Often flocks to open places and to gardens in mountain valleys in late winter.

Food: Conifer seeds, herb and grass seeds, insects.

Breeding habits: April–August, 1–2 broods; nest made of grasses, roots, moss and lichen, lined with plant fibres and feathers; usually sited high up in conifers. Often nests in clearings with isolated coniferous trees.

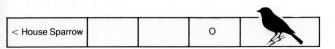

| < House Sparrow | | | O | |

Greenfinch *Carduelis chloris*
Family: Finches Fringillidae
F Verdier d'Europe
G Grünling. Grünfink

Distinctive character: Large, yellow-green finch.
Features: Yellow wing patches, especially conspicuous in flight. ♀ (drawing) mainly grey-green with less conspicuous yellow on wings and tail. Juvenile heavily streaked.
Voice: On take-off a loud musical *djudjudju* alarm call nasal *diu* or *tsvooeet*; in conflicts a jarring *tsrr*. Song consists of Canary-like ringing notes and trills, interspersed with Nuthatch-like piping and drawn-out wheezy calls such as *dyayeei*.
Occurrence: Breeds commonly in light mixed woodland, at woodland edges, in hedges, parks, orchards and wooded avenues; also in gardens, even in urban areas.
Behaviour: Sociable. Often visits bird tables. Has bat-like display flights, with slowed-down wingbeats.
Food: Seeds, buds, flowers, insects,

Greenfinch
♀

sunflower seeds.
Breeding habits: April–August, 2–3 broods; loose nest, usually half way up in a thick bush or tree; also in flower-boxes on balconies.

	– House Sparrow	P, W	I–XII	

Goldfinch
Carduelis carduelis
Family: Finches Fringillidae
F Chardonneret élégant
G Stieglitz

Distinctive character: Remarkably colourful. In flight, broad yellow wing-bars prominent.
Features: Juv. lacks black, white and red head colours, but does have the characteristic yellow wing-bars.
Voice: Vocal. High-pitched rapid ringing *deedelit* or *tseedit*; alarm call a nasal drawn-out *vayee* in intra-specific conflicts a rattling *chrrr*. Song consists of high-pitched, rapidly delivered twittering and trilling phrases and nasal notes, usually introduced by *deedelit* calls.

Occurrence: Breeds in parks, orchards, open country with hedge-rows, wooded avenues and gardens. Often found in villages with old deciduous trees. Outside breeding season found in open country and along waysides.
Behaviour: Very sociable. Usually sings high up in tree. Often feeds in small flocks on weedy wasteland with thistles and other seed-bearing plants.
Food: Seeds of thistles, dandelions and deciduous trees; in breeding season also small insects, especially aphids.
Breeding habits: May–August, 2–3 broods; ♀ builds a thick-walled matted nest made of plant fibres, moss and grass, usually high up in branch fork of broadleaf tree.

< House Sparrow	P	I–XII		

Siskin *Carduelis spinus*
Family: Finches Fringillidae
F Tarin des aulnes
G Zeisig

Distinctive character: Melancholy flight calls.

Features: Very small, with relatively slim, pointed bill. Plumage greenish-yellow, wings black with broad yellow bars. ♂ has black crown and small black chin patch. ♀ grey-green, more heavily streaked and without black on head. Juv. browner above and even more heavily streaked.

Voice: Flight call is a melancholy *toolee, tseau* or *deeay*, accented on the first syllable, often also a short *tet* or *tetetet*. Song a hurried twitter, often interspersed with *toolee* calls, imitations of other birds and ending in a drawn-out wheeze.

Occurrence: Breeds in spruce forests and mixed woods, especially in the mountains, up to the tree-line. Common in lowlands in winter. Populations fluctuate widely from year to year. Very local breeder in Britain, but often widespread in winter and then often visits gardens.

Behaviour: Forages acrobatically in birch and alder trees, often hanging upside down. Sociable and often found in large flocks outside breeding season. Sings from end of January, often high up in treetops or in bat-like song-flight.

Food: Seeds of broadleaf and coniferous trees, insects, fine seeds, nuts, suet.

Breeding habits: April–July, 2 broods; nest made of stems, moss and lichens, usually high in conifers.

	< House Sparrow	R, W, M	I–XII	

354

Redpoll *Carduelis flammea*
Family: Finches Fringillidae
F Sizerin flammé G Birkenzeisig

Distinctive character: Flight call.
Features: Very small. Horn-coloured, pointed bill. Plumage mainly streaked brownish, with deep red forehead and black chin. Breeding ♂ has reddish-pink breast. Juv. lacks red.
Voice: Typical flight call is a rapid far-carrying *che-che-che*; alarm call a nasal, drawn-out *vayee* or *wooeet*. Song is a sustained dry twitter mixed with buzzing notes, whistled notes and flight calls.

Occurrence: Breeds in open coniferous woodland up to the tree-line and in boggy areas in mountain foothills, also in alder and willow scrub and in lowland coniferous plantations. Expanding its range into towns.
Behaviour: Very sociable. In winter often in large flocks in alders and birch trees. Often sings in normal flight, or in song-flight with slower wingbeats.
Food: Seeds of trees and herbs, insects, fine seeds, nuts, suet.
Breeding habits: May–August, 1–2 broods; nest made of twigs, moss and stems, at variable height in bush or tree.

| < House Sparrow | P, W | I–XII | | 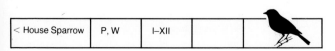 |

Twite *Carduelis flavirostris*
Family: Finches Fringillidae
F Linotte à bec jaune
G Berghänfling

Distinctive character: Mostly seen in flocks at coast in winter.
Features: Very similar to ♀ Linnet, but has less white on wings and tail and browner plumage, and with buff (not whitish) throat. ♂ has pink rump. In winter bill yellowish.
Voice: Flight call *chip-ip-ip*, softer than Linnet's; also a drawn-out squeaky *kyay kyay kyaya* or *chitoo*. Song, heard as early as late winter, is a jolting twitter with varied calls and drawn-out twanging sounds; slightly slower than Linnet's.
Occurrence: Breeds in rocky, sparsely vegetated coastal sites, uplands, moorland and heaths in northern Europe, including northern Britain. Regular on coastal meadows, saltmarsh and stubblefields in winter, in British Isles, North Sea and Baltic. Rarer inland.
Behaviour: Very sociable: in winter often forages in large, dense flocks on weedy plants and on the ground.
Breeding habits: May–August, 1–2 broods; relatively large nest made of grasses, stalks, wool and hair, usually in ground vegetation or in a cavity.

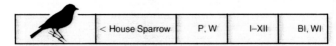

| | < House Sparrow | P, W | I–XII | BI, WI |

Linnet *Carduelis cannabina*
Family: Finches Fringillidae
F Linotte mélodieuse
G Hänfling, Bluthänfling

Distinctive character: Nasal calls.
Features: Breeding ♂ has bright red forehead and breast; duller generally in winter, with no red on head. ♀ (drawing) always lacks red, is streaked and dark brown above. Juv. more heavily streaked.
Voice: Flight call nasal stuttering *chichichi*; when nervous a nasal drawn-out *duuye* or *gluu*. Song is nasal but attractive, beginning with an accelerating series of typical calls, and developing into rapid trills, with fluty and noisy sounds.
Occurrence: Breeds in open cultivated country with hedges and copses, in cemeteries, vineyards, heathland, parks and gardens, often on the edge of villages; in mountains to tree-line. Often in large, dense flocks in open country outside breeding season.

Linnet,
♀

Food: Seeds of weedy plants and trees, insects.
Breeding habits: April–September, 2–3 broods; nests low down in hedges, bushes and young trees; often small colonies of several pairs.

< House Sparrow	P, W	I–XII		

Scarlet Rosefinch
Carpodacus erythrinus
Family: Finches Fringillidae
F Roselin cramoisi
G Karmingimpel

Distinctive character: Carmine-red head, chin, throat, breast and rump of male from 2nd year.
Features: Wings and tail dark brown, two narrow wing-bars. ♀ (drawing) and immature ♂ unobtrusive brown with paler underparts and streaked breast.
Voice: Song memorable and far-carrying – a stereotyped, rather Golden Oriole-like yet pure piping *see-weedyu-weedyee*, the last syllable rising noticeably.
Occurrence: Breeds in bushy damp areas, especially in willows or alders near water, in light herb-rich swampy woodland, in open country with scattered trees and in plantations. Eastern species, spreading west into northern Europe. Breeds in south Finland, and locally in southern Scandinavia,

Scarlet Rosefinch, ♀

Austria, Switzerland and Germany. Very scarce but regular visitor to Britain, mostly in autumn, but has bred.
Food: Insects, their larvae, buds, shoots, berries, seeds.
Breeding habits: May–July, 1 brood; loose nest of stems and grasses, lined with rootlets and hair, usually 0.5–2m up in thick scrub.

	– House Sparrow	(S), (M)	V–X	BR

Distinctive character: Powerful bill with mandibles crossed at tip.
Features: Dumpy and large-headed, with short, forked tail. ♂ brick-red after 2nd year, ♀ olive-green with yellowish rump (drawing). Juv. with heavy dark streaking.
Voice: Vocal. Hard *jip jip jip* or *klip klip klip*, often in flight; also a softer *tjook* or *tjuk*. Song: many different loud, clear phrases, repeated 2–3 times, and mixed with the typical *jip* calls and harder sounds.
Occurrence: Breeds in coniferous woodland, especially in mountain spruce forests, up to tree-line. Local breeder in Britain; periodic invasions from Continent.
Behaviour: Sociable. Clambers parrot-like amongst cones.
Food: Mainly spruce seeds.
Breeding habits: Throughout year,

Crossbill,
♀

mostly Dec–June, 1–2 broods; sturdy nest made of twigs, moss and lichens, high in spruce tree.
Scottish Crossbill *Loxia scotica*, found only in Caledonian pine forest of Scotland, has slightly deeper and blunter bill and slightly deeper call.

> House Sparrow	R, M	I–XII		

359

Bullfinch *Pyrrhula pyrrhula*
Family: Finches Fringillidae
F Bouvreuil pivoine
G Gimpel, Dompfaff

Distinctive character: Bright pink-red underparts of ♂.
Features: Plump and dumpy, with powerful black conical bill. ♀ (drawing) brownish-grey below. Juv. brownish, without black cap. In flight white rump prominent.
Voice: Soft, quiet call, a slightly falling *dju* or *pew*, easy to imitate; also a soft *puut puut* on take off. Song: soft, piping and twittering, chatter, including calls and wheezing notes.
Occurrence: Breeds in coniferous and mixed woodland, in spruce clearings, at woodland edges, in parks, gardens and cemeteries with many bushes.

Behaviour: Often very shy and secretive, and normally lives in pairs. Outside breeding season pairs may join up into small groups; often sit fluffed up in berry-bearing bushes in winter, and visit bird tables.

Bullfinch, ♀

Food: Seeds and buds of trees and herbs; berries, also insects.
Breeding habits: May–August, 2 broods; loose nest hidden in thick bushes or young conifers.

	> House Sparrow	R, (M)	I–XII

Hawfinch
Coccothraustes coccothraustes
Family: Finches Fringillidae
F Gros-bec cassenoyaux
G Kernbeißer

Distinctive character: Stout bird with large head and massive bill.

Features: Bill steel-blue in summer, horn-coloured in winter (photo). ♀ less striking, has drabber plumage. Juv. brownish with heavy dark mottling. Looks thick-set in flight and shows translucent areas on wings and white tip to tail.

Voice: A shrill, sharp *tsiks*, *tsick*, *tsi-kik* or a high-pitched *srree*. Song (rarely heard) is a jerky, tinkling assortment of call notes and nasal sounds. Song very poorly developed and so has scarcely any territorial function.

Occurrence: Breeds in broadleaf and mixed woodland, especially with beech and maple, and in parks and gardens with tall deciduous trees. Widespread but sparse and local.

Behaviour: Fairly shy. In summer stays mainly in crowns of trees, but does visit bird tables in winter in some areas. Flight rapid and direct, often in wide curves, and usually at tree-top height.

Food: Seeds of deciduous trees, especially hornbeam and maple; kernels of stone fruit (which it breaks open), buds, insects.

Breeding habits: April–June, 1–2 broods; spacious nest of twigs, roots and stems, usually high up in deciduous tree.

> House Sparrow	R	I–XII		

Snow Bunting
Plectrophenax nivalis
Family: Buntings Emberizidae
F Bruant des neiges
G Schneeammer

Distinctive character: Conspicuous white wing patch, especially in ♂.
Features: Breeding ♂ has white head and underparts, black wings with large white patch, and black bill; ♀ has less contrasting plumage with browner upperparts. In winter (photo ♂), back brownish with black markings, cap and cheek orange-brown, indistinct orange-brown breast-band; ♀ light brown above, with more brown on head, breast and flanks, and smaller area of white on wings; some young ♀ lack white on wings.

Voice: Flight call a trilling *tirr* or *teeu*. Landing flocks often make a sharp *tssr*. Song: clear trilling, lark-like phrase with rapid changes of pitch.
Occurrence: Breeds on rocky and stony mountain and tundra areas in northern Europe, including Scotland. Regular on north European coasts in winter, on open areas with low vegetation, and sometimes at lake margins and on waste ground inland.
Behaviour: Moves around in small flocks, keeping close to ground; fairly tame.
Food: Insects, spiders; seeds in winter.
Breeding habits: May–August, 1–2 broods; ground nest of tundra plants lined with feathers and wool, usually in rock crevice or under stones.

	> House Sparrow	(R), W, M	I–XII	BR

Lapland Bunting *Calcarius lapponicus*
Family: Buntings Emberizidae
F Bruant lapon
G Spornammer

Distinctive character: In winter has chestnut greater wing-coverts bordered by two thin white wingbars.
Features: Breeding ♂ (photo) very strikingly coloured and difficult to confuse. In winter ♂ (drawing) similar to Reed Bunting, but has longer wings and shorter tail; note also the characteristic wing pattern and (in ♂) remnants of rust-brown on nape. Bill yellowish. Juv. ♀ often have brownish-yellow colour on head.
Voice: On migration a dry rattling *prrrt* or *chuprrrt*; on breeding grounds *dyuee*, sometimes alternating with *cheeu*. Song resembles Snow Bunting's but sounds more jolting.

Occurrence: Breeds in low scrub above tree-line in mountains of northern Europe; has bred a number of times in Scotland. In winter regular visitor to coastal meadows, pasture

Lapland Bunting, winter

and crop fields around southern North Sea and southern Baltic. Only rarely seen inland.
Behaviour: Usually on the ground during migration, running about rapidly in a crouched posture amongst low cover.
Food: Mostly seeds, insects.

> House Sparrow	(S), W, M	mainly VIII–V	BR	

Yellowhammer *Emberiza citrinella*
Family: Buntings Emberizidae
F Bruant jaune G Goldammer

Distinctive character: Striking yellow colour on head and underparts of ♂.
Features: Slim and long-tailed, with cinnamon-brown rump. ♀ (drawing) and juv. less yellow, and also with much dark streaking on head and underparts. White outer tail feathers obvious on take-off.
Voice: Vocal *tsrik* or *trs*, and a trilling *tirr* on take-off. Song: short, melancholy phrase *tsitsitsitsitsitsitsitsee-duh* ('little bit of bread and *no* cheese'), often shortened.
Occurrence: Common almost everywhere in varied cultivated country with hedgerows, copses and bushy woodland margins, and in young spruce plantations; in mountains to

about 1,200 m. Also in villages, mainly in winter.
Behaviour: Often flicks tail; sings from tops of bushes, wires or similar

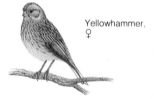

Yellowhammer, ♀

perch, even in high summer. In winter seen in small flocks.
Food: Insects, spiders, seeds, grain, green parts of plants.
Breeding habits: April–August, 2–3 broods; nest usually low down amongst low plants, in a small tree, or in path-side scrub.

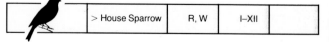

| | > House Sparrow | R, W | I–XII |

x

Cirl Bunting *Emberiza cirlus*
Family: Buntings Emberizidae
F Bruant zizi G Zaunammer

Distinctive character: Very unobtrusive.
Features: ♂ yellow below with greenish breastband, dark streaks on flanks, and with prominent yellow and black markings on head and neck. ♀ much drabber, very like ♀ Yellowhammer, but with less yellow and with grey-brown (not cinnamon-brown) rump.
Voice: Similar call to Yellowhammer, but has a thin, high-pitched *tsiih* or *tzi*, and a short, hard *tik* or *tsittit*. Rattling song somewhat reminiscent of Lesser Whitethroat's, but higher-pitched and more ringing, often all on one note.
Occurrence: Breeds in open and bushy country with isolated taller trees, in vineyards, in south Europe especially on dry, sunny slopes. Mainly south and western Europe, and Mediterranean area. Rare breeder in Britain, Switzerland, Austria and southern Germany.
Behaviour: Much less conspicuous than Yellowhammer, and usually hard to spot. Sings from higher perches, often into autumn. Outside breeding season often associate with Yellowhammers in mixed flocks on farmland.
Food: Mainly seeds; feeds insects to young.
Breeding habits: May–August, 2–3 broods; nests in thick bushes or in young trees, usually close to ground.

> House Sparrow	R	I–XII	BR	

Ortolan Bunting
Emberiza hortulana
Family: Buntings Emberizidae
F Bruant ortolan
G Ortolan, Gartenammer

Distinctive character: Pale yellow eye-ring and pink bill.
Features: Breeding ♂ has grey-green head, yellow throat and yellow moustachial stripe. ♀ paler, less greenish, and with dark streaks on breast. Autumn ♂ resembles ♀. Juv. has heavy dark streaking.
Voice: When agitated a *psip* or *pslee-e*, often alternating with *chu*. Song: a short, rather melancholy phrase – *tsree-tsree-tsree-tsree-dyu-dyu-dyu*, or similar; each ♂ has as

many as four different phrase types.
Occurrence: Breeds in areas with a mild, fairly dry climate. Prefers mixed cultivated country with orchards, avenues of trees, or scattered trees in fields, woodland margins, often close to wet areas. Decline in many areas due to habitat destruction and cold, wet summers. Scarce migrant in Britain.
Behaviour: Often sings from top of tree or bush. Mainly in small flocks outside breeding season.
Food: Mostly seeds; also insects in breeding season.
Breeding habits: May–July, 1–2 broods; nest made of grass, stems and roots, lined with fine grasses and animal hair; usually on ground between shrubs or under a bush.

|  | > House Sparrow | (M) | IV–VI, VIII–X | O |

Rock Bunting *Emberiza cia*
Family: Buntings Emberizidae
F Bruant fou G Zippammer

Distinctive character: Ash-grey head with narrow black stripes and silver-grey throat.
Features: Plumage mainly cinnamon-brown, rump unstreaked rust-brown, tail with white outer feathers. ♀ has browner-grey head with dark brown stripes. Juv. lightly streaked; young ♀ often very plainly coloured but still with red-brown rump.
Voice: Short *tsip* or high-pitched *tsee*. The rather monotonous squeaky, hurried song – often introduced by *tsip* – is somewhat reminiscent of Dunnock's.

Occurrence: Breeds on dry, sunny, often very steep slopes, with a rich mixture of bushes, rocky areas and small patches of low weedy vegetation; often in abandoned vineyards. Southern species. Rare breeder in Austria, Hungary, Switzerland and south Germany. Declined in central Europe due to habitat destruction, reduction of grazing and climate change. Rare vagrant to Britain.
Behaviour: Rather shy, often taking flight even at a distance. Sings from elevated perch.
Food: Seeds; in breeding period mainly insects.
Breeding habits: April–July, 1–2 broods; nest made of grasses, stems and roots, usually built in a cleft in rocks.

> House Sparrow	V	II–X	O	

Reed Bunting
Emberiza schoeniclus
Family: Buntings Emberizidae
F Bruant des roseaux
G Rohrammer

Occurrence: Breeds in overgrown lake and river margins, with reed and sedge beds and damp willow scrub, also in drier places (coastal bushes, young conifers). Widespread.

Reed Bunting, ♀

Distinctive character: Common bunting in wet areas.

Features: Breeding ♂ has black head, chin and throat, with white collar and moustachial stripe; in winter head and neck pattern are mostly obscured by brownish feather tips. ♀ (drawing) and juv. have camouflaged plumage with conspicuous black and white moustache.

Voice: Sharp, slightly rising *tseei*, or *tseeu*, deeper than (aerial) alarm call of Blackbird or Robin; also a short dull *chuh* or *pse*. Song: a short stammering, often clipped phrase – *tche tche tui tsiri*, *tsip tsip tete tsink tet* or *dip dip dip tier tete*.

Food: Insects, small crustaceans, snails, grass seeds.

Breeding habits: April–August, 2–3 broods; builds a large nest of reed leaves and stems, often low down in reedy scrub.

	– House Sparrow	R, W, M	I–XII	

Corn Bunting *Miliaria calandra*
Family: Buntings Emberizidae
F Bruant proyer G Grauammer

Distinctive character: Inconspicuous lark-like plumage; often sings from exposed perch.
Features: Looks dumpy and ungainly. Plumage has no striking markings. Cream-coloured below, with brown streaks on breast and flanks, no white in tail.
Voice: Flight call a short *tick*, often repeated 2–3 times. Song consists of short ticking notes, running together and culminating in a jangling final section – *tik-tik-tik-tikzikzik-zree-zisrizzis*.
Occurrence: Breeds in dry, open country with cereal crops, meadows and isolated trees and bushes, on dry slopes and downland and on waste land. Patchy distribution; numbers declining in Britain.
Behaviour: Often flies with shallow wingbeats with legs dangling. Sings with bill held wide open, often from exposed perch on a wire or top of bush, especially alongside country roads. Outside breeding season often associates with other buntings and larks.
Food: Insects, small snails, seeds, green parts of plants.
Breeding habits: May–August, 1–3 broods; loose nest made of grass and roots, in a hollow on the ground or in ground vegetation, more rarely in a hedge or thick scrub.

> House Sparrow	R, W	I–XII		

Ducks in Flight

Mallard

♀

Gadwall

♂

Garganey

♀

♂

Teal

♂

♀

Wigeon

♂

♀

Shoveler

♂

♂

Pintail

♀

Ferruginous Duck

♂

♂

♀

Red-crested Pochard

♀

Pochard

Ducks in Flight

Tufted Duck

♂

♀

♂

Scaup

♂

♀

♂

♀

Goldeneye

Common
Scoter

♀

♀

♂

Velvet Scoter

Long-tailed
Duck

♂

♀

♀

Eider

♂

♀

Smew

♂

Shelduck

♂

♀

Goosander

♂

♂

♀

Red-breasted Merganser

Birds of Prey in Flight

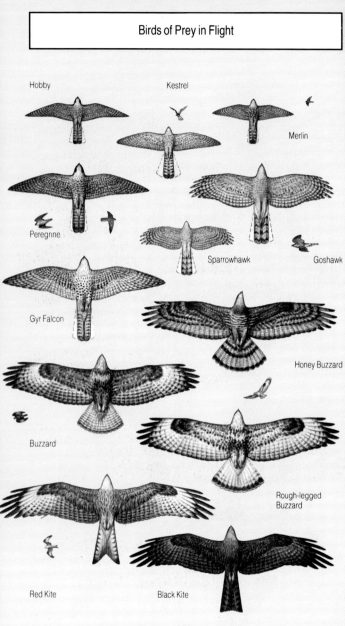

Hobby

Kestrel

Merlin

Peregrine

Sparrowhawk

Goshawk

Gyr Falcon

Honey Buzzard

Buzzard

Rough-legged Buzzard

Red Kite

Black Kite

Birds of Prey in Flight

Montagu's Harrier

♂

♀

juv.

Marsh Harrier

♂

♀

Hen Harrier

♀

Osprey

Golden Eagle

White-tailed Eagle

Ringed Plover

Kentish Plover—♂

Little Ringed Plover

Curlew Sandpiper

Knot,
winter

winter

Dunlin

Breeding
plumage

Sanderling

winter

Purple Sandpiper,
winter

Little Stint,

winter

Temminck's Stint,

winter

Spotted Redshank, winter

Greenshank, breeding plumage

Redshank

Green Sandpiper

Turnstone, breeding plumage

Wood Sandpiper

Common Sandpiper

Ruff–♂ winter

ad.

Herring
Gull

ad.

1st
winter

2nd
winter

1st
winter

2nd
winter

Lesser
Black-backed
Gull

ad.

juv.

ad

Great Black-backed
Gull

Common Gull

juv.

ad.

juv.

Kittiwake

ad.
summer

ad.
summer

juv.

ad.
winter

Black-headed
Gull

juv.

Little Gull

ad.
winter

Arctic Tern

Common Tern

Little Tern

Caspian Tern

Black Tern

White-
winged
Black
Tern

Sandwich
Tern

Whiskered
Tern

Index of English Names

Numbers in *italic*
refer to illustration
only.

Accentor,
  Alpine 279
Avocet 170

Bee-eater *4–5*, 244
Bittern *14*, 82
  Little 83
Blackbird *33*, 226
Blackcap *33*, 307
Bluethroat 281
Brambling 349
Bullfinch *50*, 360
Bunting
  Cirl 365
  Corn 369
  Lapland 363
  Ortolan 366
  Reed 368
  Rock 367
  Snow 362
Bustard, Great 163
Buzzard *64*, *123*,
  136
  Honey *41*, *65*,
    138
  Rough-legged
    137

Capercaillie *67*,
  147, 153
Chaffinch *26*, *33*,
  348
Chiffchaff 314
Chough 340
  Alpine *340*
Coot *24*, *32*, 162
Cormorant 81
Corncrake 160
Crake
  Baillon's 159
  Little 159
  Spotted 158
Crane 164

Crossbill *51*, 359
  Scottish 359
Crow
  Carrion *46*, 342
  Hooded *55*, 342
Cuckoo *26*, 229
Curlew *42*, 195
  Stone 169

Dabchick (Little
  Grebe) 77
Dipper *36*, 276
Diver
  Black-throated
    72
  Great Northern
    73
  Red-throated 73
Dotterel 175
Dove
  Collared 226
  Rock 228
  Stock *43*, 224
  Turtle 227
Duck
  Long-tailed 115
  Ruddy 111
  Tufted 112
Dunnock *26*, 278

Eagle
  Booted 140
  Golden *34*, 139
  Imperial 139
  Lesser Spotted
    141
  Short-toed 130
  Spotted 144
  White-tailed 127
Egret
  Great White 86
  Little 87
Eider *24*, *26*, 114

Falcon, Red-
  footed 143
Fieldfare 298

Finch
  Citril 351
  Snow 345
Firecrest 317
Flycatcher
  Collared 287
  Pied *25*, 286
  Red-breasted 28
  Spotted *66*, 284
Fulmar 80

Gadwall 103
Gannet *2–3*, 78
Garganey 105
Godwit
  Bar-tailed 196
  Black-tailed 197
Goldcrest 316
Goldeneye 118
Goldfinch *50*, 353
Goosander 121
Goose
  Barnacle 99
  Bean 95
  Brent 100
  Canada 98
  Greylag *40*, *67*, 9
  Lesser White-
    fronted 97
  Pink-footed 95
  White-fronted 97
Goshawk 34, 134
Grebe
  Black-necked 76
  Great Crested
    32, 74
  Little
    (Dabchick) 77
  Red-necked 75
  Slavonian 76
Greenfinch *46*, 352
Greenshank 188
Grouse
  Black 152
  Hazel *42*
  Red 150
Guillemot *24*, 218

Black 220
Gull
  Black-headed 55,
    65, 205
  Common 206
  Glaucous 209
  Great Black-
    backed 209
  Herring 63, 207
  Iceland 207
  Lesser Black-
    backed 43,
    208
  Little 204
  Mediterranean
    205

Hawfinch 26, 33,
  53, 361
Harrier
  Hen 132
  Marsh 34, 131
  Montagu's 133
Heron
  Grey 34, 64, 67,
    84
  Night 88
  Purple 85
Hobby 144
Hoopoe 246

Jackdaw 339
Jay 54, 336

Kestrel 24, 41, 65,
  142
Kingfisher 38, 221,
  243
Kite
  Black 128
  Red 129
Kittiwake 32, 43,
  203
Knot 179

Lapwing 24, 54,
  178
Lark
  Crested 260
  Shore 263
Linnet 357

Magpie 35, 56, 338
Mallard 40, 108
Mandarin 122
Martin
  Crag 265
  House 36, 267
  Sand 38, 264
Merganser, Red-
  breasted 120
Merlin 146
Moorhen 42, 161

Nightingale 282
  Thrush 283
Nightjar 242
Nutcracker 51, 337
Nuthatch 26, 37, 326

Oriole, Golden 34,
  331
Osprey 126
Ouzel, Ring 297
Owl
  Barn 25, 44, 64,
    65, 239
  Eagle 236
  Little 66, 238
  Long-eared 39,
    55, 65, 230
  Pygmy 235
  Scops 237
  Short-eared 231
  Snowy 236
  Tawny 43, 44, 65,
    232
  Tengmalm's 234
  Ural 233
Oystercatcher 41,
  168

Partridge
  Grey 84, 154
  Red-legged 156
Peregrine 145
Petrel
  British Storm 78
  Leach's 78
Phalarope
  Grey 193
  Red-necked 193
Pheasant 50, 67, 156

Pigeon, Feral 228
Pintail 107
Pipit
  Meadow 268
  Rock 270
  Tawny 271
  Tree 269
  Water 270
Plover
  Golden 176
  Grey 177
  Kentish 174
  Little Ringed 25,
    42, 165, 172
  Ringed 23, 173
Pochard 110
  Red-crested 109
Ptarmigan 151
Puffin 217

Quail 155

Rail, Water 157
Raven 341
Razorbill 219
Redpoll 355
Redshank 187
  Spotted 186
Redstart 46, 289
  Black 288
Redwing 299
Reeve 185
Robin 45, 57, 280
Roller 245
Rook 35, 343
Rosefinch,
  Scarlet 358
Ruff 185
Saker 145
Sanderling 180
Sandpiper
  Common 191
  Curlew 182
  Green 190
  Marsh 186
  Purple 184
  Wood 189
Scaup 113
Scoter
  Common 116
  Velvet 117

Serin 350
Shag 81
Shearwater
  Manx 79
  Sooty 79
Shelduck *40*, 101
Shoveler 106
Shrike
  Great Grey *66*, 335
  Lesser Grey 334
  Red-backed *33*, *49*, *66*, 332
  Woodchat 333
Siskin 354
Skua
  Arctic 201
  Great (Bonxie) 201
  Long-tailed 202
  Pomarine 202
Skylark *49*, 262
Smew 119
Snipe 199
  Great 200
  Jack 200
Sparrow
  House *50*, 346
  Tree 347
Sparrowhawk *54*, 135
Spoonbill *49*, 344
Starling 89
Stilt, Black-winged 171
Stint
  Little 181
  Temminck's 181
Stonechat 291
Stork
  Black *35*, 91
  White *64*, 90
Swallow *34*, *45*, 266
Swan
  Bewick's 94

Mute *24*, *26*, *69*, 92
  Whooper 93
Swift 24
  Alpine 241

Teal 104
Tern
  Arctic *43*, 214
  Black 216
  Caspian 210
  Common 214
  Little 213
  Roseate 211
  Sandwich 212
Thrush
  Mistle 294
  Rock 293
  Song *25*, *33*, *46*, *48*, *49*, 295
Tit
  Bearded 318
  Blue *46*, 324
  Coal 322
  Crested 323
  Great 325, 324
  Long-tailed *36*, 319
  Marsh 320
  Penduline *36*, 330
  Willow 321
Treecreeper 329
  Short-toed 328
Turnstone 192
Twite 356

Wagtail
  Grey 273
  Pied 274
  Yellow 227
Wallcreeper 327
Warbler,
  Aquatic 305
  Barred 308
  Cetti's 303

Dartford 312
Fantailed 300
Garden 309
Grasshopper 30
Great Reed 304
Icterine *25*, 306
Marsh *23*, 302
Melodious 306
Moustached 30
Orphean 307
Reed *31*, 303
River 301
Savi's 301
Sedge 305
Willow 315
Wood 313
Waxwing 275
Wheatear 292
Whimbrel 194
Whinchat 290
Whitethroat 310
  Lesser 311
Wigeon 102
Woodcock 198
Woodlark *45*, 261
Woodpecker
  Black *51*, *52*, 25
  Great Spotted *4*, *51*, *52*, *56*, 252
  Green *49*, 249
  Grey-headed 24
  Lesser Spotted 255
  Middle Spotted 254
  Syrian 253
  Three-toed *52*, 256
  White-backed 25
Woodpigeon *54*, *55*, 225
Wren *36*, *45*, 277
Wryneck *67*, 247

Yellowhammer *45*, 364

380

Index of Scientific Names

Acanthis cannabina 357
  A. flammea 355
  A. flavirostris 356
Accipiter gentilis 134
  A. nisus 135
Actitis hypoleucos 191
Acrocephalus arundinaceus 304
  A. melanopogon 305
  A. paludicola 305
  A. palustris 302
  A. schoenobaenus 305
  A. scirpaceus 303
Aegithalos caudatus 319
Aegolius funereus 234
Aix galericulata 122
Alauda arvensis 262
Alca torda 219
Alcedo atthis 243
Anas acuta 107
  A. clypeata 106
  A. crecca 104
  A. penelope 102
  A. platyrhyncos 108
  A. querquedula 105
  A. strepera 103
Anser albifrons 97
  A. anser 96
  A. brachyrhynchus 95
  A. erythropus 97
  A. fabialis 95
Anthus campestris 271
  A. petrosus 270
  A. pratensis 268
  A. spinoletta 270
  A. trivialis 269
Apus apus 240
  A. melba 241
Aquila chrysaetos 139
  A. clanga 141
  A. heliaca 139
  A. pomarina 141
Ardea cinerea 84
  A. purpurea 85
Arenaria interpres 192
Asio flammeus 231
  A. otus 230
Athene noctua 238
Aythya ferina 110
  A. fuligula 112
  A. marila 113

Bombycilla garrulus 275
Botaurus stellaris 82
Branta bernicala 100
  B. canadensis 98
  B. leucopsis 99
Bubo bubo 236
Bucephala clangula 118
Burinus oedicnemus 169
Buteo buteo 136
  B. lagopsis 137

Calcarius lapponicus 363
Calidris alba 180
  C. alpina 183
  C. canutus 179
  C. ferruginea 182
  C. maritima 184
  C. minuta 181
  C. temminckii 181
Caprimulgus europaeus 242
Carduelis cannabina 357
  C. carduelis 353
  C. chloris 352
  C. flammea 355
  C. flavirostris 356
  C. spinus 354
Carpodacus erythrinus 358
Casmerodius albus 86
Cepphus grylle 220
Certhia brachydactyla 328
  C. familiaris 329
Cettia cetti 303
Charadrius alexandrinus 174
  C. dubius 172
  C. hiaticula 173
  C. morinellus 175
Chlidonias niger 216
Cinclus cinclus 276
Cisticola juncidis 300
Circaetus gallicus 130
Ciconia ciconia 90
  C. nigra 91
Cinclus cinclus 276
Circus aeruginosus 131
  C. cyaneus 132
  C. pygargus 133
Clangula hymenalis 115
Coccothraustes coccothraustes 361
Columba livia 228
  C. oenas 224
  C. palumbus 225
Coracias garrulus 245

Corvus corax 341
    C. corone
    corone 342
    C. frugilegus 343
    C. monedula 339
Coturnix coturnix
    155
Crex crex 160
Cuculus
    canorus 229
Cygnus bewickii 94
Cygnus columbianus
    94
    C. cygnus 93
    C. olor 92

Delichon urbica 267
Dryocopus martius
    250

Egretta alba 86
    E. garzetta 87
Emberiza calandra
    369
    E. cia 367
    E. cirlus 365
    E. citrinella 364
    E. hortulana 366
    E. shoeniclus
    368
Eremophila alpestris
    263
Erithacus
    rubecula 280
Falco cherrug 145
    F. columbarius
    146
    F. perigrinus 145
    F. subbuteo 144
    F. tinnunculus
    142
    F. vespertinus
    143
Ficedula albicollis
    287
    F. hypoleuca 286
    F. parva 285
Fratercula arctica
    217
Fringilla coelebs
    348

F. montifringilla
    349
Fulica atra 162
Fulmarius glacialis
    80

Galerida cristata
    260
Gallinago gallinago
    199
    G. media 200
Gallinula chloropus
    161
Garrulus glandarius
    336
Gavia arctica 72
    G. immer 73
    G. stellata 73
Glacidium
    passerinum 235
Grus grus 164

Haematopus
    ostralegus 168
Haliaeetus albicilla
    127
Hieraaetus pennatus
    140
Himantopus
    himantopus 171
Hippolais icterina
    306
    H. polyglotta 306
Hirundo rustica 266
Hydrobates pelagicus
    78

Ixobrytus minutus
    83

Jynx torquilla 247

Lagopus lagopus
    150
    L. mutus 151
Lanius collurio 332
    L. excubitor 335
    L. minor 334
    L. senator 333
Larus argentatus
    207

L. canus 206
L. fuscus 208
L. glaucoides
    207
L. hyperboreus
    209
L. marinus 209
L. melanocephale
    205
L. minutus 204
L. ridibundus 20
Limosa lapponica
    196
    L. limosa 197
Locustella fluviatilis
    301
    L. luscinioides
    301
    L. naevia 300
Loxia curvirostra
    359
    L. scotica 359
Lullula arborea 26
Luscinia
    luscinia 283
    L. megarhynchos
    282
    L. svecica 281
Lymnocryptes
    minimus 200
Lyrurus tetrix 152

Melanitta fusca 11
    M. nigra 116
Mergus albellus 11
    M. merganser
    121
    M. serrator 120
Merops apiaster
    244
Miliaria calandra
    369
Milvus migrans 128
    M. milvus 129
Monticola saxatilis
    293
Montifringilla
    nivalis 345
Motacilla alba 274
    M. cinerea 273
    M. flava 272

Muscicapa striata 284

Netta rufina 109
Nucifraga caryocatactes 337
N. macrorhynchos 337
Numenius arquata 195
N. phaeopus 194
Nyctea scandiaca 236
Nycticorax nycticorax 88

Oceanodroma leucorrhoa 78
Oenanthe oenanthe 292
Oriolus oriolus 331
Otis tarda 163
Otus scops 237
Oxyura jamaicensis 111

Pandion haliaetus 126
Panurus biarmicus 318
Parus ater 322
P. caeruleus 324
P. cristatus 323
P. major 325
P. montanus 321
P. palustris 320
Passer domesticus 346
P. montanus 347
Perdix perdix 154
Pernis apivorus 138
Phalacrocorax carbo 81
Phalaropus lobatus 193
Phasianus colchicus 156
Philomachus pugnax 185
Phoenicurus ochruros 288

P. phoenicurus 289
Phylloscopus collybita 314
P. sibilatrix 313
P. trochilus 315
Pica pica 338
Picoides leucotos 251
P. major 252
P. medius 254
P. minor 255
P. syriacus 253
P. tridactylus 256
Picus canus 248
P. viridis 249
Platalea leucorodia 89
Plectrophenax nivalis 362
Pluvialis apricaria 176
P. squatarola 177
Podiceps auritus 76
P. cristatus 74
P. grisegena 75
P. nigricollis 76
Porzana parva 159
P. porzana 158
P. pusilla 159
Prunella collaris 279
P. modularis 278
Ptyonoprogne rupestris 265
Puffinus griseus 79
P. puffinus 79
Pyrrhocorax graculus 340
P. pyrrhocorax 340
Pyrrhula pyrrhula 360

Rallus aquaticus 157
Recurvirostra avosetta 170
Regulus ignicapillus 317
R. regulus 316

Remiz pendulinus 330
Riparia riparia 264
Rissa tridactyla 203

Saxicola rubetra 290
S. torquata 291
Scolopax rusticola 198
Serinus citrinella 351
S. serinus 350
Sitta europaea 326
Somateria mollissima 114
Stercorarius longicaudus 202
S. parasiticus 201
S. pomarinus 202
Stercorarius skua 201
Sterna albifrons 213
S. caspia 210
S. dougallii 211
S. hirundo 214
S. paradisaea 215
S. sandvicensis 212
Strepopelia tutur 227
S. decaoto 226
Strix aluco 232
S. uralensis 233
Sturnus vulgaris 344
Sylvia atricapilla 307
S. borin 309
S. communis 310
S. curruca 311
S. hortensis 307
S. nisoria 308
S. undata 312

Tachybaptus ruficollis 77
Tadorna tadorna 101

Tetrao tetrix   152
   T. urogallus   153
Tichodroma muraria
   327
Tringa erythropus
   186
   T. glareola   189
   T. nebularia   188
   T. ochropus   190

   T. totanus   187
Troglodytes
   troglodytes   277
Turdus iliacus   299
   T. merula   296
   T. philomelos
      295
   T. pilaris   298
   T. torquatus   297

   T. viscivorus   29
Tyto alba   239

Upupa epops   246
Uria aalge   218

Vanellus vanellus
   178

Photographic Acknowledgements

Adam (49 br, 200, 248), **Bracht** (80, 131), **Brandl** (32 al, 34 al, 41 br, 43 br, 44 r, 93, 103, 238, 260, 308), **Brossette** (49 ml, 49 bl), **Cotteridge** (78), **Czimmeck** (320), **Danegger** (98, 102, 105, 106, 122, 142, 170, 173, 176, 195, 205, 206, 273, 294, 325, 352), **Diedrich** (25 br, 26 b, 42 bl, 55 br, 117, 123, 177, 180, 184, 189, 215, 290, 296, 298, 309, 336, 338, 347), **Dierker** (160), **Eichhorn/Zingel** (83, 159, 175, 214, 237, 240, 246, 369), **Fürst** (39, 335, 344), **Fürst/Stahl** (89, 226, 261, 277, 281, 314, 334), **Groß** (53 br, 289), **Hautala** (80, 127), **Hiller** (251), **Humperdinck** (138, 279), **Klees** (45 br, 46 ar, 47, 107, 112, 156, 157, 208, 221, 243, 272, 278, 321, 340, 363), **König** (51 bl), **Kujala** (132), **Layer** (105, 229, 239, 280, 285, 322, 342), **Limbrunner** (4/5, 24 ar, 24 bl, 25 r, 31, 33 r, 34 bl, 36 l, 36 br, 38 br, 40 al, 40 bl, 40 br, 41 al, 41 ar, 41 m, 42 ml, 42 br, 43 ml, 44 l, 50 ar, 51 al, 51 mr, 52 mr, 52 b, 54 a, 54 m, 57, 59, 60, 61, 62, 63, 64 bl, 65 al, 65 r, 65 ml, 65 al, 66 al, 66 mr, 66 b, 67 a, 67 ml, 67 mr, 67 br, 69, 101, 111, 133, 143, 163, 198, 210, 211, 231, 241, 266, 269, 275, 276, 297, 301, 303, 333, 339, 341), **Löhrl** (43 mr, 327), **Maier** (90, 127, 155, 192), **Moosrainer** (36 bl, 147, 271, 307, 329, 351), **Natural Image/Gibbons** (217), **Nature Photographers/Blackburn**, (312, 319), **Nature Photographers/Carver** (111, 272), **Nature Photographers/Ennis** (211), **Nature Photographers/Fisher** (340), **Nature Photographers/Smith** (270), **Nature Photographers/Sterry** (title spread, contents spread), 79, 171, 274), **Nature Photographers/Tidman** (150), **Partsch** (74, 110, 348), **Pott** (95, 97, 99, 112, 114, 115, 116, 120, 171, 187, 203, 228), **Quedens** (24 al, 25 br, 32 bl, 40 ar, 42 ar, 45 mr, 46 mr, 65 mr, 135, 161, 162, 207, 247, 316), **Reinhard/Angermayer** (236), **Reinichs** (190, 256), **Rohdich** (35 b, 90, 264, 326), **Schmidt** (45 al, 46 al, 140, 306, 367), **Schrempp** (24 bl, 33 ml, 33 mr, 33 bl, 35 m, 36 al, 36 ar, 37 a, 37 b, 38 a, 46 ml, 46 b, 48, 49 al, 49 ar, 49 r, 51 ar, 53, 54 b, 64 ar, 65 ar, 65 br, 232, 312, 356), **Schulze** (201, 224, 253, 292, 302, 305, 315, 321, 349), **Schwammberger** (25 ml, 41 bl, 50 al, 50 m, 50 bl, 50 br, 51 ml, 56 a), **Silvestris** (87, 169, 178, 219, 244, 291), **Silvestris/Arndt** (332), **Silvestris/Gerlach** (286), **Silvestris/Lane** (94, 299), **Silvestris/Meyers** (109), **Silvestris/Willner** (274), **Singer** (25 ar, 32 ml, 33 al, 34 br, 35 a, 42 mr, 45 ml, 55 mr, 55 bl, 64 al, 108), **Storsberg** (174, 287), **Synatzschke** (26 al, 26 ar, 32 mr, 33 ar, 45 ar, 55 ml, 64 br, 66 ar, 66 ml, 67 bl, 204), **Walz** (2/3, 34 ml, 75, 96, 164, 181, 183, 188, 191, 220, 262, 364), **Weber** (267), **Wendl** (45 bl, 130, 154, 225, 227, 230, 234, 282, 324, 343, 353, 354, 359), **Wernicke** (23, 25 al, 43 al, 43 ar, 43 r, 73, 101, 119, 121, 153, 179, 182, 193, 199, 202, 209, 212, 218, 362), **Wothe** (34 ar, 38 bl, 56 b, 139, 165, 197, 233, 265, 293, 300, 310, 311, 368), **Young** (95), **Zeininger** (25 mr, 32 ar, 33 ar, 34 mr, 42 al, 45 r, 52 al, 55 a, 72, 76, 77, 81, 84, 85, 86, 88, 91, 118, 126, 128, 134, 136, 137, 141, 144, 145, 146, 150, 151, 152, 158, 172, 186, 194, 196, 216, 217, 235, 242, 245, 249, 250, 252, 254, 255, 257, 263, 268, 270, 283, 284, 288, 295, 304, 313, 317, 318, 319, 323, 328, 330, 337, 345, 346, 350, 355, 357, 358, 360, 361, 365, 366), **Ziesler/Angermayer** (168, 185).